Game Audio
Programming 2

Game Audio Programming 2
Principles and Practices

Edited by
Guy Somberg

CRC Press
Taylor & Francis Group
Boca Raton London New York

CRC Press is an imprint of the
Taylor & Francis Group, an **informa** business

CRC Press
Taylor & Francis Group
6000 Broken Sound Parkway NW, Suite 300
Boca Raton, FL 33487-2742

First issued in paperback 2022

© 2019 by Taylor & Francis Group, LLC
CRC Press is an imprint of Taylor & Francis Group, an Informa business

No claim to original U.S. Government works

ISBN 13: 978-1-03-240179-9 (pbk)
ISBN 13: 978-1-138-06891-9 (hbk)

DOI: 10.1201/b22247

Library of Congress Cataloging-in-Publication Data
LoC Data here

Visit the Taylor & Francis Web site at
http://www.taylorandfrancis.com

and the CRC Press Web site at
http://www.crcpress.com

To Emily and Mila

The most important people in my life.

Contents

Foreword

INTRODUCTION

Welcome to the second volume of *Game Audio Programming: Principles and Practices*! This second book in the series is particularly heartwarming to me, because of both the number of new contributors who have stepped up to share their knowledge and the number of returning contributors who have shared their enthusiasm. Books like this come about as a result of labors of love from all the individual contributors, who have all gone above and beyond to create some truly incredible works.

Before I began writing Volume 1 of this series, I knew of only one other audio programmer in the world. A large and vibrant community of audio programmers has appeared in the years between when I started work on the first volume and when this second volume has come to fruition. There are dedicated audio programming roundtables at the game developers conference, articles discussing the details of game audio programming techniques are becoming more and more prevalent, and now this book is entering a landscape that is far different from—and better than—when Volume 1 was published.

I was fortunate in my career to be at the right place and at the right time with the right interests to jump into audio programming right when the game industry as a whole started realizing that there is a need to have programming resources dedicated to audio. Many of the techniques and tricks that I and my contemporaries at the time developed out of whole cloth have become common practice. In fact, many of the features that we had to invent and build painstakingly a decade ago have become the de facto starting point for many modern audio engines.

All this technological explosion means that the bar for what is modern audio technology has been raised substantially. Many of the techniques in this book were surprising to me, and I learned a lot while editing them. I know that I am eager to try out some of these techniques in my current project.

THIS BOOK

I am excited about all of the content in this book. There are chapters that are subject surveys of high-level topics and technical topics ranging from the simple to the incredibly complex. Some chapters will touch on simple grade-school algebra, and a couple will stress your college-level calculus. Additionally, a number of the chapters have downloadable materials (source code, Unreal and Unity projects, etc.) that are available to download from the book's CRC Press website: https://www.crcpress. com/Game-Audio-Programming-2-Principles-and-Practices/Somberg/p/ book/9781138068919.

Here are brief summaries of all of the chapters in this book (in alphabetical order):

- **Advanced FMOD Studio Techniques**—This chapter delves deep into the features that FMOD provides. Learn how to light up various features of both the FMOD low-level and FMOD Studio APIs, and how to write auditing scripts to validate the correctness of your content.

- **Approximate Position of Ambient Sounds of Multiple Sources**— Follow the course of a river as it meanders through an environment, and all the different sound sources that we use to represent it. Calculus ahead!

- **A Rare Breed: The Audio Programmer**—There are a myriad of tasks that encompass the role of "audio programmer." This chapter will take you on a survey of what audio programmers do and how they do it.

- **Audio Resampling**—So much has been written about audio resampling and how it works, and so much of it is completely incomprehensible. Hopefully, this chapter will clarify all of the haze and provide an intuition for how resampling works.

- **Data-Driven Sound Limitation System**—Setting up rules for limiting the number of sounds that can be played at once is a common task, and one that is never-ending. By creating a simple data-driven script that describes behaviors, you can empower your sound designers to control the mix without needing a programmer. Check out the downloadable materials for a copy of this chapter in Japanese!

- **Designing a Channel-Agnostic Audio Engine**—Ambisonics and other channel formats can throw a wrench in the works of well-written audio engines. This chapter describes a technique for writing a channel-agnostic audio engine that can handle a mix of arbitrary channel formats.

- **Designs for Ambiences in Open-World Games**—There is a lot that goes into the ambiance of a game—more than most gamers will realize! This chapter provides an overview of the sorts of tools that have been implemented in the Dunia engine that powers the Far Cry games.

- **Distance-Delayed Sounds**—See how the speed of sound can increase the audio immersion of your game and how to implement a distance delay effect, with examples in both Unity and Unreal Engine.

- **Implementing Volume Sliders**—It is so easy to get volume sliders wrong, and so many games do it wrong. This chapter describes what happens when volume sliders go wrong, why it happens, and how to do them right!

- **Introduction to DSP Prototyping**—Python is an immensely practical language, and one which has a wealth of tools and libraries available for experimenting with authoring DSP effects. Learn techniques to experiment quickly with DSP algorithms in Python before implementing them in your game engine.

- **Life Cycle of Game Audio**—Track the lifetime of the audio designers on a large project. See what challenges they face at each step in the production pipeline and the sorts of tools that they use to improve their lives.

- **Multithreading for Game Audio**—Using multiple threads is one of the cornerstones of an audio engine. This chapter builds up a multithreaded audio engine from first principles.

- **Note-Based Music Systems**—We so rarely reach for note-based music systems like MIDI in modern times. But, with a proper back end and proper tooling (and a bit of music theory), a note-based music system can be extraordinarily effective.

- **Obstruction, Occlusion, and Propagation**—See how propagation techniques can be used to improve immersion in a game and how they can be used to solve obstruction and occlusion problems.

- **Practical Applications of Simple Filters**—Introduces the biquad filter and several use cases for it. This chapter is heavy on practical uses and implementations.

- **Practical Approaches to Virtual Acoustics**—Introduces a signal chain for a game audio engine that describes the acoustics of a room with high accuracy and with a heavy dose of practicality. This chapter also discusses using diffusion as a solution to obstruction and occlusion issues.

- **Realtime Audio Mixing**—Learn a number of very useful techniques that have been used in shipping games to control the mix and make sure that the most important sounds are what the player hears.

- **Synchronizing Action-Based Gameplay to Music**—It can be scary for a game designer to let the music engine drive the timing of the action. But with the application of the techniques in this chapter, it can be extremely powerful and empowering by creating a connection between the audio and the video.

- **Techniques for Improving Data Drivability of Gameplay Audio Code**—Learn how programming patterns originally designed for user interfaces can be applied to audio code, and those applications can increase the power that your sound designers have to control the audio.

- **Understanding Wwise Virtual Voices**—The virtual voice system in Wwise is a complex beast with a number of edge cases. This chapter describes it all in detail and helps you to make an informed decision about how to use them.

- **Using Orientation to Add Emphasis to a Mix**—See how to model microphone pickup patterns in code in order to emphasize the important sounds in a mix based on the relative position and orientations of the listener and the sound source.

This volume has four more chapters than Volume 1, which makes me incredibly happy. The sheer variety of topics is overwhelming, and we still haven't plumbed the depths of the collected knowledge of the contributors. Nevertheless, we are slowly but surely making a dent in that 20,000-page monster tome that I alluded to in the Foreword to Volume 1.

PARTING THOUGHTS

It is books like this that provide a medium both for audio programmers to share their knowledge, and for up-and-coming engineers and sound designers to learn what audio programming is all about. There are so many aspects to audio programming, and the amount of enthusiasm that the community has shown is inspiring. I hope that this book is as inspiring to you, the reader, as it has been to me.

Guy Somberg

Acknowledgments

Thanks to the awesome community of audio programmers who have sprung up in the past few years.

Thanks once again to Tyler Thompson, who has now hired me four times and always made sure that I had time for audio code. (But never enough.)

Thanks to David Steinwedel, Jordan Stock, Andy Martin, Pam Aranoff, Michael Kamper, Michael Csurics, and Erika Escamez—the sound designers who have accompanied me on my audio programming journey, and from whom I have learned and grown.

Thanks to Rick Adams, Jessica Vega, and the whole team from CRC Press, who followed up, followed through, answered obscure questions involving text formatting and Unicode characters, and made this volume a reality.

Thanks also to my wife Emily, who has always been my number one fan and whose passion and patience with my work on this book has been invaluable.

Editor

Guy Somberg has been programming audio engines for his entire career. From humble beginnings writing a low-level audio mixer for slot machines, he quickly transitioned to writing game audio engines for all manner of games. He has written audio engines that shipped AAA games such as *Hellgate: London*, *Bioshock 2*, and *The Sims 4*, as well as smaller titles such as *Minion Master, Tales From the Borderlands*, and *Game of Thrones*. Somberg has also given several talks at the Game Developer Conference and at CppCon.

When he's not programming or writing game audio programming books, he can be found at home reading, playing video games, and playing the flute.

Contributors

Robert Bantin has been writing audio software for most of his career. While at school, he was an active member of the Amiga demo scene and helped put together a handful of demos. At university, he studied acoustics and digital signal processing, and upon graduating was contacted by Philips ASA Labs in Eindhoven in order to recruit him for the MPEG technology program. After returning to the United Kingdom, he worked at Thorn-EMI on their Sensaura game audio middleware, and later at Yamaha and FXpansion on several well-known DAW plug-ins such as BFD2. He also wrote some of the first shippable code at Auro Technologies. Bantin has worked on a number of AAA games such as Guitar Hero Live and Dirt 4. He has also spoken at Develop Conference in Brighton. When he's not programming, he can be found at home building models with his son, shredding on extended range electric guitars, and playing video games when nobody's looking.

Stéphane Beauchemin's education pathway could seem quite chaotic. He made several program changes: from music to science, to music, to mathematics, to music technology, and finally to computer science. Given that he now works as an audio programmer in the video game industry, suddenly all that makes sense. Beauchemin has been working for more than 10 years as an audio programmer. He began his career at Audiokinetic as a software developer, and he is now working for a major gaming company as the lead audio programmer.

Matthieu Dirrenberger has been a sound programmer for 8 years at Ubisoft Montreal. He mainly worked on the Far Cry brand with the Dunia engine. After an MSc in math and graphic computing at the University of Strasbourg, he quickly started to work in the video game industry as a sound specialist. Over the last 12 years, he developed different projects related to audio: VST synthesizers, mastering effects based on Motorola DSP, and MIDI sequencer based on eLua platform. As a musician, he released few electronic and death metal albums (last-to-date Karnon second EP).

Michael Filion has been developing video games for his entire career of 10 years with Ubisoft Québec, with the majority in the world of audio. When explaining his work and passion to friends and family, he often oversimplifies by stating that he is "responsible for ensuring the bleeps and bloops are functional in video games." He has had the opportunity to work with many talented people on games such as *Assassin's Creed*, *Child of Light*, and *Tom Clancy's The Division*. In between delivering great titles, he enjoys traveling with his daughter and searching out different craft brews from around the world.

Florian Füsslin had a 10-year music background when entering the game industry with Crytek in 2006. During the past 12 years, he has contributed to the audio pipeline of CRYENGINE and shipped all major Crytek titles including the Crysis Franchise, Ryse: Son of Rome, several Warface Missions, the VR titles The Climb and Robinson, and the Early Access title HUNT: Showdown. Being a dedicated gamer and living the passion for game audio, he is leading the audio team in the role of an audio director as well as teaching game audio at the Hochschule Darmstadt and School of Audio Engineering in Frankfurt.

Jorge Garcia has been working in the audio field for more than a decade under different roles in broadcasting, music, and more recently, games. He has participated in the programming and engineering of game franchises such as Raiders of the Broken Planet, FIFA, and Guitar Hero. His passions, interests, and skill set span from R&D to digital signal processing, tools, and engine design and development.

Ethan Geller is an audio programmer working on the Unreal Engine, which is used by several games. Prior to working at Epic Games, Geller has worked at Dolby and PlayStation, received his master's degree from CCRMA at Stanford, and went to undergrad for music composition at Indiana University. Geller's primary research interests are HRTF personalization, optimal filter design, and wave field capture/synthesis. He also plays drums.

Nathan Harris graduated with a degree in computer science from the University of British Columbia, and with no delay launched into a career that combined his passion for music and his aptitude as a programmer—developing audio in the video game industry. Seeking a greater challenge, Harris shifted focus from game development to middleware and moved to Montreal to work at Audiokinetic—a company at the forefront of the industry whose technology is deployed in hundreds of games across the globe. As part of the research and development team, Harris is one of the masterminds behind the latest generation of 3D audio products including Wwise Spatial Audio and Wwise Reflect. Harris has a black belt in Brazilian jiu jitsu, and when not on the mats or solving problems for tomorrow's most immersive video games, he enjoys building gadgets for brewing beer and roasting coffee.

Charlie Huguenard is a musician who learned how to code. For about a decade, he made video games and other interactive experiences at companies such as Telltale Games, Magic Leap, Anki, and Funomena. As the Sound Technology Lead at Meow Wolf, he is working on new software and hardware tools to realize large-scale, immersive, interactive sound installations. In his free time, he can be found poking around the wilderness with a backpack and a hammock or taking in the beauty of the southwest from the highway.

Akihiro Minami has been an audio programmer at Square Enix for his entire career. He designed and implemented the audio engine and tools adopted in many Square Enix titles including Final Fantasy XV, Final Fantasy XIV, and Final Fantasy XIII trilogy.

Jon Mitchell has worked as an audio programmer for United Front Games, Radical Entertainment, and Codemasters, and is currently working with the wonderfully talented and friendly people at Blackbird Interactive. He lives in Vancouver with his partner and two adorable (but destructive) cats.

Dan Murray wants to live in a world where every game sounds as good as it can; to that end, he spends his time preaching about performance, complaining about compression, and disagreeing with sound designers. When he's not waiting for link.exe you can find Murray at the bouldering hall. He wants to be a real audio programmer when he grows up.

Tomas Neumann discovered his passion for interactive audio while he was studying computer graphics in Braunschweig, Germany. For more than 5 years, he worked at Crytek prominently on the Crysis series. He started as a junior programmer, and when he left as the technical audio lead, he had developed systems and workflows which are still in use in CryEngine and its licensed games. In 2010, he joined Blizzard as the first dedicated audio programmer and contributed to Overwatch and World of Warcraft to eliminate the gap between the game and the audio ranging from asset deployment, multiple sound features, a criteria-based voice-system, localization, and more.

Yuichi Nishimatsu is an audio programmer at Square Enix. He has been involved in major Square Enix titles such as Dragon Quest XI, Final Fantasy XIV, and Kingdom Hearts HD 1.5 Remix. He is also a recreational viola player who loves video game music.

Kory Postma obtained his BS in physics (summa cum laude) and his MS in computer science from Washington University in St. Louis. He has worked on military simulations, scheduling systems, and data analysis for Boeing, The Johns Hopkins University Applied Physics Laboratory, and the USGS Landsat program. He is a shareholder and a programmer for Squad by Offworld Industries, Ltd., based out of Vancouver, British Columbia, Canada. When Postma is not working, he spends his time with his wife and four children or playing video games with friends or the kids. He donates his time and/or money to charitable causes, especially in the Philippines.

Nic Taylor has 10 years working experience on audio engines in the video game industry. He started programming writing casual games for Windows in the late 1990s as well as audio plug-ins for his own music projects. Taylor's first audio engine integration from scratch was for Red 5 Studio's custom MMO engine, which was an early adopter of Wwise. Taylor has since done other audio engine integrations and feature work using well-known engines. He currently works at Blizzard Entertainment splitting his time between audio and engine work. On the side, he continues to produce music applying his interest in DSP and room acoustics.

Colin Walder earned a BSc in physics with space science and technology and an MA in music technology. He sought to realize his thesis "Intelligent

Audio for Games" by entering the industry as an audio programmer at Free Radical Design. In the 12 years since he has had the good fortune to work on a number of AAA games, including Haze, Max Payne 3, GTA V, Red Dead Redemption 2, The Witcher 3: Wild Hunt, and Cyberpunk 2077. Throughout his career, Walder has passionately sought to promote the role of audio in games and sought to develop technologies that allow interactive audio to be implemented and experienced in new ways. He is currently lead programmer for audio and localization at CD Projekt Red.

CHAPTER 1

Life Cycle of Game Audio

Florian Füsslin

Crytek GmbH

CONTENTS

1.1 PREAMBLE

Two years have passed since I had the pleasure and opportunity to contribute to this book series – two years in which game audio has made another leap forward, both creatively and technically. Key contributors and important components to this leap are the audio middleware software companies and their design tools, which continue to shift power from audio programmers to audio designers. But as always, with great power comes great responsibility, so a structured approach to audio design and implementation has never been more important. This chapter will provide ideas, insight, and overview of the audio production cycle from an audio designer's perspective.

1.2 AUDIO LIFE CYCLE OVERVIEW

"In the beginning, there was nothing." This pithy biblical phrase describes the start of a game project. Unlike linear media, there are no sound effects or dialog recorded on set we can use as a starting point. This silence is a bleak starting point, and it does not look better on the technical side. We might have a game engine running with an audio middleware, but we still need to create `AudioEntity` components, set `GameConditions`, and define `GameParameters`.

In this vacuum, it can be hard to determine where to start. Ideally, audio is part of a project from day one and is a strong contributor to the game's overall vision, so it makes sense to follow the production phases of a project and tailor it for our audio requirements. Game production is usually divided in three phases: preproduction, production, and postproduction. The milestone at the end of each phase functions as the quality gate to continue the development.

- Preproduction → Milestone First Playable (Vertical Slice)

- Production → Milestone Alpha (Content Complete)

- Postproduction → Milestone Beta (Content Finalized)

The ultimate goal of this process is to build and achieve the audio vision alongside the project with as little throwaway work as possible. The current generation of game engines and audio middleware software cater to this requirement. Their architecture allows changing, iterating, extending, and adapting the audio easily, often in real time with the game and audio middleware connected over the network.

All of these tools treat the audio content and the audio structure separately. So, instead of playing back an audio file directly, the game triggers a container (e.g. `AudioEvent`) which holds the specific `AudioAssets` and all relevant information about its playback behavior such as volume, positioning, pitch, or other parameters we would like to control in real time. This abstraction layer allows to change the event data (e.g. how a sound attenuates over distance) without touching the audio data (e.g. the actual audio asset) and vice versa. We talk about a data-driven system where the audio container provides all the necessary components to play back in the game engine. Figure 1.1 shows how this works with the audio controls editor in CryEngine.

In CryEngine, we are using an `AudioControlsEditor`, which functions like a patch bay where all parameters, actions, and events from the game are listed and communicated. Once we create a connection and wire the respective parameter, action, or event to the one on the audio middleware side, this established link can often remain for the rest of the production while we continue to tweak and change the underlying values and assets.

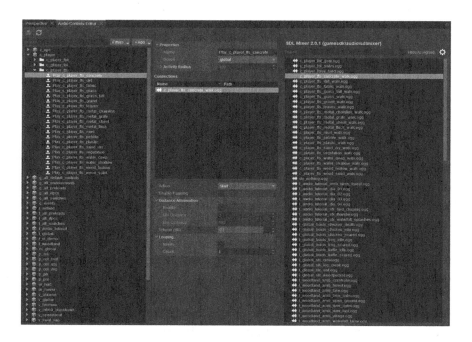

FIGURE 1.1   The audio controls editor in CryEngine.

1.2.1 Audio Asset Naming Convention

Staying on top of a hundred `AudioControls`, several hundred `AudioEvents`, and thousands of containing `AudioAssets` requires a fair amount of discipline and a solid naming convention. We try to keep the naming consistent throughout the pipeline. So the name of the `AudioTrigger` represents the name of the `AudioEvent` (which in turn reflects the name of the `AudioAssets` it uses), along with the behavior (e.g. Start/Stop of an `AudioEvent`). With the use of one letter identifier (e.g. `w_` for weapon) and abbreviation to keep the filename length in check (e.g. `pro_` for projectile), we are able to keep a solid overview of the audio content of our projects.

1.2.2 Audio Asset Production

In general, the production chain of an audio event follows three stages:

- Create audio asset
    An audio source recorded with a microphone or taken from an existing library, edited and processed in a DAW, and exported into the appropriate format (e.g. `boss_music_stinger.wav, 24 bit, 48 kHz, mono`).
- Create audio event
    An exported audio asset implemented into the audio middleware in a way a game engine can execute it (e.g. `Play_Boss_Music_Stinger`)
- Create audio trigger
    An in-game entity which triggers the audio event (e.g. "Player enters area trigger of boss arena").

While this sequence of procedures is basically true, the complex and occasionally chaotic nature of game production often requires deviating from this linear pipeline. We can, therefore, think of this chain as an endless circle, where starting from the audio trigger makes designing the audio event and audio asset much easier. The more we know about how our sound is supposed to play out in the end, the more granular and exact we can design the assets to cater for it.

For example, we designed, exported, and implemented a deep drum sound plus a cymbal for our music stinger when the player enters the boss arena. While testing the first implementation in the game, we realized that the stinger happens at the same moment that the boss does its loud scream. While there are many solutions such as delaying the scream until the stinger has worn off, we decided to redesign the asset and get rid of the cymbal to not interfere with the frequency spectrum of the scream to begin with.

1.3 PREPRODUCTION

1.3.1 Concept and Discovery Phase— Let's Keep Our Finger on the Pulse!

Even in the early stages of development, there are determining factors that help us to define the technical requirements, choose the audio palette, and draft the style of the audio language. For example, the genre (shooter, RTS, adventure game), the number of players (single player, small-scale multiplayer, MMO), the perspective (first-person, third-person), or the setting (sci-fi, fantasy, urban) will all contribute to the choices that you will be making.

Because we might not have a game running yet, we have to think about alternative ways to prototype. We want to get as much information about the project as possible, and we can find a lot of valuable material by looking at other disciplines.

For example, our visually-focused colleagues use concept art sketches as a first draft to envision the mood, look, and feel of the game world. Concept art provides an excellent foundation to determine the requirements for the environment, character movement, setting, and aesthetic.

Similarly, our narrative friends have documents outlining the story, timeline, and main characters. These documents help to envision the story arc, characters' motivations, language, voice, and dialog requirements. Some studios will put together moving pictures or video reels from snippets of the existing concept art or from other media, which gives us an idea about pacing, tension, and relief. These cues provide a great foundation for music requirements.

Combining all this available information should grant us enough material to structure and document the project in audio modules, and to set the audio quality bar.

1.3.2 Audio Modules

Audio modules function both as documentation and as a structural hub. While the user perceives audio as one experience, we like to split it in the three big pillars to manage the production: dialog, sound effects, and music. In many games, most of the work is required on the sound effects side, so a more granular structure with audio modules helps to stay on top. Development teams usually work cross-discipline and therefore tend to structure their work in features, level sections, characters, or missions, which is not necessarily in line how we want to structure the audio project.

Here are some examples of audio modules we usually create in an online wiki format and update as we move through the production stages:

- **Cast**—characters and AI-related information
- **Player**—player-relevant information
- **Levels**—missions and the game world
- **Environment**—possible player interactions with the game world
- **Equipment**—tools and gadgets of the game characters
- **Interface**—HUD-related requirements
- **Music**—music-relevant information
- **Mix**—mixing-related information

Each module has subsections containing a brief overview on the creative vision, a collection of examples and references, technical setup for creating the content, and a list of current issues.

1.3.3 The Audio Quality Bar

The audio quality bar functions as the anchor point for the audio vision. We want to give a preview how the final game is going to sound. We usually achieve this by creating an audio play based on the available information, ideally featuring each audio module.

Staying within a linear format, utilizing the DAW, we can draw from the full palette of audio tools, effects, and plugins to simulate pretty much any acoustic behavior. This audio play serves three purposes: First, it creates an audible basis for the game to discuss all audio requirements from a creative or technical perspective. Second, it shows the palette and tools we are going to need to achieve the very same audio vision in the final software. Third, it generates shippable quality audio assets we can implement into the audio middleware for the first in-game prototypes in the upcoming milestone.

1.3.4 The Audio Prototypes

The audio prototypes function as test scenarios for the different audio modules. Unlike the audio quality bar, we use the audio tools and the audio middleware software available in the actual game engine to achieve the audio vision. We build small test cases with a clear focus to define the triggers, parameters, and conditions we want to extract from the game for the audio middleware software to respond to. We also use this to establish a naming convention and folder structure for assets, events, and triggers, as well as the audio signal flow (e.g. mixing bus structure) and technical setup of the audio data (e.g. memory pools, sound bank preloading).

The feature prototypes also serve as a common ground and reference across all game disciplines to describe, test, and verify all feature-related issues and improvements.

Here are some examples of audio prototype scenarios we build and update as we move through the production stages. As most of them are very helpful for all disciplines, it is not necessarily the audio team that creates and maintains these:

- **Surface types** – material types available. See Figure 1.2 for an example.

- **Reverb areas** – environmental reverbs. See Figure 1.3 for an example.

- **Distance alley** – a corridor with distance markers for audio attenuation. See Figure 1.4 for an example.

- **Equipment zoo** – available gadgets and tools the player can interact with

- **Vehicle zoo** – available vehicles the player can interact with

- **Environment zoo** – available game world interactions

- **NPC zoo** – available non-player characters

While all disciplines are prototyping during the concept phase, the game design team requires the fastest turnaround for their ideas, including requests for audio. These ideas can often change faster than audio can support them. By the time we have designed an audio asset, put it into an event, and created a trigger for it, it may already be outdated or need major overhaul. In order to not continuously play catchup, we often produce the

FIGURE 1.2   An example of a surface-type stage.

FIGURE 1.3   An example of reverb areas.

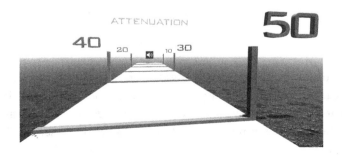

FIGURE 1.4   An example of a distance alley.

sounds by recording ourselves for an almost instantaneous asset and keep audio middleware setup and parameters as simple as possible. Once the trigger is implemented and we see the placeholder sound working, we can improve the asset and work on the audio middleware setup accordingly.

We usually follow a layered approach to audio design:

- Feedback

- Immersion

- Emotion

- Experience

For *feedback*, we describe a simple acoustic event that something has happened. This applies to the self-recorded quick placeholder as well as other debug audio such as white noise or beeps.

Take an example from game audio history: Let's think of the short beep sound in PONG from 1972. It triggers whenever the player reflects the ball or the ball bounces at the edge of the screen. Not very beautiful, but it adds an additional sense and readability layer to our game. Modern games are much more detailed and come with a lot more narrative, lore, and story—our beloved pixels from PONG matured into Andre Agassi and Boris Becker on a Wimbledon tennis court. That requires our beep sound to follow that *immersion* and morph into the typical flick sound a tennis ball does when we hit it with a racket. This is the stage where we probably want to alter the sound based on game parameters such as travel speed or direction as well as completely switch it based on the type of strike such as backhand or forehand. On top, we want to enter the *emotional* layer and use information such as the current score to adapt the sound whether the protagonist is leading or losing. Last but not least, there is an *experience* layer, which targets the user actually playing the game. This includes things such as the controller rumble when hitting the ball or mixing the racket hit sounds louder over time depending on the length of the current rally.

While we are still in the preproduction phase, we want to emphasize on the options, possibilities, and richness that audio can bring to the game. The audio prototype stages and zoo levels are a good showcase to advocate and advertise our ideas to the rest of the development team as we are moving toward the first important milestone.

1.3.5 First Playable

The preproduction phase usually ends with a first playable version of the game: a limited and condensed vertical slice showcasing the potential of the final product. We therefore focus on the core mechanics: a small but in-depth set of features which outline how the game is going to be experienced. Taking a first-person shooter, for example, we will have the actions for gunplay present (select, aim, fire, melee, reload, holster), but maybe we just show it working one gun (assault rifle) with two fire modes (rapid and single) and two ammunition types (full metal jacket and blanks). The final product will consist of a lot more weapons with a wide array of attachments, fire modes, magazines, and reload styles, but it is enough to prove that we are able to build the system to begin with.

For audio, this means we have a stable audio implementation and tools available to place, define, execute, and debug our `AudioEvents`, and cover the feedback layer, as well as a solid idea of the immersion layer in regard to asset design.

It can totally happen that a sound that was designed and set up for the vertical slice stands up to expectations and ships in the final version. But we usually expect that audio is going to follow the iterative nature of game development and will change and adapt during the upcoming phases. That said, we still want audio to be a very strong contributor to this milestone and spearheading quality as much as possible even in this early stage of production.

1.3.6 Preproduction Summary

By the end of the preproduction cycle, we want to have a solid understanding of the game's creative and technical requirements. The audio modules provide documentation and break down the workload into manageable tasks. The audio quality bar provides us with an audio vision we can use to start implementing into the actual game environment using our chosen audio middleware. With the vertical slice at the end of the milestone, we completed the asset production cycle once from concept to asset creation to implementation and mixing. Running through this process gives us a solid estimate of how long it will take to complete the rest of the audio entering the next stage.

1.4 PRODUCTION

1.4.1 Proof of Concept Phase—Let's Build the Game!

In production, we build on the audio modules that we previously prototyped during the preproduction stage. The goal is to get full audio coverage and all audio modules implemented into the game properly. The nature of this phase requires a fair amount of iteration and flexibility. We have a solid idea what we would like to achieve, but as the game takes shape, we will need to solve challenges which can result in creative and technical redesign.

The focus, therefore, shifts toward the creative use of the audio middleware and designing the event and data structures of the final game. We want to keep the asset design representative with a strong feedback layer for solid audio readability, but put the most effort into the iconic elements and signature sounds of each audio module to establish the immersion and emotional layer. These iconic sounds function as the reference point for mixing of each audio module. By mixing everything according to the EBU R128 Loudness Recommendation Standard,[1] we can maintain a solid premix throughout the whole production, which allows both the QA and game design departments to give valuable feedback on how the game sounds pretty much at all times.

The audio prototype levels remain the key for solid progress: they allow us to focus solely on one audio module from a creative and technical perspective without getting distracted, blocked, or cluttered by the shape and status of the actual game. This focus is especially helpful to make members of other disciplines understand our audio requirements and to provide a common ground where everybody can run feature tests or performance profiling.

Therefore, instead of looking at the full game where there is a chance of getting distracted, we review just one feature and can clarify immediately what might still be missing, show potential issues live, and verify that previously discussed improvements and bug fixing were actually successful.

One way to speed up the iteration process is to invent a clear placeholder language, introduced via a console command or debug key. It replaces the actual game audio with a spoken version of the event or audio trigger, making it very easy to verify implementation, especially for non-audio people. For example, NPCs can voice the state they are in (`see_player_first_time`), character dialog can speak the event name or the trigger (`player_m01_ab02_mission_objective`), sound effects can speak the action (`wood_door_open`), or music signaling the intensity level and current piece playing (`Intro_Ambient_Low`).

We also establish special debug placeholder sounds which we trigger when a certain game state or game parameter is missing or not specified. For example, when the player character walks on an undefined surface type, it will trigger a beep sound instead of footsteps to highlight that this hasn't been properly tagged yet. Or when setting up a new weapon, we populate the event with obviously placeholder assets to create the final event structure, while still highlighting the assets which have not been designed yet without delaying functionality testing.

We continue to work on asset design and implementation improvements, now putting more emphasis on the immersive and emotional component. We try to get toward a shippable audio experience and reduce the dependencies on other game disciplines. Ideally, we want all the information available before we finalize our asset design and audio setup. Asking the right questions and demanding the appropriate answers can help a great deal to achieve this.

For example, ambiences can be finalized once we know about the game play space, time of day, and weather conditions. Footsteps can be finished once we know about the shoe types, walking cadences, travel speeds, and surface types. Movement Foley can be completed as soon as we know the variety of character clothing and player actions. Game world physics such as collisions and destruction can be designed once we know the amount of player and world interaction.

There will remain enough gaps and holes where we won't get a decisive answer until the content is actually completed, but it should help to narrow down the possibilities and options to a manageable number of remaining tweaks and adjustments when this phase of development comes to an end.

1.4.2 The Alpha Milestone

The production phase usually ends with declaring the game to be content complete. This means all features are working and we are able to play the product from start to finish without game-breaking issues such as a software crash or progress blocker. For audio, this means we have completed a bulk of the work: we have designed all required assets, implemented all the relevant audio triggers, and made sure that all game parameters are set and updating correctly. The audio mix is in a representative state, which means we can fully focus on the audio experience while we enter the last phase of the development.

1.4.3 Production Summary

By the end of the production cycle, we want to have all audio events and all audio triggers available and working, ideally in a shippable state. Each audio module has received a premix pass for consistency, and the overall mix is balanced to the EBU R128 Loudness Standard.

We also want to have a solid understanding of which audio modules still need attention, and a good idea of the bugs, issues, and improvements we would like to tackle in the next stage.

1.5 POSTPRODUCTION

1.5.1 Optimization, Beautification, and Mixing— Let's Stay on Top of Things!

During the postproduction phase, the focus shifts to the overall audio experience of the whole game. We are still working on the audio modules, fixing bugs, cleaning up the project, optimizing performance, and polishing assets. However, the main goal is to establish the final mix and to declare a release candidate which eventually becomes the final product.

The Audio Prototype levels continue to play an important role, as we are now utilizing them for sanity checks. Whenever possible, we utilize automated testing and log potential audio warnings. For example, spawn the player with all tools and gadgets and execute the "use" action, triggering the respective audio events. Or a console command which automatically plays all dialog lines of a story character or cycles through all available NPC states and variations. We can script a fly-through to test all reverb areas working properly, and to make sure ambiences are playing correctly. At this point, QA is a big contributor to spot audio issues as well as the (automated) search for errors or warnings in the audio logs from playtest sessions.

All of this testing is critical, but the most important part is the final mix, which requires that the audio designers play the full game just like the end users would. We usually perform mixing in tandem, so one person plays and one person mixes with the audio middleware connected to the game in real time. Whenever possible, we try to mix as a trio, with one additional passive listener taking notes and entering issues to the bug tracker we encounter. The trio has proven useful, especially when mixing in VR with headphones, which only the person wearing the head-mounted display can fully experience. The uneven number also helps in breaking disputes in mixing decisions, especially those where it is a matter of taste. In addition, we have an open door policy, so everybody is welcome to join the mixing sessions. The final say on mixing decisions remains with the audio team, but feedback from other disciplines can be an inspiring influence, or can put a finger on a spot we might not have touched otherwise.

At the end of the postproduction phase, making changes becomes more and more restrictive. Luckily, audio is usually considered risk-free as the audio middleware pre-compiles the data including an error check. As the project nears completion, we mix from only one machine (and therefore only one changing factor), which allows us to mix the product almost until the very last moment.

1.5.2 The Beta Milestone

Usually, the postproduction phase ends with the declaration of a release candidate, which is tested against the technical certification requirements. If it passes, this version is declared the gold master and becomes the final product. While it is quite common to continue to work on the product and fix the remaining issues for a patch on the actual release date, audio is usually not considered a part of this process and therefore our job is done.

1.5.3 Postproduction Summary

Audio in games caters to three things: acoustic feedback for the player, building immersion of a believable game world, and helping to drive the emotions of the player. To really finish the audio for a product, it needs to be in this final and fully playable state because only then we can finalize what is perceived by the consumer as one audio experience.

1.6 CONCLUSION

There has been no project in my career we hadn't wished to have started things earlier, defined something more clearly, or just given it another round of polish. But there is only so much time in a project's development cycle! Therefore, the time spent during the beginning of the life cycle of game audio thinking about the layout, must-haves, nice to haves, and possible one-way streets is equally important as the time spent building the actual content or toward the end of the production when polishing the last steps right before finalization.

That's why regardless of the length, complexity, and size of a project, the tools to help stay on top of the flood of content are to generate structures, build modules, create feature and test levels, set production stages, and define quality gates. These tools are especially important for games with longer development cycles, where features and scope of a product can change quite drastically, and we constantly need to adjust schedules, deliverables, and priorities. Following the production phases and adding an audio-specific definition, we increase awareness and transparency for the audio team and the dependencies which improve the overall communication between the audio and the development team.

Done properly, the lifecycle of audio will be never ending, as coming out of one product just means we take over the structure, the assets, the setup and all the experience we gained, all the lessons we learned, and all the things we still want to accomplish to dive into the next audio journey.

1.7 POSTSCRIPT

Making games and game audio remains a very complex task. There are many experts and specialists required to get a product build and shipped, and it requires each and everyone involved to make use of all available skills: social, creative, and technical. Making games can be challenging at the very least, hard at times, and sometimes even purely frustrating. But if you see it through, it is most exciting and satisfying to see a project form and the audio vision come to life. Therefore, I want to take this opportunity to thank everyone in my team and at the company for trying to achieve this day by day.

NOTE

1 https://tech.ebu.ch/docs/r/r128.pdf.

CHAPTER 2

A Rare Breed

The Audio Programmer

Stéphane Beauchemin

CONTENTS

2.1 AUDIO PROGRAMMERS—THE UNICORN MYTH

I am always amazed by how audio programmers are perceived by the people who are looking for one. How do you find an audio programmer when you don't really know what is the audio programmer role? Even when you talk to different audio programmers you realize that there are many definitions for the role, and if it was not enough, all of them have a different educational background. If you add on the top of that the resource scarcity you may come to the conclusion that audio programmers are just like unicorns: mythical beasts that everyone wants, but which don't actually exist.

While talking to other audio programmers at GDC 2017, I realized that a clarification was badly needed, and I was encouraged by my peers to write this chapter to educate people about the role. In this chapter, I will try to depict a clear picture of the audio programmer's role so you can have an understanding of what an audio programmer's day-to-day work is like. At the end of this chapter, you should be able draw the composite sketch of the perfect audio programmer, and it won't look like a unicorn (Figure 2.1).

FIGURE 2.1 An audio programmer.

We will begin by getting an understanding of audio in video game development. Once we have established the different areas where audio is needed in video game development, we will break down the different subjects of audio programming. Then, we will discuss the relationship of the audio programmer to the other members of the team: sound designers, other programmers, and producers. Finally, we will talk about good strategies for audio feature development.

2.2 AUDIO IN VIDEO GAME DEVELOPMENT

2.2.1 Sound as Gameplay Feedback

What is the purpose of sound in a video game? What is the importance of sound in a video game? Those simple questions could be answered in length. However, I will try to provide a simple answer: sound in a video game is nothing more than gameplay feedback to the player. Just like video or haptic feedback (like controller rumble), sound is a sensory feedback that is delivered to the player. The different stimuli created by the video game system are picked up by the brain, which analyzes it so that the player can react and input an action into the game with the controller.

Now, think of all the different types of gameplay feedback that can travel through sound. With dialogue, information can be given about a mission. With 3D sound positioning, the player can know where their enemies are hiding. With music, a mood or a feeling is established. With simple audio cues, the player can recognize that he is getting close to danger or that there is an important gameplay element in the surrounding area. Those are only a few examples, but you can see that the gameplay information given by sound is only bounded by the creativity of game designers and audio designers—in other words, it is pretty much infinite.

2.2.2 Sound Is Ever-Present, but Behind the Curtain

Sound is always present in a video game. When the game is silent, it is usually an artistic choice from the audio director, or simply a technical constraint (i.e. during loading screen, it might be better not to use streaming bandwidth for music so the level loads faster). With all the information that can be broadcasted using sound, how do you keep the interest of the player in the soundtrack of your game? How do you keep the player from getting bored or—even worse—annoyed?

Games that don't take time to provide sound variations for certain common events risk this boredom. Hearing the same sound over and over again can become very frustrating and make you want simply turn off the sound completely. Interestingly, most players will quickly recognize that the audio in a game is poorly implemented, but few will actually acknowledge the quality of audio when it is done well. The audio will simply make the game feel more cohesive and this is why working in audio for video games can be ungratifying.

2.2.3 Sound Is Everywhere

Sound touches nearly every system of a game: gameplay, AI, VFX, cinematic sequences, menus, animations, physics, etc. It is probably easier to list the subjects that don't involve audio. Accordingly, the audio department needs to interact with a lot of disciplines. Given all of these connections to other departments, the scale and complexity of the audio can quickly become unmanageable if the audio department does not take care. The audio programmer is one key factor in keeping this complexity and scale under control—although by no means the only factor. Let's dive into the audio programming role definition.

2.3 WHAT IS AN AUDIO PROGRAMMER, AND WHO NEEDS ONE?

At the GDC 2014 talk entitled "Lessons Learned from a Decade of Audio Programming," Guy Somberg discusses the difficulty that companies have finding audio programmers [1]. Why are audio programmers so hard to find? It turns out that the answer to that lies in how you define the role of the audio programmer. It is fascinating that some people are looking for an audio programmer without really knowing what role they are trying to fill. Contrariwise, as an audio programmer, I often find myself doing the job of a tools programmer, a gameplay programmer, or a systems programmer. Unless you are developing your own sound engine, there are really few tasks that can be considered pure audio programming.

2.3.1 Types of Audio Programming Tasks

Being an audio programmer in the context of a game production can mean a lot of things. Let's examine some of the different areas of audio programming in the context of a video game production, and identify the main challenges.

2.3.1.1 Audio Tools
Audio tools are the glue in between the different parts of your audio integration pipeline. From the moment a wave file has been exported from a

DAW to the moment it is ready for playback in your game engine there are a lot of steps. You can see an audio tool as something that will free the sound designers' time from repetitive tasks and let them do creative work instead. These tools range from small to medium programs that will make the audio integration process a cohesive experience.

Most of these tools simply convey data from one step of the pipeline to another, and they are conceptually easy to understand and usually easy to program. They are often made with scripting language (like python) or a managed programming language like C#. Those languages in particular are good for audio tools because there are a lot of libraries available to deal with managing files on disk, XML and JSON parsing, versioning system control (Perforce, Git, Subversion, etc.), and audio processing libraries. It is important to select a language that offers enough features out of the box, because you want to get the job done with as little effort as possible without reinventing the wheel.

It is impossible to list all the particular tasks that audio tools need to accomplish because each project has different needs. A few examples of such tools are automated wav audio data import from sound engine to game engine, audio bank generation, audio data cooking, batch processing of wav files (normalization, DSP processing for dialogue, etc.), audio data reports, and so on.

Audio tools could be developed by the audio programmer or by a tools programmer. However, the audio programmer should still be the owner of the development to make sure that audio tools that are being developed fulfill their stated purpose. Audio tools have direct impact on the productivity of the sound designers, and to some extent on the productivity of the audio programmer. Normally, you are able to evaluate the quality of the audio tools by answering these questions:

- How much time does it take to a sound designer to put a sound in the game?

- How often do the audio tools break? Are the sound designers able to find the problem themselves without the need of a programmer?

- How much time do you spend debugging the audio pipeline on average per week?

That is why audio tools should be developed keeping in mind the following ideas: stability, ease of use, and low maintenance. I know that a tool that I wrote is successful when I can forget about that is used every day in the audio integration pipeline. Usually, this means that the tool is mature and I can focus on more interesting audio tasks.

2.3.1.2 Audio Integration

Once the sounds have been created by the sound designer, it is ready to be integrated into the game. Modern game engines are sufficiently data-driven such that most of the time, you don't need the intervention of a programmer to hook sounds up, and sound designers can integrate the sound into the game themselves.

However, there might be exotic gameplay moments where custom integration of sound will need to be done in code. For example, during a boss fight there may be special rules for triggering and stopping sound that are more complex than during normal gameplay. Even if your sound designers have access to a scripting language during these exotic moments, it can be faster to integrate—and often more performant—to hook in code directly. In these situations, the work of the audio programmer should be to provide a simple API for the gameplay programmers to integrate sound in the game code or game scripting language.

This way of working is the most efficient because it will usually take just minutes for a gameplay programmer to put sound hooks at the right place in code, while it could take hours for an audio programmer to understand the gameplay code and put the hook at the right place. Moreover, there are generally a lot more gameplay programmers than there are audio programmers on a production floor.

2.3.1.3 Audio Gameplay Systems

Audio gameplay systems are systems that dynamically affect sounds that are playing in the game. Simple examples include sound propagation (occlusion, obstruction, reverberation) and a virtual voices system, but there are more complex sound integration scenarios such as vehicle sounds, weather, crowds, ambiance, dynamic music, etc. The exact systems that you need to build depend greatly on the game you are making. Generally, the audio gameplay systems that need to be developed need to match the audio direction pillars and also the game direction pillars.

All audio gameplay systems should be consumer-facing features. We always want to achieve the highest-quality audio experience we can without falling into feature creep. It can be easy to get lost in these features, so it is important to measure their return on investment (ROI). We will talk about measuring ROI for audio features later in this chapter.

2.3.1.4 Handling Dialogue

There are two places where an audio programmer could be involved with dialogue: tools and run-time systems.

2.3.1.4.1 Dialogue Tools   Dialogue tools generally involve tasks such as: generating text-to-speech temporary files, automating the integration process of dialogue lines after a recording session, tracking what lines have not been recorded yet, managing a database of content for the writer, etc. I have seen AAA titles that have shipped with around 50,000 lines of dialogue (not including localized languages). There is also a trend in the industry toward creating branching storylines, which can explode the number of dialogue lines to record.

For games with more modest numbers of dialogue lines, it may be possible for the audio programmer to own the dialogue tools. However, as the number of lines balloons into the thousands or tens of thousands, it might be worthwhile to delegate the task of dialogue tools to a dedicated tools programmer.

One thing that often gets overlooked when dealing with dialogue is subtitles and localization. Most sound middleware already handles the localization of dialogue files and provides functionality to deal with switching out files. This integration makes the task easier, but managing all the data and providing a streamlined pipeline for this process can still be a challenge. Although localization happens at the end of a production, we will ideally want to start the localization process before the game is finished. Starting the process too early can introduce risk that the dialogue lines that are in process of being translated can be changed or removed. The tools that are provided to the localization and narrative team need to help them track obsolete lines or lines that have changed.

2.3.1.4.2 In-Game Dialogue System   While subtitles and localization can be a hard task on the tools side, they are relatively simple to handle at run-time. Most sound middleware already handles dialogue localization, and providing the text for the dialogue line that is currently playing for the subtitle is usually an easy task as well. However, these systems can become tricky when the dialogue is triggered systemically by the game. In these situations, sounds can be played at any time with any number of other sounds and dialogue lines.

A good solution to resolve this complexity is to implement a priority system to deal with concurrency. Any given character in the game can only deliver one line for the obvious reason that a character has only one mouth! It can also be annoying to have two different unrelated conversations playing at the same time. In those situations, we want the player to hear the conversation that provides the most important gameplay feedback. Using a dynamic mixing technique such as a ducking system can also help to alleviate these problems.

There are few things more annoying than a dialogue line that plays over and over again with no variation. One way to provide variation in the dialogue that the player hears is to implement a randomized or conditional dialogue container system that allows the system to intelligently select from among the available variations of a specific line. The system could be simply randomized, but providing some intelligence based on the gameplay conditions can create a far richer experience. For more information, there are interesting videos available on the subject on the GDC vault [2, 3].

2.3.1.5 Middleware Integration

Unless your studio has developed an in-house audio engine, the audio programmer will need to perform and maintain the integration of audio middleware into the game engine. Most major audio middleware such as FMOD Studio, Audiokinetic Wwise, and Criware ADX2 provide integration for game engines such as Unreal Engine or Unity. Those integrations are a good starting point to get you up and running, but there is still a lot of work to be done to customize it for your needs. If your game is using an in-house game engine, the middleware integrations for the well-known engines can be a good reference for the sorts of things that you need to implement.

One complaint that some people have is that audio middleware has become the de facto solution in the industry, and that fewer studios are developing internal audio engines. While a customized audio engine certainly can provide value for the right game, audio middleware engines are great tools for audio programmers, and prevent us having to reinvent the wheel each time we start on a new project.

2.3.1.6 Low-Level Audio Systems

Low-level audio systems are the ones that actually deal with things such as the audio hardware, file streaming, memory usage, mixing, codecs, hardware codec decompression, code vectorization, multithreading, and more. Some of these tasks require deep knowledge of digital audio but also require expertise with file I/O, interaction with hardware, and optimizing CPU performance.

Studios that implement their own audio engine will require a lot of this expertise, but those that use audio middleware have the luxury of outsourcing a majority of this work to the middleware company. However, this does not mean that an audio programmer working on a game production doesn't need to know about low-level audio systems, it simply means that these low-level tasks won't be the main focus.

It is not uncommon for AAA game production to modify the source code of a middleware audio engine for performance reasons or to add a custom feature. Even when using middleware, there are a number of systems that need to be integrated with the game engine such as routing file I/O requests and memory allocations through the game engine's systems.

2.3.1.7 DSP and Plugins

DSP programming involves manipulating the audio data in order to modify the signal and create audio effects. In an interactive medium such as a video game, it is important to be able to alter the audio signal based on what's happening in the game. Being able to code DSP effects is an important skill for the audio programmer, but it is not mandatory for many audio programmer roles. Nevertheless, even if DSP programming is not the primary focus, a good audio programmer needs to have at least a basic understanding of how digital signal processing works.

2.4 AUDIO PROGRAMMERS AND OTHER PROGRAMMERS

By now, you can see that audio programming tasks involve numerous different subjects, and you can see the gigantic scope of audio integration into a game project. With all the tasks that need doing, it is important to enlist the aid of the other programmers on the team to help take care of audio programming tasks and audio integration in the game.

Generally speaking, creating hooks for sound designers to play audio in the game should be a trivial task for other programmers: one line of code should be enough to let anyone in the game to trigger a sound. If it is more complex than that, the job of integrating audio in the game will fall back to the audio programmer. Similarly, debugging sounds that are not playing (by far the most common bug in any game project) also takes a lot of time. Providing audio debugging tools to other programmers and teaching them how to use them will free up valuable development time.

2.5 WORKING ON NEW AUDIO FEATURES

2.5.1 Measuring the Return on Investment (ROI)

One big challenge of working on audio features is measuring the ROI to determine whether or not it is worth implementing the feature in the first place. When discussing new features with an audio designer, it can seem that every single feature is critical. But if an audio programmer implements all of the requests from all the audio designers, the audio engine will become overly complex, and it will be more time-consuming both in implementation time and in cognitive overhead for the audio designers. Ultimately, though, what is important is the results in the game.

Before starting to work on any audio feature you must ask a number of questions. What will this new feature bring? Is there an easier way to achieve the same result? What is the impact on the player? How hard is this feature to use once the tools are in place?

Let's take as an example a sound obstruction/occlusion system. It seems that such a system is absolutely necessary for any 3D game, but that might not be absolutely true. What is important is whether or not an obstruction/occlusion system can give informational cues to the player. Being able to tell that an enemy is close or behind a wall may be crucial information, and the game will appear broken without any sort of obstruction system. On the other hand, if your game doesn't have any kind of stealth gameplay, then maybe it is not worth investing the time in an elaborate sound occlusion/obstruction system. That same development time could instead go toward building (for example) a dynamic music system. In order for an audio engine feature to be worthwhile, you must be able to link it to the gameplay of your game.

2.5.2 What is the Problem, Exactly?

It is important to have a deep understanding of the problem you are trying to solve before jumping into an implementation of the solution. Often the audio designers will come up with a well-thought-out solution, and they will ask for a given feature without telling you what the problem is that they are trying to solve. Even if the solution outlined by the audio designer might seem to solve the problem in a reasonable fashion, it does not mean that it is the best solution in terms of implementation time, risk, maintainability, and ease of use. By taking a step back and examining the problem, you can formulate a solution that can often be better.

On a project I worked on, one sound designer came to me with a request to add a feature that he called "atomic soundbanks." He defined an atomic soundbank as one bank per play event, which contains all the media for the play event in question. Conceptually, this is a great feature because it automates the creation of soundbanks for the game. On the other hand, this way of breaking the data can be suboptimal: it can cause extra disk seeks, and might also waste disk space by duplicating assets that are used in multiple play events.

The audio designer came up with this solution because he had worked a project where they had implemented the feature, and it seemed to solve the problem at hand. Instead of going ahead and implementing the feature, I asked him what the real problem was that he was trying to solve. He told me that moving play events from one bank to another was a time-consuming task, and that atomic soundbanks seemed like a good solution.

At this point, I realized that we did not really needed atomic sound-banks for our game, but we did need to work on improving the ease of use of bank management. I created tools that automated the creation of soundbanks in an optimal fashion for our game, while still allowing the possibility of overriding it manually for special situations. In the end, the sound designer was happy with the solution I delivered to him even if I did not solve the problem the way he expected.

2.5.3 Expectations

Remember that you will need to be dealing with the complete life cycle of a feature: creation, support, maintenance, documentation, and optimization. When planning out a project with a sound designer and/or a producer, it is best to define a set of clear goals, and schedule them out on a timeline. Make sure to leave plenty of time for unplanned events and other overhead, but do not skimp on features. By delivering your features on time and as promised, you will foster a good working relationship with your clients. This will probably translate into more leeway from producers for future projects, which is always good.

2.5.4 Life Cycle of a New Feature

Two things to keep in mind when working on a new feature are "fail early and fail fast" and "be wrong as fast as you can" [4]. It is much better to discover that a given feature won't make it into the game after one week of development rather than after four months. Ideally, you should tackle a new feature in the following order:

- **Proof of concept**: Do the minimum amount of work to prove that the feature will work. It doesn't have to be pretty or perfect, but it should convince you that the feature will work.
- **Solve technical constraints**: The proof of concept will often uncover some systems that need to change in order to proceed to the implementation. Making that change first is important, as it will make the implementation go more smoothly.
- **Implementation**: At this point, there should be no obstructions to implementing the feature.
- **Improve ease of use and iteration time**: Consider how the sound designers will be using the feature, and what their workflow will be with it. Make tools, keyboard shortcuts, and other quality-of-life improvements to make their job easier.
- **Optimization**: Make sure that the feature uses as little CPU and memory as possible.

2.5.5 Hard-to-Solve Problems

Audio, as with other disciplines, has a number of problems that are notoriously difficult to solve.

Speaking to other audio programmers working from different companies, I have found that there are features that people fail to implement no matter what they try. A couple of examples are automatic footstep tagging in animations and automatic reverb zone definition in open world games. When tackling these sorts of features, it is important to bear in mind the difficulty of the problem at hand—you could be pouring your energy into a bottomless pit.

Even if you do solve the problem, it may end up being a pyrrhic victory. Let's say that you manage to implement a system that tags footsteps in animations automatically. If the system is not perfect, then a human will have to go in and audit every single automatically generated event and retouch it. At that point, have you really saved any time over doing it by hand?

Note that this does not mean we should not attempt to solve these problems, but we do need to make it clear with the sound designers that we are trying to solve a hard problem, and have an alternative plan if this fails.

2.6 CONCLUSION

The role of the audio programmer is often misunderstood by the rest of team because a lot of the work is behind the scenes. If you do your job right, then nobody really notices, but if you do it wrong then it is abundantly clear. Because audio programmers have to juggle so many different specialized aspects of development, it's not hard to see why many generalist programmers shy away from audio programming tasks. Also, because there are currently so few audio programmers in the industry, it is important to be able to communicate what the role is. When the rest of the team understands your goals and challenges, they can become partners to achieve quality audio in your game.

Generally speaking, audio programmers account for less than a fraction of a percent of all game developers. Even if we include audio designers, the percentage of all audio specialists in the industry is still marginal. I believe that getting people to understand what the role of the audio programmer is will help raise the quality of the candidates in the industry. You can now spread the word and reach out to other people to teach them what the role of the audio programmer is. This will help the new candidates to know what they are getting into but also help people that are looking for one.

REFERENCES

1. Guy Somberg, 2014, Lessons Learned from a Decade of Audio Programming, www.gdcvault.com/play/1020452/Lessons-Learned-from-a-Decade.
2. Elan Ruskin, 2012, www.gdcvault.com/play/1015528/AI-driven-Dynamic-Dialog-through.
3. Jason Gregory, 2014, www.gdcvault.com/play/1020951/A-Context-Aware-Character-Dialog.
4. Edwin Catmull, 2014, Creativity, Inc. Transworld Publishers Limited.
5. Nicolas Fournel, 2011, Opinion: Putting the Audio Back in Audio Programmer, www.gamasutra.com/view/news/125422/Opinion_Putting_The_Audio_Back_In_Audio_Programmer.php.

SECTION I

Low-Level Topics

CHAPTER 3

Multithreading for Game Audio

Dan Murray

Id Software

CONTENTS

3.1 GOTTA GO FAST

Game audio is asynchronous by nature. Whatever the rate at which you draw frames to the screen, process user input, or perform physics simulations—audio is doing its own thing. Any time we spend synchronizing audio with other systems is time we could have spent doing useful work. However, we do need to communicate among threads, and so we should endeavor to minimize the cost, complexity, and overhead of this communication so that we do not waste resources. In this chapter, we will discuss audio device callbacks and callback etiquette; frame buffering, managing threads, and inter-thread communication in the context of game audio; and how to present a fast and efficient sound engine interface to the rest of the game. While you read this chapter, I strongly recommend that you write, compile, and test all of the code. At the end of each section,

I have included a list of search engine-friendly terms. If you encounter terminology or techniques that are new to you or you do not quite understand you can easily start researching them online by searching for these terms. For reference all of the code shown in this chapter and more can be downloaded on the book's website at www.crcpress.com. Special thanks to Karl "Techno" Davis for his help putting together this chapter.

3.2 AUDIO DEVICE CALLBACKS

Everything starts with the audio device or soundcard we are sinking buffers of audio into. The audio device notifies the kernel each time it needs another buffer of data. The application or applications responsible for providing the data are notified in turn, typically in the form of a callback. From there, the audio data flows through the system in a number of steps.

Each application is expected to supply its audio data such that an entire buffer can be provided to the audio device. The format of the audio data supplied by each application may differ. For example, one application may submit data at a lower sample rate than another, one application may submit data as a stream of signed 24-bit integers or signed 16-bit integers, and so on.

The interval of these callbacks is typically equal to the playback time of the audio represented by the buffer. For example, if we are sinking buffers of audio data 512 frames at a time where one second of data is represented by 48,000 frames then each buffer represents 10.7 ms of audio data, and we can expect the period of callback to be the same. A frame of 1,024 samples, at the same sample rate, represents 21.3 ms, and so on.

Once the application has filled its buffer with data, the data is re-sampled, interleaved, deinterleaved, dithered, or scaled as needed such that a single buffer of audio data—in the format that the audio device expects—can be provided to the audio device.

This is a typical callback function signature:

```
void callback(float *buffer, int channels, int frames, void *cookie);
```

Here, the application is expected to write channels * frames samples of audio data into the region of memory pointed at by buffer. It is important that you know the format of the data you are reading or writing in a callback—for example, whether the samples in buffer need to be interleaved (LRLR) or deinterleaved (LLRR). Upon receipt of a callback, you are expected to write the next buffer of output data to the supplied region of memory and immediately return.

It is crucial that you do not waste time when handling callbacks, in order to minimize the latency between the audio device requesting a frame of audio and the application providing it.

It is very common for callbacks to take an opaque piece of pointer-width user data, sometimes called a cookie, in the form of a `void*`. When registering to receive a callback you will usually be given the option of supplying this argument, which will be passed back to you each time you receive the callback. Here is an example of how we might use this to call a member function:

```
struct sound_engine {
  static void callback(float *buffer,
                       int channels,
                       int frames,
                       void *cookie) {
    sound_engine *engine = (sound_engine *)cookie;
    engine->write_data(buffer, channels, frames);
  }
  void write_data (float *buffer, int channels, int frames) {
    memcpy(buffer, data, channels * frames * sizeof(float));
  }
  float *data;
}
```

This example callback function signature is both a simplification and generalization. The exact signature of the callback, format of the buffer into which you write, and how you register and receive these callbacks is platform- and API-specific.

Search engine-friendly terms for this section:

sound card, c function pointer syntax, callback (computer programming), void* pointer in c, wasapi, advanced linux sound architecture, core audio apple, audio resampling, audio dither, 24 bit audio, direct sound windows, pulseaudio linux, sdl mixer documentation, low latency audio msdn, audio graphs msdn

3.3 ABSTRACT AUDIO DEVICE

For the purposes of this chapter, we will define an interface to and the behavior of an abstract audio device, which will serve as a replacement for a real audio device during this chapter.

```
struct audio_device {
  audio_device(int samplerate, int channels, int frames,
               void (*func)(float *, int, int, void *),
               void *cookie);
};
```

An audio_device expects:

- The sample rate of the data you are going to supply.

- The number of channels in the stream of data.

- The number of frames of audio data you are going to supply per callback.

- A function pointer to the callback function you wish to be called whenever data is required.

- (Optionally) an opaque pointer-width piece of user data.

A typical callback might look like this:

```
void callback(float *buffer, int channels,
  int frames, void *cookie) {
  for (int i = 0; i < channels * frames; i++) {
    buffer[i] = 0.0f;
  }
}
```

Here we are just writing zeros into the buffer for the example; we will fill this function in with real code later in the chapter. You can create an audio_device using the callback function like this:

```
int samplerate = 48000; // 48kHz
int channels = 2;       // stereo
int frames = 512;       // 10.7ms
audio_device device(samplerate, channels, frames, callback, NULL);
```

The supplied callback function will now be called each time the audio device needs more data. In this example, it will be approximately every 10.7 ms. callback is expected to write channels * frames (1,024 in this example) samples into buffer each time it is called back. buffer will be interpreted as 512 frames of data at a sample rate of 48 kHz, with each frame containing two channels worth of samples.

3.4 BUFFERING

At this point, we could construct a simple sound engine with our audio device. Each time our callback is invoked we could read data we need from disc, convert the audio data from one format to another, sample and resample buffers of audio data, perform DSP, mix various buffers to construct final buffer for this frame, and then finally copy it into `buffer` and return. However, doing so would be a violation of the callback etiquette established earlier in this chapter.

Instead, we will separate out the basics of what this callback needs to do—copy the final buffer into `buffer` and return—from everything else. The simplest way to do this copy is to buffer the data so that the data needed by the callback has already been computed and is available slightly before it is required. A single frame, or double buffer, is the simplest form of buffering:

```
struct double_buffer {
  double_buffer(int samples) :
    read_(NULL), write_(NULL) {
    read_ = (float *)malloc(samples * 2 * sizeof(float));
    memset(read_, 0, samples * 2 * sizeof(float));
    write_ = read_ + samples;
  }

  ~double_buffer() {
    if (read_ < write_) {
      free(read_);
    } else {
      free(write_);
    }
  }

  void swap() {
    float *old_read = read_;
    read_ = write_;
    write_ = old_read;
  }
  float *read_;
  float *write_;
};
```

`double_buffer` consists of a single allocation split into two regions (`read_` and `write_`), each of which is `samples` in length. When an application has finished writing to the write buffer, it can swap the double buffer, which changes the `read_` and `write_` pointers so that `read_` points to what was the write buffer and `write_` points to what was the read buffer.

Using this structure, we can copy the read buffer into the callback buffer and return from our callback:

```
void callback(float *buffer, int channel,
  int frames, void *cookie) {
  double_buffer *dbl_buffer = (double_buffer *)cookie;
```

```
  int bytes = sizeof(float) * channels * frames;
  memcpy(buffer, dbl_buffer->read_buffer(), bytes);
}
```

For this example, I've assumed that we passed a pointer to a double buffer as the optional user data when we created our `audio_device`.

Using a buffer allows us to drive the generation of audio from our device callbacks, without having to compute the frame of data inside of the callback. Let's see how to make that happen:

Initially the read buffer is empty, which represents a frame of silence. Double-buffering naturally imposes a single frame of delay in the form of this single frame of silence. When we receive our first callback we supply the contents of the read buffer to the callback. We know that the read buffer contains our frame of silence, so this is valid even though we haven't computed any data yet.

Now we know that we need to generate the first frame of data. We know that we will get called back again and we know roughly how long until that happens, so before returning from the callback we should make note of the need to compute the next frame of data and begin working on it. Critically, we won't block and do this work inside the callback; we will do this somewhere else at another time.

Computing the next frame of data must take less time than the period of the callback minus the time we spent copying the read buffer into the output, such that when a completed frame is ready and waiting when we receive the next callback. After we have finished writing our next frame of data into the write buffer we call `swap` and wait for the callback to occur. Now when we receive the callback for the next frame the read buffer will contain to our new frame data, and we can just copy it into the output buffer and start the whole process over again.

Why do we need a double buffer in the first place? After all, we could accomplish this algorithm using a single combined read/write buffer:

- When we receive the first callback buffer of data it expects us to fill out is set to all zeros, using `memset`, for example.

- Make a note of the need to compute the next frame and return.

- Write the next frame into the combined read/write buffer.

- From now on when we receive a callback we read the contents of the combined read/write buffer.

This approach breaks down when you are not able to finish writing the next frame of data before the callback attempts to read it. Suppose that in order to write a particular frame you have to do some expensive computation which varies in duration from frame to frame. If one frame takes longer to compute than the period of the callback, then the callback will start reading from the combined read/write buffer while you are still writing to it.

The double buffer above also breaks when generating one frame takes longer than the period, but in a different way. Suppose you have taken too long and are still writing the next frame to the write buffer when the callback starts to read. The next callback will be re-reading the previous frame's read buffer because swap has not been called since the last callback. In this case, we can see that the difference between a single buffer and a double buffer is mostly semantic: they both suffer when you have a single long frame.

A triple buffer allows us to deal with these problems:

```
struct triple_buffer {
  triple_buffer(int samples)
     : buffer_(NULL), samples_(samples),
        read_(samples), write_(0) {
    buffer_ = (float *)malloc(samples * 3 * sizeof(float));
    memset(buffer_, 0, samples * 3 * sizeof(float));
  }

  ~triple_buffer() { free(buffer_); }

  float *write_buffer() { return buffer_ + write_; }

  void finish_write() { write_ = (write_ + samples_) % (samples_ * 3); }

  float *read_buffer() { return buffer_ + read_; }

  void finish_read() { read_ = (read_ + samples_) % (samples_ * 3); }

  float *buffer_;
  int samples_;
  int read_;
  int write_;
};
```

triple_buffer consists of a single allocation split into three regions each of which is samples in length. read_ and write_ indicate which of the three regions are the read and write buffers. Most notably, triple_buffer differs from double_buffer by having finish_write and finish_read rather than a combined swap.

finish_read changes the read_ index so that the region after the current read buffer is now the new read buffer and finish_write changes the write_ index so that the region after the current write buffer is now the new write buffer. read_ and write_ are initialized such that read_ is one region ahead of write_.

Now when the application takes too long to write the next frame the callback will see two distinct and valid read buffers before it starts reading from the current write buffer. This allows for one frame to borrow some time from the next frame such that if the total time to write two frames is never longer than twice the callback period the callback always sees a valid and completed frame of data. In practice, this means we can have one frame which takes a long time to compute without any issues.

These buffers are specific implementations of the more general concept of having an arbitrary number of frames buffering the data from your application to the audio device. The number of buffers will vary based on your application's needs, such that the buffer is always sufficiently full. Both double_buffer and triple_buffer increase the latency by delaying data by one or two frames between your application and the audio device, as well as creating an additional memory cost in the form of storage space for these additional frames. Even more additional frames of buffering will provide you with additional tolerance to long frames at the cost of additional further latency and even more memory.

We can represent this concept generically with a ring buffer:

```
struct ring_buffer {
  ring_buffer(int samples, int frames)
      : buffer_(NULL), samples_(samples),
        max_frames_(frames), read_(0),
        write_(0), num_frames_(frames) {
    buffer_ = (float *)malloc(samples_ * max_frames_ * sizeof(float));
    memset(buffer_, 0, samples_ * max_frames_ * sizeof(float));
  }

  ~ring_buffer() { free(buffer_); }

  bool can_write() { return num_frames_ != max_frames_; }

  float *write_buffer() { return buffer_ + (write_ * samples_); }

  void finish_write() {
    write_ = (write_ + 1) % max_frames_;
    num_frames_ += 1;
  }
```

```
  bool can_read() { return num_frames_ != 0; }

  float *read_buffer() { return buffer_ + (read_ * samples_); }

  void finish_read() {
    read_ = (read_ + 1) % max_frames_;
    num_frames_ -= 1;
  }

  float *buffer_;
  int samples_;
  int max_frames_;
  int read_;
  int write_;
  int num_frames_;
};
```

ring_buffer consists of a single allocation split into N regions, where N is equal to the value of frames, each of which is samples in length. read_ and write_ indicate which of the N regions are the read and write buffers. A ring_buffer with frames equal to 2 would behave like a double_buffer and a ring_buffer with frames equal to 3 would behave like a triple_buffer.

ring_buffer differs from triple_buffer by having methods for checking if there are available frames to read and or write. can_write checks if num_frames_ is not equal to max_frames_, meaning that we have an available frame to write to. can_read checks if num_frames_ is not equal to zero, meaning that we haven't yet read all of the available frames.

With ring_buffer our callback from earlier might look like this:

```
void callback(float *buffer, int channel,
              int frames, void *cookie) {
  ring_buffer *rng_buffer = (ring_buffer *)cookie;
  if (rng_buffer->can_read()) {
    int bytes = sizeof(float) * channels * frames;
    memcpy(buffer, rng_buffer->read_buffer(), bytes);
    rng_buffer->finish_read();
  }
}
```

Search engine-friendly terms for this section:

buffer (computer programming), buffering audio, double buffer, triple buffer, multiple buffering, ring buffer, circular buffer, circular queue, cyclic buffer

3.5 DEVICE-DRIVEN FRAME GENERATION

What we have been discussing so far can be called device-driven frame generation, in which the output device periodically requests frames of data, and the application responds to these requests by computing and supplying the data. In order to compute frames of data without blocking our callback, we will need to create a thread. We will build a sound engine use the standard threading library for the purposes of this chapter.

Let's start by putting together a very basic sound engine that doesn't actually do anything yet:

```
struct sound_engine {
  sound_engine() :
    update_thread_(&sound_engine::update, this) {}

  void update() {
    for (;;) {
      // wait to be notified of the need to compute a frame
      // compute a frame
      // loop
    }
  }

  std::thread update_thread_;
};
```

In this example, we create a thread which will call into the member function `sound_engine::update()`. The thread function loops, and we will fill in the code throughout this section. Let's combine it with our abstract audio device from Section 3.3:

```
struct sound_engine {
  sound_engine()
      : update_thread_(&sound_engine::update, this),
        device_(48000, 2, 512, callback, this) {}

  static void callback(float *buffer, int channels,
                       int frames, void *cookie) {
    sound_engine *engine = (sound_engine *)cookie;
    engine->write_data_to_device(buffer);
  }

  void write_data_to_device(float *buffer) {
    // notify the update thread of the need to compute a frame
    // copy the current read buffer
    // return
  }

  void update() {
    for (;;) {
```

```
        // wait to be notified of the need to compute a frame
        // compute a frame
        // loop
      }
    }

  std::thread update_thread_;
  audio_device device_;
};
```

Now we have two clear points where work happens. The audio device call-back is going to pull frames of data and in doing so notify us of the need to replenish the data in the pipeline that it has consumed. In response to this the update thread will push frames of data into the pipeline so that it is sufficiently full. In order to communicate how many frames of audio data we need, we will have both threads share a variable which indicates the number of frames of data the update thread needs to compute:

```
struct sound_engine {
  sound_engine()
      : frames_requested_(0),
        update_thread_(&sound_engine::update, this),
        device_(48000, 2, 512, callback, this) {}

  static void callback(float *buffer, int channels,
                       int frames, void *cookie) {
    sound_engine *engine = (sound_engine *)cookie;
    engine->write_data_to_device(buffer);
  }

  void write_data_to_device(float *buffer) {
    // notify the update thread of the need to compute a frame
    frames_requested_.fetch_add(1);
    // copy the current read buffer
    // return
  }

  void update() {
    for (;;) {
      // wait to be notified of the need to compute a frame
      int frames_to_compute = frames_requested_.exchange(0);
      // compute as many frames as we need to
      for (int i = 0; i < frames_to_compute; ++i) {
        // compute a frame
      }
      // loop
    }
  }

  std::atomic<int> frames_requested_;
  std::thread update_thread_;
  audio_device device_;
};
```

The issue with approach is that our update thread is constantly checking if it needs to do work (busy-waiting, or spinning), which is a waste of resources. A better alternative would be to have the thread yield to the kernel, and only get scheduled to run when there is work to do. In order to do this, we need a way for our audio device callback to notify our update thread that it should wake and start computing data. We will use an event/semaphore:

```
struct update_event {
  update_event() {
#ifdef _WIN32
    event = CreateEvent(0, 0, 0, 0);
#elif __linux__
    sem_init(&semaphore, 0, 0);
#endif
  }

  ~update_event() {
#ifdef _WIN32
    CloseHandle(event);
#elif __linux__
    sem_destroy(&semaphore);
#endif
  }

  void signal() {
#ifdef _WIN32
    SetEvent(event);
#elif __linux__
    sem_post(&semaphore);
#endif
  }

  void wait() {
#ifdef _WIN32
    WaitForSingleObject(event, INFINITE);
#elif __linux__
    sem_wait(&semaphore);
#endif
  }

#ifdef _WIN32
  HANDLE event;
#elif __linux__
  sem_t semaphore;
#endif
};
```

By using an `update_event`, our `update_thread_` can wait for the audio device callback to signal that it should wake up. Let's see what it looks like in practice:

```
struct sound_engine {
  sound_engine()
      : update_thread_(&sound_engine::update, this),
        device_(48000, 2, 512, callback, this) {}

  static void callback(float *buffer, int channels,
                       int frames, void *cookie) {
    sound_engine *engine = (sound_engine *)cookie;
    engine->write_data_to_device(buffer);
  }

  void write_data_to_device(float *buffer) {
    // copy the current read buffer
    // notify the update thread of the need to compute a frame
    event_.signal();
    // return
  }

  void update() {
    for (;;) {
      // wait to be notified of the need to compute a frame
      event_.wait();
      // compute as many frames as we need to
      while (/* have frames to compute */) {
        // compute a frame
      }
      // loop
    }
  }

  update_event event_;
  std::thread update_thread_;
  audio_device device_;
};
```

Note that when `event_.wait()` returns we need to check exactly how many frames of data we are expected to compute as we may have consumed multiple frames and been signaled multiple times. Now we will add the ring buffer from Section 3.4:

```
struct sound_engine {
  sound_engine()
      : buffers_(1024, 3),
        update_thread_(&sound_engine::update, this),
        device_(48000, 2, 512, callback, this) {}

  static void callback(float *buffer, int channels,
                       int frames, void *cookie) {
    sound_engine *engine = (sound_engine *)cookie;
    engine->write_data_to_device(buffer);
  }

  void write_data_to_device(float *buffer) {
```

```
    // copy the current read buffer
    if (buffers_.can_read()) {
      int bytes = buffers_.samples_ * sizeof(float);
      memcpy(buffer, buffers_.read_buffer(), bytes);
      buffers_.finish_read();
    }
    // notify the update thread of the need to compute a frame
    event_.signal();
    // return
  }

  void update() {
    for (;;) {
      // wait to be notified of the need to compute a frame
      event_.wait();
      // compute as many frames as we need to
      while (buffers_.can_write()) {
        int bytes = buffers_.samples_ * sizeof(float);
        memset(buffers_.write_buffer(), 0, bytes);
        buffers_.finish_write();
      }
      // loop
    }
  }

  update_event event_;
  ring_buffer buffers_;
  std::thread update_thread_;
  audio_device device_;
};
```

The available capacity of the ring buffer—the number of frames that we can write before `can_write` returns false—conveys the amount of data our update has to push into the pipeline so that it is sufficiently full. But now we have a problem: we have multiple threads reading and writing to members of the ring buffer, which introduces a race condition.

We need to synchronize access and modification so that both threads see the correct values and behavior. To start with we will use a simple spin lock:

```
struct spin_lock {
  spin_lock() : state_(unlocked) {}

  void lock() { while (state_.exchange(locked) == locked){} }

  void unlock() { state_.store(unlocked); }

  typedef enum { unlocked, locked } state;
  std::atomic<state> state_;
};
```

A thread trying to call lock() will only return once it is able to exchange the value of state_ with locked when it was previously unlocked. That is, it must be the first to lock state. A thread trying to lock when another thread has already done this will spin in the while loop waiting for the value of state_ to be unlocked. When the thread which successfully locked the spin_lock is ready to allow other threads to access the region it protects, it should call unlock(). Unlocking a spin_lock will set the value of state_ to unlocked which allows another thread to escape the while loop. Let's add the spin_lock to our sound engine to protect our ring buffer:

```
struct sound_engine {
  sound_engine()
     : buffers_(1024, 3),
       update_thread_(&sound_engine::update, this),
       device_(48000, 2, 512, callback, this) {}

  static void callback(float *buffer, int channels,
                    int frames, void *cookie) {
    sound_engine *engine = (sound_engine *)cookie;
    engine->write_data_to_device(buffer);
  }

  void write_data_to_device(float *buffer) {
    lock_.lock();
    // copy the current read buffer
    if (buffers_.can_read()) {
      int bytes = buffers_.samples_ * sizeof(float);
      memcpy(buffer, buffers_.read_buffer(), bytes);
      buffers_.finish_read();
    }
    lock_.unlock();
    // notify the update thread of the need to compute a frame
    event_.signal();
    // return
  }

  void update() {
    for (;;) {
      // wait to be notified of the need to compute a frame
      event_.wait();
      lock_.lock();
      // compute as many frames as we need to
      while (buffers_.can_write()) {
        int bytes = buffers_.samples_ * sizeof(float);
        memset(buffers_.write_buffer(), 0, bytes);
        buffers_.finish_write();
      }
      lock_.unlock();
      // loop
    }
```

```
  }
  update_event event_;
  spin_lock lock_;
  ring_buffer buffers_;
  std::thread update_thread_;
  audio_device device_;
};
```

Note that we do not hold the lock while waiting for the event as this would prevent the audio device callback from ever acquiring the lock.

While using a spin lock like this will correctly protect concurrent access to the ring buffer, it is nevertheless problematic because now our update thread can block our callback thread. Instead, we will remove the spin lock and modify the ring buffer to be lock- and wait-free:

```
struct ring_buffer {
  ring_buffer(int samples, int frames)
      : buffer_(NULL), samples_(samples),
        max_frames_(frames), read_(0),
        write_(0), num_frames_(frames) {
    size_t alloc_size = samples_ * max_frames_ * sizeof(float);
    buffer_ = (float *)malloc(alloc_size);
    memset(buffer_, 0, alloc_size);
  }

  ~ring_buffer() { free(buffer_); }

  bool can_write() { return num_frames_.load() != max_frames_; }

  float *write_buffer() { return buffer_ + (write_ * samples_); }

  void finish_write() {
    write_ = (write_ + 1) % max_frames_;
    num_frames_.fetch_add(1);
  }

  bool can_read() { return num_frames_.load() != 0; }

  float *read_buffer() { return buffer_ + (read_ * samples_); }

  void finish_read() {
    read_ = (read_ + 1) % max_frames_;
    num_frames_.fetch_sub(1);
  }

  float *buffer_;
  int samples_;
  int max_frames_;
  int read_;
  int write_;
  std::atomic<int> num_frames_;
};
```

The easiest way to understand the changes is to compare the new code with the ring buffer from Section 3.4. We have added a single atomic variable num_frames_ which keeps track of the number of written frames. num_frames_ ensures we only write if we have space and that we only read if we have available frames to read. This code works because we have a single producer and single consumer, and therefore we can make assumptions about read_ and write_ not being changed by another thread. The writing thread is the only thread to modify the value of write_, and the reading thread is the only thread to modify the value of read_. When we read the value of write_ in write_buffer() and finish_write() we can safely assume that it will not be modified. Similarly, when we read the value of read_ in read_buffer() and finish_read() we can safely assume that it will not be modified.

Now that we no longer need external access control for the ring buffer, the sound_engine itself can be reverted to its previous form by removing the spin_lock.

Search engine-friendly terms for this section:

thread (computer science), c++ std thread, win32 thread api, posix thread api, lock (computer science), mutual exclusion, mutex, spin lock (software), synchronization (computer science), c++ std atomic, lock free (computer science), wait free (computer science), interlocked variable access win32, busy wait, semaphore, createevent win32, linux manual pages sem_init

3.6 INTERFACING WITH THE GAME

Now that we have established the heartbeat rhythm of our audio frame generation, we need to allow the game to communicate with the sound engine so it can dictate what should be rendered to each buffer. It is important that we stick to our principle of minimizing the cost of communication here as well. Game code calling into the sound engine should not be penalized by having to interact with a poorly designed and expensive API.

We will use a lock- and wait-free message-based interface where individual commands are represented as a small set of plain data stored in a tagged union in order of arrival. Our message type and some very simple example message types might look like this:

```
struct play_message {
  int sound_id;
};
```

```
struct stop_message {
  int sound_id;
};

enum class message_t { play, stop };

union message_params {
  play_message play_params;
  stop_message stop_params;
};

struct message {
  message_t type;
  message_params params;
};
```

play_message and stop_message both have a single parameter: the unique identifier of the sound that should be played or stopped. In general, we try to keep the amount of data required for any one message's parameters as small as possible to avoid wasted space in other message types.

Let's see an example of pushing a message onto the queue:

```
void play_sound(int sound_id) {
  message m;
  m.type = message_t::play;
  m.params.play_params.sound_id = sound_id;
  // push m into message queue
}
```

So far, we've just been creating the messages on the stack in the game thread, but we still need some sort of mechanism to send messages across threads. We will create a message queue, which will work in a similar way to our final ring_buffer implementation. Here, we are assuming that the game is talking to the sound engine from a single thread, so our single-producer single-consumer model can be reused:

```
struct message_queue {
  message_queue(int messages)
      : messages_(NULL), max_messages_(messages),
        num_messages_(0), head_(0), tail_(0) {
    size_t alloc_size = max_messages_ * sizeof(message);
    messages_ = (message *)malloc(alloc_size);
  }

  ~message_queue() { free(messages_); }

  bool push(message const &msg) {
    if (num_messages_.load() != max_messages_) {
```

```
      int new_head = (head_ + 1) % max_messages_;
      messages_[head_] = msg;
      head_ = (head_ + 1) % max_messages_;
      num_messages_.fetch_add(1);
      return true;
    }
    return false;
  }

  bool pop(message &msg) {
    if (num_messages_.load() != 0) {
      msg = messages_[tail_];
      tail_ = (tail_ + 1) % max_messages_;
      num_messages_.fetch_sub(1);
      return true;
    }
    return false;
  }

  message *messages_;
  int max_messages_;
  int head_;
  int tail_;
  std::atomic<int> num_messages_;
};
```

The game will be push()ing messages from all over the codebase throughout the frame, but the sound engine will drain a single frame's worth of messages from the queue all in one go. In order to prevent the sound engine from reading too many messages, we need to mark the point at which the sound engine should stop draining messages. We will use a special frame message to say that "messages after this point represent the next frame's messages and may not represent a complete frame of messages yet":

```
void update() {
  message frame_msg{message_t::frame};
  queue_.push(frame_msg);
}
```

The loop for draining the messages will look like this:

```
for (;;) {
  message msg;
  if (!queue_.pop(msg)) {
    break;
  }
  if (msg.type == message_t::frame) {
    break;
  }
  switch (msg.type) {
  case message_t::play: {
```

```
    int sound_id = msg.params.play_params.sound_id;
    // play the sound represented by sound_id
    break;
  }
  case message_t::stop: {
    int sound_id = msg.params.stop_params.sound_id;
    // stop the sound represented by sound_id
    break;
  }
  default: { break; }
  }
}
```

This draining code will run on the sound engine thread prior to writing each frame. We first check to see if the message type is frame, which tells us that we have reached the end of the audio messages for this frame and that we should exit the loop early. The play and stop cases are placeholders for the real code that you would write to start and stop sounds.

There is an issue with the code so far: what happens when we have been notified that we need to render a frame, but the game has not yet pushed a frame message? If we start pulling messages off of the queue we will most likely pop all of the messages that are currently in the queue and break out of the loop. If we attempt to render a frame of audio using this partial set of commands, it will most likely result in incorrect output. For example, if the game has pushed some (but not all) position updates for the frame, we will render a frame of audio using some positions from this frame and some positions from last frame.

To fix this issue, we will keep a count of the number of frame messages currently in the message queue.

```
void update() {
  message frame_msg{message_t::frame};
  queue_.push(frame_msg);
  frame_messages_.fetch_add(1);
}
```

Now we can attempt to drain the messages but break if there is not a frame message in the queue:

```
for (;;) {
  int frame_messages = frame_messages_.load();
  if (frame_messages_ == 0) {
    break;
  }
  message msg;
  if (!queue_.pop(msg)) {
```

```
      break;
    }
    if (msg.type == message_t::frame) {
      frame_messages_.fetch_sub(1);
      break;
    }
    switch (msg.type) {
    case message_t::play: {
      int sound_id = msg.params.play_params.sound_id;
      // play the sound represented by sound_id
      break;
    }
    case message_t::stop: {
      int sound_id = msg.params.stop_params.sound_id;
      // stop the sound represented by sound_id
      break;
    }
    default: { break; }
    }
}
```

This pattern also addresses another small issue with our previous message draining code: if multiple frames worth of messages are in the queue because we have not been able to drain them fast enough, we will now process all of them before attempting to render the frame.

Now we have our game message queue, we can put it together with the sound engine that we built in Section 3.5.

```
class sound_engine {
public:
  sound_engine(
    int samplerate, int channels, int frames, int refills)
      : buffers_(frames * channels, refills),
        queue_(64), frame_messages_(0), stop_(false),
        update_thread_(&sound_engine::process_messages, this),
        device_(samplerate, channels, frames, callback, this) {}

  ~sound_engine() {
    stop_.store(true);
    event_.signal();
    update_thread_.join();
  }

  void update() {
    message frame_msg{message_t::frame};
    queue_.push(frame_msg);
    frame_messages_.fetch_add(1);
  }

  void play_sound(int sound_id) {
    message m;
    m.type = message_t::play;
```

```
      m.params.play_params.sound_id = sound_id;
      queue_.push(m);
    }

  void stop_sound(int sound_id) {
    message m;
    m.type = message_t::stop;
    m.params.stop_params.sound_id = sound_id;
    queue_.push(m);
  }

private:
  static void callback(float *buffer, int channels,
                       int frames, void *cookie) {
    sound_engine *engine = (sound_engine *)cookie;
    engine->write_data_to_device(buffer);
  }

  void write_data_to_device(float *buffer) {
    if (buffers_.can_read()) {
      float *read_buffer = buffers_.read_buffer();
      int bytes = sizeof(float) * buffers_.samples_;
      memcpy(buffer, read_buffer, bytes);
      buffers_.finish_read();
    }
    event_.signal();
  }

  void process_messages() {
    for (;;) {
      event_.wait();
      if (stop_.load()) {
        break;
      }
      while (buffers_.can_write()) {
        for (;;) {
          int frame_messages = frame_messages_.load();
          if (frame_messages_ == 0) {
            break;
          }
          message msg;
          if (!queue_.pop(msg)) {
            break;
          }
          if (msg.type == message_t::frame) {
            frame_messages_.fetch_sub(1);
            break;
          }
          switch (msg.type) {
          case message_t::play: {
            int sound_id = msg.params.play_params.sound_id;
            printf("play %d\n", sound_id);
            break;
          }
          case message_t::stop: {
```

```
                int sound_id = msg.params.stop_params.sound_id;
                printf("stop %d\n", sound_id);
                break;
            }
            default: { break; }
            }
        }
        buffers_.finish_write();
      }
    }
  }

  update_event event_;
  ring_buffer buffers_;
  message_queue queue_;
  std::atomic<int> frame_messages_;
  std::atomic<bool> stop_;
  std::thread update_thread_;
  audio_device device_;
};
```

Search engine-friendly terms for this section:
  union type, tagged union, message passing, event loop

Appendix A
Thread Prioritization

Typically, the thread on which an audio device provides you with a call-back will run at a higher-than-normal priority. The complete set of rules that govern thread scheduling are platform specific and consist of many caveats. However, it is generally safe to assume that a pending thread of a higher priority will be scheduled by the kernel if the currently running threads are of a lower priority. You can access the native thread handle of a standard thread object using `std::thread::native_handle()`, and use it to set the priority of the thread:

```
#ifdef _WIN32
    SetThreadPriority(thread_.native_handle(),
                        THREAD_PRIORITY_ABOVE_NORMAL);
#elif __linux__
    sched_param sch;
    sch.sched_priority = 20;
    pthread_setschedparam(thread_.native_handle(), SCHED_FIFO, &sch);
#endif
```

It is important to consider the relative priority of each of the threads not just within a self-contained sound system, but also with the context of your entire application. It is a reasonable simplification to assume that if your thread wishes to be scheduled now that it will be scheduled in the near future. However, for work where the latency between wanting to be scheduled and actually running on the CPU should be minimal, you can specify that the thread or threads which perform this work are of a higher priority than other threads.

A higher priority thread can interrupt other threads more readily than threads of the same priority, which causes those threads to stop their work temporarily in favor of the work of the higher-priority thread. These interruptions, called context switches, are not free and should be avoided if possible. As a general rule, the thread that is responsible for the production of the audio frame data (the `sound_engine` update thread in our example) should come onto core as quickly as possible and then stay there until the frame has been submitted, and therefore should be of a higher priority than other threads.

Search engine-friendly terms for this section:

scheduling (computing), process and thread functions (windows), pthreads linux manual pages

Appendix B
Application-Driven
Frame Generation

Throughout this chapter, we have discussed device-driven frame generation, where the audio device callback pulls frames in whenever it needs them. Application-driven frame generation leaves the decision about when to push data into the pipeline, and how much data to push, to the application. This mechanism gives the application more flexibility as it can now decide how many samples it wants to produce, and can even vary the amount of samples produced from frame to frame.

With this additional flexibility you could, for example, render an amount of audio which is equal to the time it took to compute your last game or render frame, varying this as your frame time varies. However, with this flexibility comes added responsibility. Previously our system was self-sustaining: the act of consuming data caused the production of data to replace it. Data will still be consumed by the device at a steady rate no matter what, but now the responsibility of keeping the pipeline full has shifted to the application.

Suppose we do push one game frame's worth of audio data per game frame into our system. What happens if we have a very long frame? Our buffering will help to a certain extent in much the same way that it helps when we take too long to write frames of audio, but now the interval at which we can push data not only depends on the time it takes to compute the audio frame itself but on the entire game frame.

Application-driven frame generation also lets us precisely control the data that is used to generate each frame. Consider what happens when once per game frame the game supplies the position of the listener and the positions of each of the sound objects to the audio system. If the device wakes up and starts computing a frame after we have submitted some of these but before we have submitted them all then we will render this frame with a mix of old and new positions. However, if we wait until we've communicated all of this frames' data to the sound engine we can ensure that every sample is rendered with a complete and coherent set of data matching the image shown on screen. In Section 3.6, we worked around this by using a count of the number of frame messages. This solves the problem, but at the cost of increasing the worst-case latency by up to a frame.

Appendix C
Platform-Specific
Implementations
of Audio Device

Windows with WASAPI:

```
#define WIN32_LEAN_AND_MEAN
#include <windows.h>
#include <mmdeviceapi.h>
#include <audioclient.h>
#include <audiosessiontypes.h>
#include <atomic>
#include <cstdlib>
#include <thread>

struct audio_device {
  audio_device(int samplerate, int channels, int frames,
               void (*func)(float *, int, int, void *),
               void *cookie) {
    CoInitialize(NULL);
    event_ = CreateEvent(0, 0, 0, 0);
    IMMDeviceEnumerator *enumerator = NULL;
    CoCreateInstance(
      __uuidof(MMDeviceEnumerator), NULL, CLSCTX_ALL,
      __uuidof(IMMDeviceEnumerator), (void **)&enumerator);
    enumerator->GetDefaultAudioEndpoint(
      eRender, eConsole, &device_);
    device_->Activate(__uuidof(IAudioClient), CLSCTX_ALL, NULL,
                      (void **)&client_);
    REFERENCE_TIME defaultPeriod, minPeriod;
    client_->GetDevicePeriod(&defaultPeriod, &minPeriod);
    WAVEFORMATEX *format = NULL;
    client_->GetMixFormat(&format);
    format->nSamplesPerSec = samplerate;
    format->nChannels = channels;
```

```
    client_->Initialize(AUDCLNT_SHAREMODE_SHARED,
                        AUDCLNT_STREAMFLAGS_EVENTCALLBACK,
                        defaultPeriod, 0, format, NULL);

    CoTaskMemFree(format);
    client_->SetEventHandle(event_);
    client_->GetService(__uuidof(IAudioRenderClient),
                        (void **)&render_);
    client_->Start();
    stop_ = false;
    audio_thread_ = std::thread(
    [this, func, cookie, channels, frames]() {
      while (!stop_) {
        WaitForSingleObject(event_, INFINITE);
        BYTE *output_buffer;
        render_->GetBuffer(frames, &output_buffer);
        if (output_buffer) {
          func((float *)output_buffer, channels, frames, cookie);
          render_->ReleaseBuffer(frames, 0);
        }
      }
    });
    SetThreadPriority(audio_thread_.native_handle(),
                    THREAD_PRIORITY_ABOVE_NORMAL);
  }

  ~audio_device() {
    stop_ = true;
    audio_thread_.join();
    render_->Release();
    client_->Stop();
    client_->Release();
    device_->Release();
    CloseHandle(event_);
  }

  HANDLE event_;
  IMMDevice *device_;
  IAudioClient *client_;
  IAudioRenderClient *render_;
  std::atomic<bool> stop_;
  std::thread audio_thread_;
};
```

Linux with ALSA:

```
#include <alsa/asoundlib.h>
#include <atomic>
#include <cstdlib>
#include <pthread.h>
#include <thread>

struct audio_device {
  audio_device(int samplerate, int channels, int frames,
```

```
                    void (*func)(float *, int, int, void *),
                    void *cookie) {

    buffer_ = (float *)malloc(sizeof(float) * channels * frames);
    snd_pcm_open(&handle_, "default", SND_PCM_STREAM_PLAYBACK,
                SND_PCM_NONBLOCK | SND_PCM_ASYNC);
    snd_pcm_hw_params_t *hardware_params;
    snd_pcm_hw_params_alloca(&hardware_params);
    snd_pcm_hw_params_any(handle_, hardware_params);
    snd_pcm_hw_params_set_access(handle_, hardware_params,
                        SND_PCM_ACCESS_RW_INTERLEAVED);
    snd_pcm_hw_params_set_format(handle_, hardware_params,
                        SND_PCM_FORMAT_FLOAT);
    snd_pcm_hw_params_set_rate(handle_, hardware_params,
                        samplerate, 0);
    snd_pcm_hw_params_set_channels(handle_, hardware_params,
                            channels);
    snd_pcm_hw_params(handle_, hardware_params);
    snd_pcm_sw_params_t *software_params;
    snd_pcm_sw_params_alloca(&software_params);
    snd_pcm_sw_params_current(handle_, software_params);
    snd_pcm_sw_params_set_avail_min(handle_,
                            software_params, frames);
    snd_pcm_sw_params_set_start_threshold(handle_,
                                software_params, 0);
    snd_pcm_sw_params(handle_, software_params);
    snd_pcm_prepare(handle_);
    audio_thread_ = std::thread(
    [this, func, cookie, channels, frames]() {
      while (!stop_) {
        snd_pcm_wait(handle_, -1);
        func((float *)buffer_, channels, frames, cookie);
        snd_pcm_writei(handle_, buffer_, frames);
      }
    });
    sched_param sch;
    sch.sched_priority = 20;
    pthread_setschedparam(audio_thread_.native_handle(),
                        SCHED_FIFO, &sch);
  }

  ~audio_device() {
    stop_ = true;
    audio_thread_.join();
    snd_pcm_close(handle_);
    free(buffer_);
  }

  float *buffer_;
  snd_pcm_t *handle_;
  std::atomic<bool> stop_;
  std::thread audio_thread_;
};
```

CHAPTER 4

Designing a Channel-Agnostic Audio Engine

Ethan Geller

Epic Games

CONTENTS

4.1 INTRODUCTION

There is a common misconception that increasing the number of channels for an audio signal increases the overall quality of that signal in some meaningful fashion. I recall a point at which Aaron (the audio programming lead at Epic) and I were testing a feature he was working on: allowing submixes to optionally have their own channel configurations. This feature was in pursuit of adding support for ambisonics[1] in Unreal. He was testing this by having an audio source moving in a circle around the listener. This source was then downmixed and sent to a 5.1 submix, then that 5.1 submix was downmixed when sent to a stereo output, which Aaron was listening to through headphones. "This sounds *better* with the 5.1 submix!" Aaron exclaimed, and I agreed. "Why does this sound *better* than just using stereo?"

It did not take us long to realize: the panning method we used in 5.1 downmixing was resulting in significantly less dramatic differences in power between the left and right channels than the equal-power panning we were using for stereo downmixes. This created a greater sense of externalization when using headphones. However, when we used desktop stereo speakers, the "softer" panning from the intermediary 5.1 submix caused the spatial mix to be too subtle, leading to issues in sound localization when the sound source was within 45° of being directly in front or behind the listener. Regardless, the end result of the intermediary 5.1 submix in this use case could be achieved easily by changing the panning algorithm for the stereo downmix without ever dealing with more than two channels of audio.

This led me to recall an experience I had when I was in college. During winter vacation, I went over a friend's house to watch *The Conjuring*. My friend's parents had set up a 5.1 system, but to my dismay, they had placed the surround left and surround right speakers on the corners of the couch we were sitting on. Meanwhile, the front left, front right, and center channels were seven feet away, and the channels had not been mixed for this esoteric set up. "This is garbage. The mix in your parents' home theater setup is incomprehensible." I stated about 30 minutes into the movie. "I don't know what's being conjured in this movie, or who is supposed to be conjuring it." My friend shrugged. "It sounds fine to me," they said. "They're obviously conjuring some kind of ghost."

I bring up these two experiences to drive home the point that multichannel audio is a difficult problem space. Assumptions that seem valid in an ideal listening situation are consistently rebuked in real-world scenarios. Imagine a hypothetical audio engine that sees six output channels and mixes everything to a presumed channel order for 5.1 audio. The panning mechanism is based on the reference angles and distances specified in ITU-R BS 775. This audio engine may take similar approaches for two channels and eight channels for stereo and 7.1, respectively (Figure 4.1).

This hypothetical audio engine has shipped games for nearly a decade without anyone having to touch the downmix code. One day, a new affordable spatial audio solution called The Orb is released. It's easy to set up and it sells like crazy. The issue is that The Orb registers as a four-channel output device, and only accepts audio encoded to first order ambisonics. Furthermore, the developers of The Orb are already working on versions of their product that use higher-order ambisonics, and occasionally

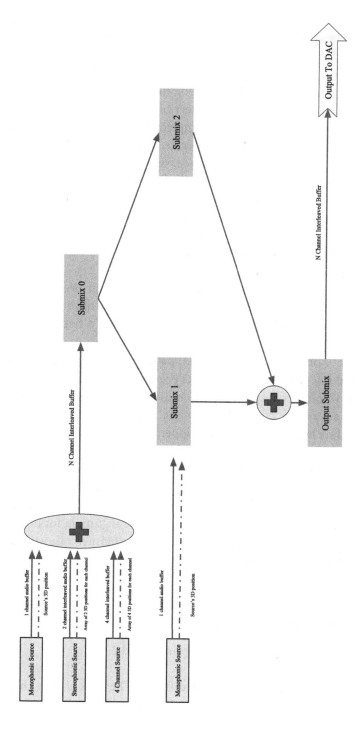

FIGURE 4.1   A fixed-channel submix graph.

mixed-order ambisonics, and The Orb API allows programs to know where speakers are placed in a user's home setup in order to better tailor their panning logic.

It doesn't take long for an executive at your company to find out you're the person responsible for their audio engine, at which point they set up a meeting with you. This meeting goes terribly: "Can we support The Orb? No? How long would it take you to implement support for The Orb for our game? *How long?!*" In a flurry of code, you write special-cased code in your critical render loop for Orb Mode, set your submixes to mix to 7.1, and write a special Orb mixdown from 7.1 to first-order ambisonics based on the Ambisonics Wikipedia page. You hope that nobody cares that you have actually negated all spatial information along the vertical axis in your mixing process. You hear the audio come out of The Orb after a week of crunching, release a sigh of relief, and live in fear of this ever occurring again.

As goofy as it sounds, the fictional Orb speaker kit presents a lot of similar issues that binaural spatialization solutions have already proposed. Do all submixes have to be post-spatialization? What if we want to apply compression to a submix? Time-varying compression will introduce a time-variant nonlinearity in our signal path, which means if we do it on a submix that has gone through an HRTF spatializer, we are distorting its finely tuned frequency response. If an audio designer is optimizing their mix to take advantage of an HRTF spatializer, they may want to make that the absolute last processing that happens on their game's audio before it reaches the speakers. Furthermore, what if you would like to send the HRTF-spatialized audio to the VR headset, but also send audio that is not HRTF-spatialized to the computer's default output audio device?

Building an audio engine that is flexible enough to handle any channel configuration or spatialization method is the core argument for designing your audio engine to be *channel-agnostic*. A channel-agnostic audio engine has three key objectives:

1. Minimizing assumptions about channel count and order.

2. Minimizing assumptions about speaker positions and angles.

3. Minimizing overhead while achieving 1 and 2.

In my experience, this is achievable but difficult. The crux of your channel-agnostic audio engine will be how you define your *Mixing Interface*.

4.2 ABSTRACTING THE MIXER

I'm going to start with an output buffer and some variables declared globally:

```
const int32 NumOutputChannels = 2;
const int32 NumOutputFrames = 512 / NumOutputChannels;

// Our stereo, interleaved output buffer.
float OutputBuffer[NumOutputFrames * NumOutputChannels];
```

I'm also going to define a struct that will define individual audio sources:

```
struct FSoundSource
{
  float AudioBuffer[NumOutputFrames];
  int32 NumFrames; // For this case will always be 256.
  int32 NumChannels; // For this case will always be 1.
  float xPos; // -1.0 is left, 1.0 is right.
}

vector<FSoundSource> AllSources;
```

Now, consider the following piece of code, in which we downmix a source to an interleaved stereo output:

```
// Begin iterating through all sources
for (auto& Source : AllSources)
{
  // iterate through all samples:
  for (int32 Index = 0; Index < NumOutputFrames; Index++)
  {
    const float LeftPhase = 0.25f * PI * (Source.xPos + 1.0f);
    const float RightPhase =
      0.5f * PI * (0.5f * (Source.xPos + 1.0f) + 1.0f);
    OutputBuffer[Index * NumOutputChannels] +=
      sinf(LeftPhase) * Source.AudioBuffer[Index];
    OutputBuffer[Index * NumOutputChannels + 1] +=
      sinf(RightPhase) * Source.AudioBuffer[Index];
  }
}
```

This works—we've iterated through all of our (presumed monophonic) sources and summed them into a stereo interleaved buffer using sinusoidal panning to approximate an equal power pan. However, we've made three assumptions here:

1. We would like to use a sinusoidal panning algorithm.

2. We will only have monophonic sources.

3. We will only have a stereo output.

Let's instead create a class called `IMixer`:

```
class IMixer
{
public:
  // Sum a monophonic source into a stereo interleaved
  // output buffer.
  virtual void SumSourceToOutputBuffer(
    float* InputAudio, float* OutputAudio, int32 NumFrames) = 0;
}
```

Let's implement our sinusoidal panning in a subclass of `IMixer`:

```
class FSinePanner : public IMixer
{
public:
  virtual void SumSourceToOutputBuffer(
    float* InputAudio, float* OutputAudio, int32 NumFrames) override
  {
    static const int32 NumOutputChannels = 2;
    for (int32 Index = 0; Index < NumFrames; Index++)
    {
      const float LeftPhase = 0.25f * PI * (Source.xPos + 1.0f);
      const float RightPhase =
        0.5f * PI * (0.5f * (Source.xPos + 1.0f) + 1.0f);
      OutputAudio[Index * NumOutputChannels] +=
        sinf(LeftPhase) * InputAudio[Index];
      OutputAudio[Index * NumOutputChannels + 1] +=
        sinf(RightPhase) * InputAudio[Index];
    }
  }
}
```

Now, let's cache a pointer to an instance of `FSinePanner`:

```
unique_ptr<IMixer> MixingInterface(new FSinePanner());
```

When we iterate through our sources, we can now just call `SumSourceToOutputBuffer()` in our loop:

```
// Iterate through all sources
for (auto& Source : AudioSources)
{
  MixingInterface->SumSourceToOutputBuffer(
    Source.AudioBuffer, Output);
}
```

With this scheme, if we wanted to use a different panning method we could just create a different subclass of `IMixer` and make `MixingInterface` point to an instance of that class instead. Let's change our `FSoundSource` struct to define a series of positions for each channel rather than just one position:

```
struct FSoundSource
{
  float* AudioBuffer; // interleaved audio buffer.
  int32 NumFrames; // The number of frames in the audio buffer.
  int32 NumChannels; // The number of channels.
  vector<float> xPositions; // The position of each channel.
}
```

Now that we have a series of positions for each channel, let's update our IMixer virtual function to take multiple input positions, and also specify a number of output channels.

```
class IMixer
{
public:
  // Sum a monophonic source into a stereo interleaved
  // output buffer.
  virtual void SumSourceToOutputBuffer(
    float* InputAudio, int32 NumInputChannels,
    const vector<float>& InputChannelPositions,
    float* OutputAudio,
    int32 NumOutputChannels, int32 NumFrames) = 0;
}
```

And now we will update our FSinePanner to match. For simplicity, the FSinePanner will only perform a stereo pan between the first two output channels for this example.

```
class FSinePanner : public IMixer
{
public:
  virtual void SumSourceToOutputBuffer(
    float* InputAudio, int32 NumInputChannels,
    vector<float>& InputChannelPositions,
    float* OutputAudio,
    int32 NumOutputChannels, int32 NumFrames) override
  {
    for (int32 Index = 0; Index < NumFrames; Index++)
    {
      for (int32 InputChannel = 0;
           InputChannel < NumInputChannels;
           InputChannel++)
      {
        const int32 InputSampleIndex =
          Index * NumInputChannels + InputChannel;
        const float LeftPhase =
          0.25f * PI * (InputChannelPositions[InputChannel] + 1.0f);
```

```
            const float RightPhase =
              0.5f * PI *
              (0.5f *
                (InputChannelPositions[InputChannel] + 1.0f) + 1.0f);
            OutputAudio[Index * NumOutputChannels] +=
              sinf(LeftPhase) * InputAudio[InputSampleIndex];
            OutputAudio[Index * NumOutputChannels + 1] +=
              sinf(RightPhase) * InputAudio[InputSampleIndex];
          }
        }
      }
}
```

Now our render loop can handle any number of input channels per source, as well as any number of output channels. It is up to whatever subclass of IMixer we use to properly handle any and all cases.

The last change I'll make to IMixer is to refactor the parameters into two structs: everything having to do with input and everything having to do with output. For input, we'll just use our FSoundSource struct, and for output, we'll create a new struct called FMixerOutputParams:

```
struct FMixerOutputParams
{
  float* OutputAudio;
  int32 NumOutputChannels;
  vector<float> OutputChannelXPositions;
  int32 NumFrames;
}

class IMixer
{
public:
  // Sum a monophonic source into a stereo interleaved
  // output buffer.
  virtual void SumSourceToOutputBuffer(
    const FAudioSource& Input, FMixerOutputParams& Output) = 0;
}
```

Notice that I also created an array of output channel positions: our FSinePanner could now potentially choose how to pan to each output speaker based on its position.

Packing our parameters into these structs gives us two critical improvements:

- SumSourceToOutputBuffer() has become much easier on the eyes, both wherever it is implemented and wherever it is used.

- If we ever decide we need additional parameters, we can add additional member variables to these structs without changing the function signature that subclasses have to implement.

There is a notable concern with this move, however: moving parameters to structs means that you could easily miss properly setting a parameter before calling one of these functions without causing any sort of compiler errors.

It may not seem like we accomplished very much, since we have essentially just extracted our panning code, but think about what this now allows us to do. We can support different panning methods, channel configurations, and multichannel sources—and best of all, we can swap them out at runtime, so long as we reset the `MixingInterface` pointer in a thread-safe way.

However, there are a few issues that we'd run into if we just stopped here:

1. Subclasses of `IMixer` currently could not maintain any sort of state between calls of `SumSourceToOutputBuffer()`. For example, if a mixer used any sort of filter, they will need to retain a cache of previous samples between buffers. How can the mixer do this if it does not know which source or output buffer that `SumSourceToOutputBuffer()` is operating on?

2. Formats that reproduce sound fields rather than sound from specific positions, like Ambisonics, would not be well-supported using `IMixer`. When The Orb (our fictional spatial audio solution) is released, we'd still be in a pretty bad place to use it.

In order to solve these two problems, we're going to give our mixer interface complete control over how our audio is represented in every dimension, from when we pass it sources to when we are sending audio to speaker channels. To do this, we are going to design the mixing process as disparate *encoding streams*, *transcoding streams*, and *decoding streams*.

4.3 MIXER STREAMS

Let's remove any terminology having to do with downmixing and upmixing, and instead treat buffers as matrices with arbitrary dimensions decided by the *mixer interface*.

In Figure 4.2, every evenly dashed arrow is a buffer of audio data entirely defined by the mixer interface. Whenever we previously were going to *downmix* a source's audio to a channel bed, we are now going to create an *encoding stream*. Wherever we previously needed to do a channel conversion (say, downmix a 7.1 submix to stereo) we will instead set up a *transcoding stream*. And whenever we were going to mix audio to a channel configuration that corresponds to physical speaker positions, we will instead set up a *decoding stream*.

The encoded stream is going to have to represent a *generalized soundfield*, rather than a set of singular channels. If you have experience in the broadcast world or recording audio in the real world with multi-mic setups, you may notice that I am using a lot of terminology used to refer to microphone configurations. For example, one could transcode a soundfield captured with a Mid-Side microphone configuration to a mono-cardioid stream or an ORTF stream. Downmixing could be considered a very basic approximation of a virtual microphone configuration. This was what fixed-channel audio engines have attempted to use downmixed 5.1/7.1 channel beds for. Our mixer interface could follow this behavior or replicate more advanced methods of soundfield capture. A mixer implementation could even emulate different actual microphone patterns. A different implementation of the mixer interface could enable an entire submix graph in ambisonics, including transcoding streams for connecting a first-order submix to a second-order submix, for example.

4.3.1 The Fixed-Channel Submix Graph Rendering Loop

Let's create a rendering loop for a fixed-channel submix graph using the mixer interface we described previously:

```
void FSubmix::ProcessAndMixInAudio(
  float* OutBuffer, int NumFrames, int NumChannels)
{
  // Loop through all submixes that input here and recursively
  // mix in their audio:
  for (FSubmix& ChildSubmix : ChildSubmixes)
  {
    ChildSubmix->ProcessAndMixInAudio(
      OutBuffer, NumFrames, NumChannels);
  }

  // Set up an FMixerOutputParams struct with our output
  // channel positions.
  FMixerOutputParams OutParams;
```

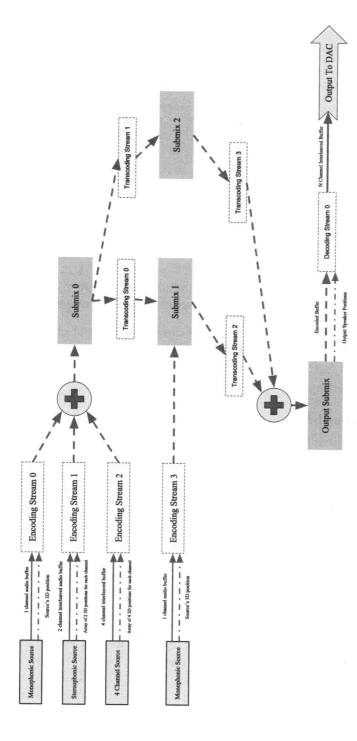

FIGURE 4.2 Basic flow of a channel-agnostic submix graph.

```
OutParams.OutputAudio = OutBuffer;
OutParams.NumOutputChannels = NumChannels;
OutParams.OutputChannelXPositions = GetDeviceChannelPositions();
OutParams.NumFrames = NumFrames;

// Loop through all sources connected to this submix and
// mix in their audio:
for ( FSoundSource& Source : ConnectedSources )
{
  MixerInterface->SumSourceToOutputBuffer(Source, OutParams);
}

// Any processing you'd want to do in a submix -
// including DSP effects like reverb - would go here.
}
```

There are some really nice things about this loop:

- It's simple.

- We're able to process our entire submix graph inline in a single buffer, meaning our submix graph uses O(1) memory usage.

- By using the mixer interface, we can specify output channel positions at runtime without having to alter our submix graph. We can support features such as changing panning laws based on runtime audio settings without rebuilding our submix graph.

As we start building our channel-agnostic submix graph, we should try to retain these qualities.

4.3.2 Incorporating Streams into Our Mixer Interface

First, let's introduce a base class to hold whatever submix settings our mixer interface would like to specify:

```
class FMixerSubmixSettingsBase
{
  // ...
};
```

I would recommend making the submix settings base class as barebones as possible so that the mixer interface implementation can define exactly what they need to know. If we are able to use reflection, we can use it to filter for this mixer interface's Settings class:

```
REFLECTED_CLASS()
class MixerSubmixSettingsBase
```

```
{
  GENERATE_REFLECTED_CLASS_BODY()
};
```

Similar to how we created `FMixerOutputParams`, let's create input and output parameter structs for our encoding, decoding, and transcoding streams:

```
// Encoder Stream Data
struct FMixerEncoderInputData
{
  // The source to encode audio from.
  FSoundSource InputSource;

  // this will point to the settings of the submix this callback
  // is encoding to.
  MixerSubmixSettingsBase* InputSettings;
};

struct FMixerEncoderOutputData
{
  // Buffer that the encoding stream will sum into.
  float* AudioBuffer;
  int NumFrames;
};

// Decoder Stream Data:
struct FMixerDecoderPositionalData
{
  int32 OutputNumChannels;

  // FVector is a struct containing three floats
  // representing cartesian coordinates in 3D space.
  vector<FVector> OutputChannelPositions;

  FQuat ListenerRotation;
};

struct FMixerDecoderInputData
{
  // Encoded stream data.
  float* AudioBuffer;
  int32 NumFrames;

  // this will point to the settings of the submix this stream
  // was encoded with.
  MixerSubmixSettingsBase* InputSettings;

  FMixerDecoderPositionalData& OutputChannelPositions;
};

struct FMixerDecoderOutputData
{
```

```
  float* AudioBuffer;
  int NumFrames;
};

// Transcoder Stream Data
struct FMixerTranscoderCallbackData
{
  // encoded stream data.
  // We already have enough space allocated here for
  // the larger of the two streams we are transcoding between.
  float* AudioBuffer;                    •

  int NumFrames;

  // Settings of the submix we are transcoding from.
  MixerSubmixSettingsBase* SourceStreamSettings;

  // Settings of the submix we are transcoding to.
  MixerSubmixSettingsBase* DestinationStreamSettings;
};
```

Now we can define our stream interfaces:

```
class IMixerEncodingStream
{
public:
  virtual ~IEncodingStream();

  // Function we call on every encode.
  virtual void EncodeAndSumIntoBuffer(
    FMixerEncoderInputData& Input,
    FMixerEncoderOutputData& Output) = 0;
};

class IMixerDecodingStream
{
public:
  virtual ~IMixerDecodingStream();

  // Function we call on every decode.
  virtual void DecodeBuffer(
    FMixerDecoderInputData& Input,
    FMixerDecoderOutputData & Output) = 0;
};

class IMixerTranscodingStream
{
public:
  virtual ~IMixerDecodingStream();

  // Function we call on every transcode.
  virtual void TranscodeBuffer(
    FMixerTranscoderCallbackData& BufferData) = 0;
};
```

Notice that we only have one buffer for both input and output for our transcoder stream. This is because we want the transcoding process to be done *in place*. Converting any interleaved buffer between two numbers of channels can be done within the same buffer as long as there is enough space for the larger of the two buffers. For example, here's a process for converting a stereo interleaved signal to a 5.1 interleaved signal by starting at the last frame:

```
void MixStereoToFiveDotOne(float* Buffer, int NumFrames)
{
  const int NumInputChannels = 2;
  const int NumOutputChannels = 6;
  for (int FrameIndex = NumFrames - 1;
       FrameIndex >= 0;
       FrameIndex--)
  {
    float* OutputFrame = &Buffer[FrameIndex * NumOutputChannels];
    float* InputFrame = &Buffer[FrameIndex * NumInputChannels];

    // Left:
    OutputFrame[0] = InputFrame[0];
    // Right:
    OutputFrame[1] = InputFrame[1];
    // Center:
    OutputFrame[2] = 0.0f;
    // LFE:
    OutputFrame[3] = 0.0f;
    // Left Surround:
    OutputFrame[4] = InputFrame[0];
    // Right Surround:
    OutputFrame[5] = InputFrame[1];
  }
}
```

By starting at the last frame, you ensure that you are not overwriting any information until you are finished with it. When going from more channels to less, you can start from the front:

```
void MixFiveDotOneToStereo(float* Buffer, int NumFrames)
{
  const int NumInputChannels = 6;
  const int NumOutputChannels = 2;
  for (int FrameIndex = 0; FrameIndex > NumFrames; FrameIndex++)
  {
    float* OutputFrame = &Buffer[FrameIndex * NumOutputChannels];
    float* InputFrame = &Buffer[FrameIndex * NumInputChannels];

    // Left:
    OutputFrame[0] = (InputFrame[0] + InputFrame[4]);
    // Right:
```

```
        OutputFrame[1] = (InputFrame[1] + InputFrame[5]);
    }
}
```

It is possible that an implementation of the mixer interface will need additional state when transcoding. We will leave it up to the mixer interface to handle this state within its implementation of the transcoding stream.

Finally, let's update our mixer API.

```
class IMixerInterface
{
public:
    // This is where a MixerInterface defines its
    // stream implementations:
    virtual IMixerEncodingStream* CreateNewEncodingStream() = 0;
    virtual IMixerDecodingStream* CreateNewDecodingStream() = 0;
    virtual IMixerTranscodingStream* CreateNewTranscodingStream() = 0;

    // This function takes advantage of our reflection system.
    // It's handy for checking casts, but not necessary
    // unless we would like to use multiple IMixerInterfaces
    // in our submix graph.
    virtual REFLECTED_CLASS* GetSettingsClass() { return nullptr; };

    // This function will let up know how much space we should
    // reserve for audio buffers.
    virtual int GetNumChannelsForStream(
      MixerSubmixSettingsBase* StreamSettings) = 0;

    // This function will allow us to only create transcoding streams
    // where necessary.
    virtual bool ShouldTranscodeBetween(
      MixerSubmixSettingsBase* InputStreamSettings,
      MixerSubmixSettingsBase* OutputStreamSettings) { return true; }
}
```

That's it—we now have a mixer interface that will allow us to have a fully channel-agnostic submix graph. Furthermore, fully implementing this in our submix code will not actually be as difficult as it may initially seem.

4.3.3 A Channel-Agnostic Submix Graph

Most of the work of supporting this new interface will be in initialization procedures. Here is our submix declaration:

```
class FSubmix
{
public:
```

```
    size_t GetNecessaryBufferSize(int NumFrames);

    // This function will traverse the current graph and return
    // the max number of channels we need for any of the submixes.
    int GetMaxChannelsInGraph();

    void Connect(FSubmix& ChildSubmix);
    void Connect(FSoundSource& InputSource);

    void Disconnect(FSubmix& ChildSubmix);
    void Disconnect(FSoundSource& InputSource);

    void Start(MixerSubmixSettingsBase* ParentSettings);

    void ProcessAndMixInAudio(float* OutBuffer, int NumFrames);

    MixerSubmixSettingsBase* SubmixSettings;
private:
    struct FSourceSendInfo
    {
      FSoundSource* Source;
      IMixerEncodingStream* EncodingStream;
      FMixerEncoderInputData EncoderData;
    };

    vector<FSourceSendInfo> InputSources;

    vector<FSubmix*> ChildSubmixes;

    //This starts out null, but is initialized during Start()
    IMixerTranscodingStream* TranscodingStream;

    // Cached OutputData struct for encoders.
    FMixerEncoderOutputData EncoderOutput;

    // Cached TranscoderData struct.
    FMixerTranscoderCallbackData TranscoderData;
};
```

In order to know how large a buffer our submix graph requires for its process loop, we'll use the maximum number of channels required by any one node in our submix graph:

```
size_t FSubmix::GetNecessaryBufferSize(int NumFrames)
{
    return NumFrames * sizeof(float) * GetMaxChannelsInGraph();
}
```

To get the maximum number of channels in our graph, we'll traverse the whole node graph with this handy recursive function:

```
int FSubmix::GetMaxChannelsInGraph()
{
  int MaxChannels =
    MixerInterface->GetNumChannelsForStream(SubmixSettings);
  for( FSubmix& Submix : ChildSubmixes )
  {
    MaxChannels = max(MaxChannels, Submix.GetMaxChannelsInGraph());
  }

  return MaxChannels;
}
```

When we connect a new submix as an input to this submix, we don't need to do anything special.

```
void FSubmix::Connect(FSubmix& ChildSubmix)
{
  ChildSubmixes.push_back(ChildSubmix);
}
```

When we connect a new audio source to our submix, we'll need to set up a new encoding stream with it:

```
void FSubmix::Connect(FSoundSource& InputSource)
{
  FSourceSendInfo NewInfo;
  NewInfo.Source = &InputSource;
  NewInfo.EncodingStream =
    MixerInterface->CreateNewEncodingStream();
  NewInfo.EncoderData.Source = InputSource;
  NewInfo.EncoderData.InputSettings = SubmixSettings;

  InputSources.push_back(NewInfo);
}
```

When we disconnect a child submix, we'll iterate through our child submixes and remove whichever one lives at the same address as the submix we get as a parameter in this function. There are both more efficient and safer ways to do this than pointer comparison. However, for the purposes of this chapter, this implementation will suffice:

```
void Disconnect(FSubmix& ChildSubmix)
{
  ChildSubmixes.erase(
    remove(ChildSubmixes.begin(),
           ChildSubmixes.end(),
           &ChildSubmix),
    ChildSubmixes.end());
}
```

We'll follow a similar pattern when disconnecting input sources, but we will also make sure to clean up our encoding stream once it is disconnected. Since we have declared a virtual destructor for IMixerEncodingStream, calling delete here will propagate down to the implementation of IMixerEncodingStream's destructor:

```
void Disconnect(FSoundSource& InputSource)
{
  auto Found = find(InputSources.begin(),
                    InputSources.end(),
                    &InputSource);
  if(Found != InputSources.end())
  {
    delete *Found;
    InputSources.erase(Found);
  }
}
```

Before we begin processing audio, we'll make sure that we set up trans-coding streams anywhere they are necessary. We will recursively do this upwards through the submix graph:

```
void Start(MixerSubmixSettingsBase* ParentSettings)
{
  if(MixerInterface->ShouldTranscodeBetween(SubmixSettings,
                                            ParentSettings))
  {
    TranscodingStream = MixerInterface->CreateNewTranscodingStream();
    TranscoderData.SourceStreamSettings = SubmixSettings;
    TranscoderData.DestinationStreamSettings = ParentSettings;
  }
  else
  {
    TranscodingStream = nullptr;
  }

  for (FSoundSubmix* Submix : ChildSubmixes)
  {
    Submix->Start();
  }
}
```

Finally, let's update our process loop. You'll notice that it doesn't actu-ally look that much different from our original, fixed-channel loop. The primary difference is that, at the end of our loop, we may possibly be transcoding to whatever submix we are outputting to. Notice that we still retain our O(1) memory growth because we handle transcoding in place.

```
void FSoundSubmix::ProcessAndMixInAudio(
  float* OutBuffer, int NumFrames)
{
  // Loop through all submixes that input here and recursively
  // mix in their audio:
  for (FSubmix& ChildSubmix : ChildSubmixes)
  {
    ChildSubmix->ProcessAndMixInAudio(OutBuffer, NumFrames);
  }

  // Set up an FMixerOutputParams struct with our output
  // channel positions.
  EncoderOutput.AudioBuffer = OutBuffer;
  EncoderOutput.NumFrames = NumFrames;

  // Loop through all sources connected to this submix and mix
  // in their audio:
  for ( FSourceSendInfo& Source : InputSources)
  {
    Source.EncodingStream->EncodeAndSumIntoBuffer(
      Source.EncoderData, EncoderOutput);
  }

  // Any processing you'd want to do in a submix-
  // including DSP effects like reverb- would go here.

  //If we need to do a transcode to the parent, do it here.
  if ( TranscodingStream != nullptr )
  {
    TranscoderData.AudioBuffer = OutBuffer;
    TranscoderData.NumFrames = NumFrames;
    TranscodingStream->TranscodeBuffer(TranscoderData);
  }
}
```

Decoding will be handled just outside of the submix graph:

```
// set up decoding stream:
unique_ptr<IMixerDecodingStream> DecoderStream(
  MixerInterface->CreateNewDecodingStream());

// Set up audio output buffer:
int NumFrames = 512;
float* EncodedBuffer =
  (float*) malloc(OutputSubmix.GetNecessaryBufferSize(512));

// Set up decoder input data with the encoded buffer:
FMixerDecoderInputData DecoderInput;
DecoderInput.AudioBuffer = EncodedBuffer;
DecoderInput.NumFrames = NumFrames;
DecoderInput.InputSettings = OutputSubmix.SubmixSettings;

// There are many ways to handle output speaker positions.
// Here I'll hardcode a version that represents a 5.1 speaker
```

```
// setup:
vector<FVector> OutputSpeakerPositions = {
  {1.0f, 1.0f, 0.0f}, // right
  {1.0f, 0.0f, 0.0f}, // center
  {0.0f, 0.0f, -1.0f}, // LFE
  {-1.0f,-1.0f, 0.0f}, // Left Rear
  {-1.0f, 1.0f, 0.0f} }; // Right Rear

FMixerDecoderPositionalData SpeakerPositions;
SpeakerPositions.OutputNumChannels = 6;
SpeakerPositions.OutputChannelPositions = OutputSpeakerPositions;
SpeakerPositions.ListenerRotation = {1.0f, 0.0f, 0.0f, 0.0f};

// Let's also set up a decoded buffer output:
FMixerDecoderOutputData DecoderOutput;
DecoderOutput.AudioBuffer =
  (float*) malloc(sizeof(float) * 6 * NumFrames);
DecoderOutput.NumFrames = NumFrames;

// Start rendering audio:
OutputSubmix.Start();

while(RenderingAudio)
{
  UpdateSourceBuffers();
  OutputSubmix.ProcessAndMixInAudio(EncodedBuffer, NumFrames);
  DecoderStream->DecodeBuffer(DecoderInput, DecoderOutput);
  SendAudioToDevice(DecoderOutput.AudioBuffer, NumFrames);
}

// Cleanup:
free(EncodedBuffer);
free(DecoderOutput.AudioBuffer);

delete DecoderStream;
```

4.3.4 Supporting Submix Effects

One of the biggest concerns with the channel-agnostic submix graph is what it means for submix effects, such as reverb or compression. My recommendation would be to propagate the submix's effect settings to the effect:

```
class ISubmixEffect
{
public:
  virtual void Init(MixerSubmixSettingsBase* InSettings) {}
  virtual void ProcessEffect(
    float* Buffer, int NumFrames,
    MixerSubmixSettingsBase* InSettings) = 0;
};
```

This way the effect can determine things such as the number of channels in the interleaved buffer using our mixer interface:

```cpp
class FAmplitudeModulator : public ISubmixEffect
{
private:
  int SampleRate;
  int NumChannels;
  float ModulatorFrequency;
public:
  virtual void Init(
    int InSampleRate,
    MixerSubmixSettingsBase* InSettings) override
  {
    SampleRate = SampleRate;
    NumChannels =
      MixerInterface->GetNumChannelsForStream(InSettings);
    ModulatorFrequency = 0.5f;
  }

  virtual void ProcessEffect(
    float* Buffer, int NumFrames,
    MixerSubmixSettingsBase* InSettings) override
  {
    // World's laziest AM implementation:
    static float n = 0.0f;
    for(int FrameIndex = 0; FrameIndex < NumFrames; FrameIndex++)
    {
      for (int ChannelIndex = 0;
           ChannelIndex < NumChannels;
           ChannelIndex++)
      {
        Buffer[FrameIndex + ChannelIndex] *=
          sinf(ModulatorFrequency * 2 * M_PI * n / SampleRate);
      }
      n += 1.0f;
    }
  }
}
```

Furthermore, if you are in a programming environment where you can utilize reflection, submix effects could support specific mixer interfaces different ways:

```cpp
class FAmbisonicsEffect : public ISubmixEffect
{
private:
  int SampleRate;
  int AmbisonicsOrder;
public:
  virtual void Init(
    int InSampleRate,
    MixerSubmixSettingsBase* InSettings) override
```

```
{
  if(MixerInterface->GetSettingsClass() ==
    CoolAmbisonicsMixerSettings::GetStaticClass())
  {
    CoolAmbisonicsMixerSettings* AmbiSettings =
      dynamic_cast<CoolAmbisonicsMixerSettings*>(InSettings);
    AmbisonicsOrder = AmbiSettings->Order;
  }
  // ...
}
// ...
}
```

Of course, implementing support for every individual mixer type could become extremely complex as the number of potential mixer interfaces grows. However, supporting a *handful* of mixer implementations separately while falling back to using just the channel count when faced with an unsupported mixer interface is viable. Allowing developers to create reverb and dynamics plugins specifically designed for The Orb will foster a healthy developer ecosystem around both The Orb and your audio engine.

4.4 FURTHER CONSIDERATIONS

This is just the start of creating a robust and performant channel-agnostic system. Building from this, we could consider

- *Consolidating streams.* In its current form, the submix graph encodes every separate source independently for each individual submix send. We could potentially only set up encoding streams so that every source is only encoded to a specific configuration once per callback, then that cached buffer is retrieved every time that source mixed into the submix process.

- *Submix sends.* The example formulation we gave of a submix graph does not support sending the audio from one submix to another submix without that submix being its sole parent. Setting up submix sends using this system, while using the requisite transcoding streams, may prove useful.

The channel-agnostic submix graph we've built here can support ambisonics, 5.1, 7.1, stereo, 7.1.4, 5.1.2, 24-channel spherical ambisonics reproduction speaker configurations, 64-channel Dolby Atmos cinemas, and even the aforementioned mystical Orb home theater audio solution. This engine supports virtually any system for recreating a sound field. By making your audio engine channel-agnostic, you will be able to develop and maintain it for many generations of developments and breakthroughs in audio spatialization and wavefield synthesis.

NOTE

1 Ambisonics is a surround format that breaks up a two- or three-dimensional sound field into discrete channels representing a spherical harmonic decomposition of a limited order, typically between first and third order.

CHAPTER 5

Audio Resampling

Guy Somberg
Echtra Games

CONTENTS

5.1 INTRODUCTION

One of the fundamental operations that an audio mixer must perform is that of sample rate conversion: taking a buffer of samples at one sample rate and converting it to another sample rate. More precisely, sample-rate conversion is the process of changing the sampling rate of a discrete signal to obtain a new discrete representation of the underlying continuous signal. While this is a nice pithy statement that accurately sums up the end result we're trying to achieve, finding concise and intuitive descriptions of the actual process of resampling is maddeningly difficult. Most of the literature either describes it using vague mathematical constructs or describes it in terms of hardware and wiring. In this chapter, we will attempt to construct an intuition for how resampling works, and derive some code for a linear resampler.

Note that, while there will be a lot of math in this section, we will not be constructing the formulas from principles, but rather describing the process, and intuiting a formulation from it.

5.2 RESAMPLING

To state the problem we are trying to solve more directly, we have a stream of samples at N Hz, and we want to perform a function on this stream that outputs an equivalent stream of samples at M Hz. Or, in code terms:

```
void Resample(int input_frequency, int output_frequency,
              const float* input, size_t input_length,
              float* output, size_t output_length)
{
    // fill code here...
}
```

Ultimately, what we will have to do in order to accomplish this is to select certain samples from the input signal and fabricate others (based on the resampling ratio). Let's make this example more concrete by selecting actual numbers: let's say that we have an input signal at 12 Hz and we want to resample it to 20 Hz. Figure 5.1 shows our input signal at 12 Hz.

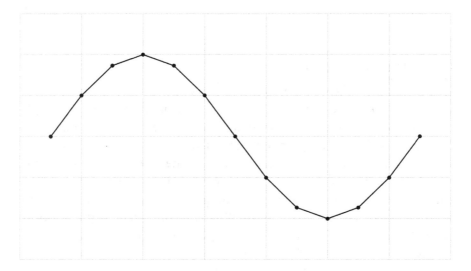

FIGURE 5.1 A signal at 12 Hz.

There is no trivial conversion from 12 Hz to 20 Hz, as there would be with (for example) 30 Hz to 15 Hz, where we could simply take every other sample. What we really need is to be able to look at our source signal in two different ways: if we squint at it *this* way it looks like 12 Hz, and if we squint at it *that* way it looks like 20 Hz. More generally, our signal is a discrete representation of a continuous signal. If we can interpret our signal as its continuous representation, then we can sample it at whatever resolution we want.

Obviously, we cannot use the continuous signal directly, since we are operating on a discrete digital signal. However, what we can do is move our signal to a convenient representation that is closer to the continuous signal: we will take the least common multiple (LCM) of the two sampling rates (an approximation of the continuous signal), up-sample the signal to that new sample rate by fabricating some samples in between, and then down-sample back to our desired sample rate. This procedure will work for any two pairs of sample rates, whether the sample rate is getting larger or smaller.

In our example, the LCM of 12 Hz and 20 Hz is 60 Hz, so we up-sample our signal to 60 Hz by linearly interpolating between the two existing samples, as in Figure 5.2. Then to get down to 20 Hz, we take every third sample, as in Figure 5.3. To do the reverse (from 20 Hz to 12 Hz), we start

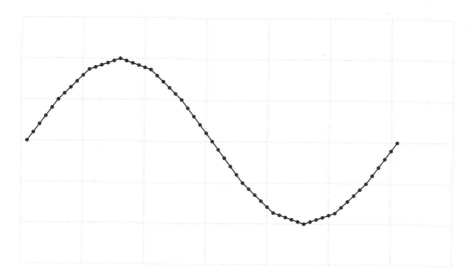

FIGURE 5.2   A 12 Hz signal up-sampled to 60 Hz.

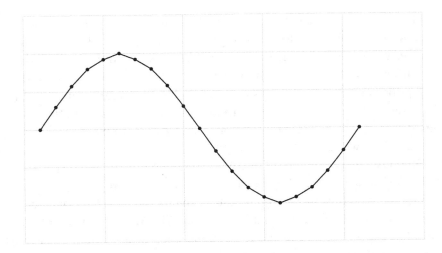

FIGURE 5.3 A 12 Hz signal up-sampled to 60 Hz, then down-sampled to 20 Hz.

with a 20-Hz signal (Figure 5.4), up-sample it to 60 Hz (Figure 5.5), and then take every fifth sample to get to 12 Hz (Figure 5.6). Note that the signal in Figure 5.4 is closer to the continuous signal than the up-sampled version from Figure 5.3 because it has been sampled from a higher sample rate source.

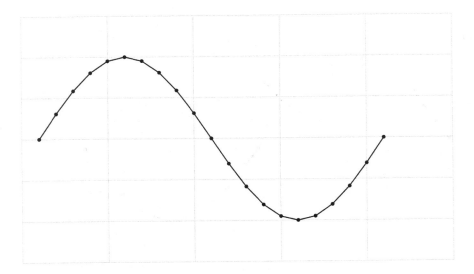

FIGURE 5.4 A 20 Hz signal.

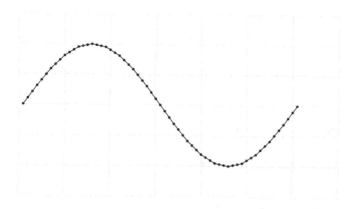

FIGURE 5.5   A 20 Hz signal up-sampled to 60 Hz.

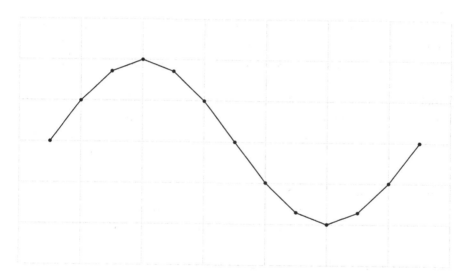

FIGURE 5.6   A 20 Hz signal up-sampled to 60 Hz, then down-sampled to 12 Hz.

5.2.1 A REQUIRED OPTIMIZATION

This algorithm works great for numbers such as 12 Hz and 20 Hz, which are small. But in reality, we'll be resampling much larger values. In extreme situations, we may even be resampling between values such as 192,000 Hz and 44,100 Hz, which have an LCM of 28,224,000. Obviously, we cannot actually resample our data up to 22 million samples per second. Not only would the data size be ridiculously large (nearly 900 megabytes for a single second of eight-channel floating-point data), it's a huge waste of processing power, since we'll be throwing out most of the samples that we generate.[1]

So, instead of performing the interpolation on all of the samples, and then selecting the ones that we need, we will perform our interpolation on the fly on just those samples that we are interested in. There are many different kinds of interpolation, but for the purposes of this chapter we will focus on the linear interpolation.

5.3 A LINEAR INTERPOLATOR

If we examine the ratios of the LCM frequency to the input frequencies, it will tell us how many samples we need to read from the input for every sample that we need to write to the output. For example, in our original example, the LCM was 60 Hz, and the ratio for the input frequency of 12 Hz is therefore 60 Hz/12 Hz = 5. Similarly, the output frequency ratio is 60 Hz/20 Hz = 3. This means that to mix from 12 Hz to 20 Hz we need to read three input samples for every five output samples. Contrariwise, to go from 20 Hz to 12 Hz, we consume five input samples for every three output samples.

Let's try that with bigger numbers: 192,000 Hz and 44,100 Hz, for which the LCM is 28,224,000 Hz. Our ratios are 28,224,000 Hz/192,000 Hz = 147 and 28,224,000 Hz/44,100 Hz = 640. So, to convert from 192,000 Hz to 44,100 Hz, we consume 640 samples for every 147 output samples.

Great! So now we know how many samples to consume and at what ratio. But what do we do with those numbers? How do we turn that into actual sample data?

First, let's take a look at the actual input values from our original 12 Hz→20 Hz conversion and see if we can intuit some relationship between the numbers.

The values in Tables 5.1 and 5.2 are as follows:

- **Output Index**—Index number of the output sample

- **From**—Beginning index from the input samples

- **To**—Next sample after *From*

- **Offset**—The number of LCM samples past the *From* index

First, we can very quickly see that the Offset column follows a pattern: (0, 2, 1) when converting from 20 Hz to 12 Hz, and (0, 3, 1, 4, 2) when converting from 12 Hz to 20 Hz. We can also see a pattern to the values in the

TABLE 5.1   Sampling from 20 to 12 Hz

Output Index	From	To	Offset
0	0	1	0
1	1	2	2
2	3	4	1
3	5	6	0
4	6	7	2
5	8	9	1
6	10	11	0
7	11	12	2
8	13	14	1
9	15	16	0
10	16	17	2
11	18	19	1

TABLE 5.2   Sampling from 12 to 20 Hz

Output Index	From	To	Offset
0	0	1	0
1	0	1	3
2	1	2	1
3	1	2	4
4	2	3	2
5	3	4	0
6	3	4	3
7	4	5	1
8	4	5	4
9	5	6	2
10	6	7	0
11	6	7	3

From column, which is that we consume three output samples for every five input samples (or vice versa). This is unsurprising, since we have constructed the data that way, but we can nevertheless see that relationship in action here.

From these values, we can intuit a relationship among the various parameters. First, let's define a few terms:

- Input frequency ($freq_{in}$)—Sample rate of the data that is being inputted into the resampler.

- Output frequency ($freq_{out}$)—Sample rate of the data that is being outputted from the resampler.

- LCM—Least common multiple of the input frequency and the output frequency.

- Input ratio (R_{in})—LCM/$freq_{in}$

- Output ratio (R_{out})—LCM/$freq_{out}$

Now, by examining the data, we can convince ourselves that

$$From = \left\lfloor \frac{index \cdot R_{out}}{R_{in}} \right\rfloor$$

$$To = From + 1$$

$$Offset = (R_{out} \cdot index) \bmod R_{in}$$

From here, it is trivial to fabricate the actual point value as:

$$Output = Lerp\left(Input_{From}, Input_{To}, \frac{Offset}{R_{in}} \right)$$

5.4 CODE FOR A LINEAR RESAMPLER

We now have enough information to fill in the code from Section 5.3:

```
float Lerp(float from, float to, float t)
{
  return (1.0f - t) * from + t * to;
}

void Resample(int input_frequency, int output_frequency,
              const float* input, size_t input_length,
              float* output, size_t output_length)
{
  auto LCM = std::lcm(input_frequency, output_frequency);
  auto InputRatio = LCM / input_frequency;
  auto OutputRatio = LCM / output_frequency;
  for(size_t i = 0; i < output_length; i++)
  {
    auto From = i * OutputRatio / InputRatio;
    auto To = From + 1;
    auto Offset = (i * OutputRatio) % InputRatio;
    Output[i] = Lerp(input[From], input[To],
                     Offset / static_cast<float>(InputRatio));
  }
}
```

Note that the calculation of the LCM is a nontrivial calculation, and you should probably move it out of this function and cache it for the duration of the playback. It is presented inline in the function for expository purposes. Note also that `std::lcm` is a C++ standard library function that is new as of C++17. If you do not have a sufficiently updated compiler or library at your disposal, you may need to write the function yourself, which is not terribly complicated (but is outside the scope of this chapter).

5.5 SIMPLIFYING THE CODE

The code in Section 5.4 is perfectly serviceable, but it's a bit inefficient. Even if we cache the results of the `std::lcm` call, there are plenty of wasted operations here. Let's see what we can do to improve this code.

5.5.1 Removing the LCM

Let's take a step back for a moment and revisit our formula for the `From` value:

$$From = \left\lfloor \frac{index \cdot R_{out}}{R_{in}} \right\rfloor$$

$$R_{in} = \frac{LCM}{freq_{in}}$$

$$R_{out} = \frac{LCM}{freq_{out}}$$

This is a formula that is ripe for simplification. Let's plug the values of R_{in} and R_{out} into the formula for `From`:

$$From = \left\lfloor \frac{index \cdot \dfrac{LCM}{freq_{out}}}{\dfrac{LCM}{freq_{in}}} \right\rfloor = \left\lfloor \frac{index \cdot \dfrac{1}{freq_{out}}}{\dfrac{1}{freq_{in}}} \right\rfloor = \left\lfloor \frac{index \cdot freq_{in}}{freq_{out}} \right\rfloor$$

And just like that, our LCM has disappeared entirely from our formula. We're still using it in the `Offset` value, but we will tackle that momentarily.

5.5.2 Simplifying the Function Declaration

Let's take another look now at our function declaration:

```
void Resample(int input_frequency, int output_frequency,
              const float* input, size_t input_length,
              float* output, size_t output_length)
```

The `input_frequency` and `output_frequency` parameters are in the units of samples per second, and their values represent the number of frames of audio data that we're going to read in one second worth of time. The `input_length` and `output_length` parameters are in the units of samples. Except, if you think about it, they're not just in samples, they're actually in units of *samples per unit of time*, where the unit of time is the duration of a single buffer of audio data.

We now have two different input parameters with units of samples per unit of time, and they are both representing the frequency of the respective buffers. It turns out, though that we don't need the actual frequencies—what we are interested in is the ratio of the two frequencies, as we saw in Section 5.5.1. It's not hard to see that, by definition:

$$\frac{freq_{in}}{freq_{out}} = \frac{length_{in}}{length_{out}}$$

We can now rewrite our function signature as:

```
void Resample(const float* input, size_t input_length,
              float* output, size_t output_length)
```

And our formula for `From` is now:

$$From = \left\lfloor \frac{index \cdot length_{in}}{length_{out}} \right\rfloor$$

5.5.3 The Simpler Code

Now that we have simplified the components of our formulas, let's put it all together into some new, better code:

```
void Resample(const float* input, size_t input_length,
              float* output, size_t output_length)
{
  float ratio = input_length / static_cast<float>(output_length);
  float i = 0.0f;
```

```
for (int j=0; j<output_length; j++)
{
  auto From = static_cast<int>(i);
  auto To = From + 1;
  float t = i - From;
  output[j] = Lerp(input[From], input[To], t);
  i += ratio;
}
}
```

There are a couple of things to note about this code, as it relates to the formulas that we have derived:

- Rather than explicitly calculating From every time through the loop, we are accumulating one ratio per iteration of the loop. This ends up having the same value, but is more efficient than calculating the value explicitly.

- Similarly, we are calculating the Offset by repeated accumulation, rather than by calculating it explicitly. Again, this iterative formulation gives us the same values in a more efficient manner.

- The code above has a couple of edge cases that will prevent it from being a "plug and play" solution. In particular, if the From is equal to input_length − 1 then this code will overflow the input buffer. To make it real, you'll need to detect this case, and potentially to shuffle a sample around from call to call to use as input.

5.6 OTHER RESAMPLERS

While a linear resampler is quite sufficient for most game purposes, you may want to experiment with other resampling options. There are innumerable interpolation functions that work in this context, and they all have different frequency response properties, typically at the cost of memory. For more details on resamplers and their properties and implementation details, I can recommend a paper by Olli Niemitalo entitled "Polynomial Interpolators for High-Quality Resampling of Oversampled Audio."[2]

5.7 CONCLUSION

Resampling is so fundamental to the operation of an audio engine, but we so rarely actually think about it and how it works. Even if you never actually write code at the level of the algorithms described in this chapter, it is important to have an intuitive understanding of what the audio engine is doing at a low level. Hopefully, this chapter has helped to create an intuition about how resampling works at a low level. The code presented in this chapter is just a starting point—there are plenty of opportunities for optimizations, and many other resampling algorithms with different aural properties.

ACKNOWLEDGMENT

Many thanks to Dan Murray (author of Chapters 3 and 7 in this volume) for helping to edit this chapter and for the code samples.

NOTES

1 Fun trivia fact: the lowest frequency you're likely to see in audio is 8,000Hz, and the highest frequency you're likely to see is 192,000 Hz. The combination of ratios with the highest LCM in that range is between 191,998 Hz and 183,999 Hz, which have an LCM of 36,863,424,002 Hz! It's highly unlikely that you'll see these two particular frequencies in your resampler, but if you do, you definitely don't want to spend the 1.18 TB of data for one second of eight-channel audio.

2 http://yehar.com/blog/?p=197.

CHAPTER 6

Introduction to DSP Prototyping

Jorge Garcia

Freelance

CONTENTS

6.1 INTRODUCTION

In this chapter, we will explore the prototyping process of DSP algorithms and techniques that support the creation of interactive soundscapes. Audio DSP is a vast and huge body of knowledge that covers (among other things) the analysis, synthesis, and processing of audio signals. We'll dive a bit into some DSP basics, but the main focus will be oriented toward the early experimental stages of development, before implementing a DSP algorithm at run time.

We will discuss some of the reasons to implement early prototypes in a game audio production cycle, and we'll see a brief list of the available languages and frameworks that can help us with DSP prototyping. Finally, we'll see some examples of low-pass filter designs in Python.

This chapter doesn't pretend to be an exhaustive and in-depth introduction to DSP theory. For that, there are several references out there we can find useful, such as DAFX[1] or Think DSP.[2] Here I aim to introduce you to some ideas for your own projects, so let's get started!

6.2 WHY PROTOTYPE

It is becoming increasingly important for many games to implement custom DSPs. More available processing power in current and upcoming platforms and higher budgets dedicated to audio make it possible to unleash a variety of runtime DSP algorithms that were expensive in the past. Trends on dynamic soundscapes, dynamic mixing approaches, and procedural audio are some of the reasons for modern games to demand more and more online and offline audio processing. In this context, being able to test and try out new ideas is very important for various reasons:

- Developing DSP can be very time-consuming, from the early design stages to the runtime implementation. Having a process to test out and reject ideas early can be more convenient than diving straight into a low-level implementation.

- Using high-level languages and frameworks helps to iterate over ideas quickly. As we will see, there are specific tools that can help us visualize and interpret data.

- Being able to test out different alternatives quickly makes it easier to find the best algorithm fit for the game context and the runtime constraints.

- Sharing a prototyping codebase across team members also empowers developers to experiment and try out different ideas for developing a proof-of-concept.

- Having prototype code makes it easier to port or implement different versions of the algorithm to various platforms or game engines. It's like having a code baseline that can then be adapted to lower level languages.

- With more isolated code, it can be easier to develop tests for algorithms.

There are also some caveats to developing prototypes in production projects:

- There is more development time that has to be invested. You can end up losing development time when a particular algorithm isn't working or ends up being too expensive for the target platform.

- Prototype code quality can be lower and perform worse than final production code, so more time has to be invested on optimizations with the target hardware in mind.

- Learning a prototyping language or framework takes time, which is not directly invested in the final product.

- It is usually harder to profile and to obtain relevant performance data from prototypes because of the abstraction layers that are involved.

- Integrating prototype code with game engines can be harder than with native code.

With all of the pros and cons in mind, we can now think about DSP prototyping across the different stages of development by taking these steps:

1. Research available algorithms. Here preliminary data and requirements are gathered, references are reviewed and initial prototype code that is available in the public domain or other appropriate license is assessed.

2. Initial prototype implementation with the framework and language of choice.

3. Iteration and optimizations of the different alternatives.

4. Evaluation of the approaches (back to step 2).

5. Initial implementation in the target language and platform.

6.3 AUDIO LANGUAGES AND FRAMEWORKS

There is a wide range of tools available for audio prototyping. In this section, I will briefly mention some of the best and well-known tools so that you can try them out for your projects.

6.3.1 Audio and Music Languages

In this category, we find pure audio programming languages such as CSound,[3] ChucK,[4] SuperCollider,[5] and FAUST.[6] SuperCollider and FAUST are based on the functional programming paradigm, whereas CSound is declarative and ChucK is imperative. These are languages that are specialized in audio, so we can find a myriad of functions and libraries part of their core that directly support processing and synthesis.

6.3.2 Dataflow

Max/MSP,[7] Pure Data,[8] and Reaktor[9] are node-based programming languages. They are inspired by visual programming instead of traditional programming. This paradigm allows quick iteration over ideas by basically connecting boxes together with wires. The flow of the signal is carried through one box to the next. Some of these languages also allow integrating patches (dataflow diagrams) in C++ applications and game engines using dedicated wrappers or optimized runtime libraries.

6.3.3 DSP Libraries and Frameworks

There are some cross-platform frameworks such as MATLAB™,[10] Anaconda,[11] Juce,[12] or Audiokit[13] that allow developing prototypes by using their high-level APIs. On one hand, MATLAB is both a programming language and a framework composed of different libraries (toolboxes) that is used widespread in the industry for scientific computing. It includes some specific tools for Audio, including a complete filter design toolbox. Anaconda is a similar toolbox (and some say it's a good alternative to MATLAB) that uses the Python language. Actually, Anaconda is a group of popular Python libraries bundled together in a friendly way.

On the other hand, the Juce framework is a C++ Audio library (multiplatform) that includes common components for developing Audio plugins and applications. It allows both prototyping and final product development. Finally, Audiokit is an audio synthesis, processing and analysis framework for iOS, macOS, and tvOS in C++, Objective-C, and Swift which is simple and easy to learn, yet powerful for developing Audio applications and plugins.

6.3.4 Python in This Chapter

In this chapter, we will be using Python as a scripting language for DSP prototyping. There are various reasons why it was chosen for the examples:

- It's a high-level language and allows fast iteration over ideas without getting into platform specifics.

- Python provides an interactive interpreter, which allows for rapid code development and prototyping.

- The code can be ported easily to C++ or other lower-level programming languages.

- The community around Python is lively and there are several open-source and free frameworks and libraries specialized in audio processing.

- Python is used across the games industry not only as a code prototyping tool but also in the development of asset pipelines and scripting in game engines, which makes it ideal for integrating it with game projects.

6.4 DSP EXAMPLE: AUDIO PLOTTING AND FILTERING

For the following example code we will be using the Anaconda framework for Python. You can download it from www.anaconda.com/download/, where you can also find installation instructions. The examples are compatible with both Python 2 and Python 3.

We will start by loading an audio file and plotting some information. For this, we are using a mono music loop at 16-bit and 44,100 Hz of sampling rate, that could be used as a gameplay soundtrack or menu music in a game. It's been downloaded from https://freesound.org/people/dshoot85/sounds/331025/ and created by the FreeSound user dshoot85.

6.4.1 Plotting Basics

The following Python code first loads the audio file into an array, then converts the 16-bit data to a floating-point range between −1 and +1 (dividing it by 32,768 = 2^{15}). Lastly, it creates a time plot with labels for the axes and a function t that is used to plot the time. As we can see, the duration of the audio file is about 4 seconds (Figure 6.1).

```
from scipy.io import wavfile
import matplotlib.pyplot as plt
import numpy as np

sr, data = wavfile.read("music.wav")

data = data / 2.**15
```

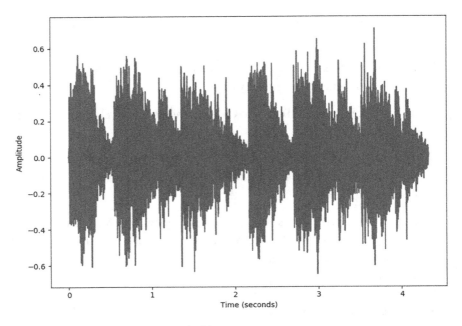

FIGURE 6.1   A plot of the sample file.

```
plt.axes(xlabel="Time (seconds)", ylabel="Amplitude")
t = np.linspace(0, len(data)/float(sr), len(data))
plt.plot(t, data)
plt.show()
```

In a second plot we create a spectrogram of the audio data. This shows the frequency evolution over time. It's using an FFT size of 512 points, so that we can have a good mix of frequency versus time resolution (Figure 6.2).

```
plt.axes(xlabel="Time (seconds)", ylabel="Frequency (Hz)")
plt.specgram(data, NFFT=512, Fs=sr, cmap=plt.cm.gist_gray)
plt.plot()
plt.show()
```

Another useful plot for us is the magnitude spectrum, which represents the overall frequency content of the audio. We represent the magnitude in a dB scale, and the frequency is in Hz (Figure 6.3).

```
plt.magnitude_spectrum(data, Fs=sr, scale='dB')
plt.show()
```

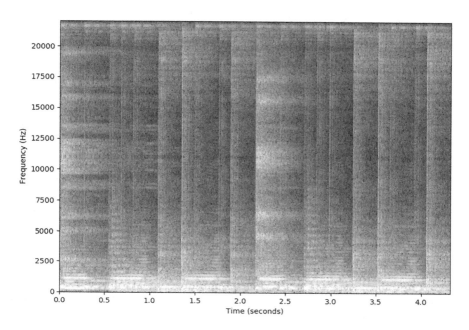

FIGURE 6.2   A frequency spectrogram of the sample file.

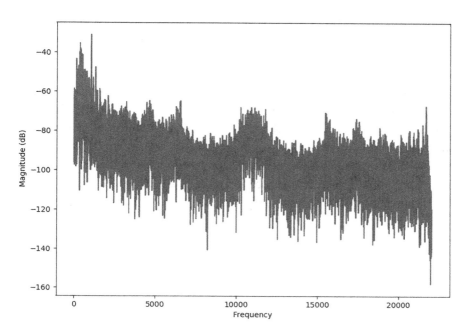

FIGURE 6.3   A magnitude spectrum plot of the sample file.

6.4.2 Effects Implementation

We can now dive into some effects implementation in Python. One of the most used audio DSP effects in games are filters, which are used to model different phenomena such as sound occlusion and obstruction, or to creatively filter out frequency content from sound effects or music while being driven by gameplay parameters.

Filter design is a whole topic on its own, so here we will only be covering some basics that will allow us to build a simple prototype. There are different types of filters, depending on the implementation and frequency response. The frequency response is how the filter alters the different frequency components and phase. We could delve deeply into the distinction between finite impulse response (FIR) and infinite impulse response (IIR) filters, but here we will only mention that there are different filter topologies and implementations depending on different parameters of choice.

Filters are implemented by combining signals with their delayed copies in different ways. FIR use delayed copies of their input, while IIR use delayed outputs. You can read more about this in *The Audio Programming Book* by Victor Lazzarini.[14] The number of delays determines the order of the filter—two delays makes a second-order filter, three delays makes a third-order filter, etc. We won't cover all the DSP theory in detail, but you can refer to the references of this chapter for some of the relevant literature in the field.

One well-known family of filter designs is Butterworth. In this section, we will implement it with the provided libraries in Python Anaconda. One key characteristic of Butterworth filters is that they have a flat passband (in other words, the frequencies that the filter passes are unaffected) and a good stop band attenuation (the frequencies that are rejected by the filter are attenuated a lot). In our case, we are going to implement a low-pass filter: a filter that passes low frequencies and attenuates higher frequencies. As we are about to see, this can be achieved with only a few lines of code in Python thanks to the Anaconda libraries:

```python
from scipy.signal import butter, lfilter

def butter_lowpass(cutoff, fs, order):
    nyquist = 0.5 * fs
    cut = cutoff / nyquist
    b, a = butter(order, cut, btype='low')
    return b, a

def butter_lowpass_filter(data, cutoff, fs, order):
```

```
    b, a = butter_lowpass(cutoff, fs, order=order)
    y = lfilter(b, a, data)
    return y
```

The cutoff frequency is the frequency where the filter starts attenuating. The function `butter` returns the filter coefficients `a` and `b`. If desired, we could use these into the equations that implement a Butterworth filter for developing a runtime version. The function `lfilter` actually filters out the signal.

The program below uses the `butter_lowpass` Python functions to implement a low-pass filter of order 8 with a cutoff frequency of 2 kHz, and applies it to the music loop we plotted previously:

```
if __name__ == "__main__":
    import numpy as np
    import matplotlib.pyplot as plt
    from scipy.signal import freqz
    from scipy.io import wavfile

    fs, data = wavfile.read("music.wav")
    data = data / 2. ** 15

    cutoff = 2000.0 #Cutoff Frequency in Hz

    # Plot the frequency response for a few different orders.
    for order in [2, 4, 8]:
        b, a = butter_lowpass(cutoff, fs, order)
        w, h = freqz(b, a)
        plt.figure()
        plt.clf()
        plt.xlabel('Frequency (Hz)')
        plt.ylabel('Gain')
        plt.grid(True)
        plt.plot((fs*0.5/np.pi)*w, abs(h), label="order = %d" % order)
        plt.legend(loc='best')

    #Filter the signal and plot spectrogram
    filtered = butter_lowpass_filter(data, cutoff, fs, 8)
    plt.figure()
    plt.clf()
    plt.axes(xlabel="Time (seconds)", ylabel="Frequency (Hz)")
    plt.specgram(filtered, NFFT=512, Fs=fs, cmap=plt.cm.gist_gray)
    plt.plot()
    plt.show()

    wavfile.write("filtered_output.wav", fs, filtered)
```

The program outputs several plots, which represent the frequency response of different orders for the low-pass filter and the spectrogram of the resulting filtered signal.

Figure 6.4 shows the frequency response for order 2, Figure 6.5 shows the frequency response for order 4, and Figure 6.6 shows the frequency response for order 8.

As we can see from the graphs, the higher the order, the steeper the slope of the filter. With this we can inspect quickly what will be the effect of applying the filter, and design accordingly. Higher order filters will also need extra processing power, so we can balance their design to fit runtime constraints. The effects of applying the filter can be observed in a spectrogram plot (Figure 6.7).

Finally, we can also listen to the resulting filtered signal by writing the output to disk.

This simple example already reflects how easy and straightforward is to design and iterate over the design of a filter.

The next step involves implementing the low-level filter in Python: we now are going to continue with the code for a second-order Butterworth filter as an example, which will actually be closer to the final C++ implementation in our game engine or audio middleware. We are using the same music wav file as in the previous sections to test the code.

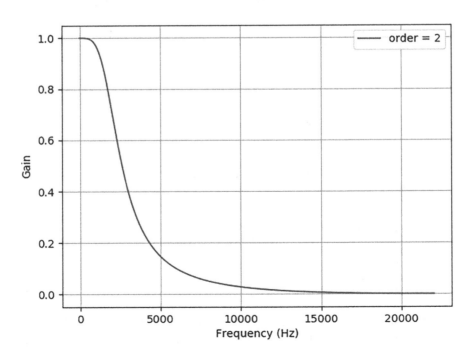

FIGURE 6.4 Frequency response of a Butterworth filter for order 2.

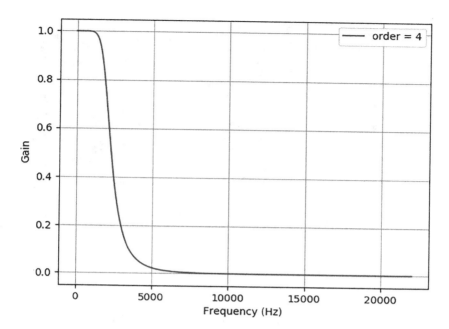

FIGURE 6.5   Frequency response of a Butterworth filter for order 4.

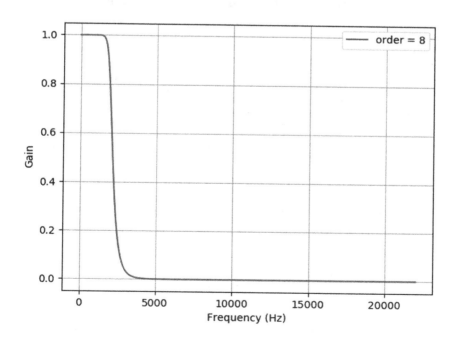

FIGURE 6.6   Frequency response of a Butterworth filter for order 8.

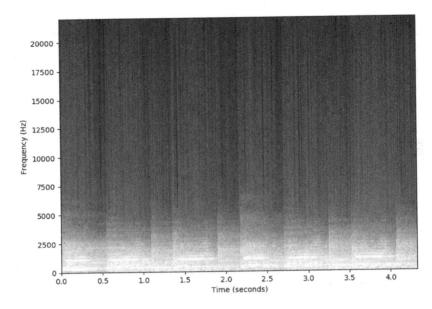

FIGURE 6.7 A spectrogram plot of a Butterworth filter applied to the sample file.

First, let's start the program and calculate the Butterworth filter coefficients:

```
# Butterworth second-order filter difference equation:
# y(n) = a0*x(n)+a1*x(n-1)+a2*x(n-2)-b1*y(n-1)-b2*y(n-2)

if __name__ == "__main__":
    import numpy as np
    import matplotlib.pyplot as plt
    from scipy.io import wavfile

    fs, data = wavfile.read("music.wav")
    data = data / 2. ** 15

    cutoff = 2000.0 #Cutoff Frequency in Hz

    # Second-order Butterworth filter coefficients
    filterLambda = 1 / np.tan(np.pi * cutoff / fs)
    a0 = 1 / (1 + 2 * filterLambda + filterLambda ** 2)
    a1 = 2 * a0
    a2 = a0
    b1 = 2 * a0 * (1 - filterLambda ** 2)
    b2 = a0 * (1 - 2 * filterLambda + filterLambda ** 2)
```

Then, we declare some variables for the filter delayed samples, allocate an output buffer (y) and apply the filter:

```
xn_1 = 0.0
xn_2 = 0.0
yn_1 = 0.0
yn_2 = 0.0

y = np.zeros(len(data))

for n in range (0, len(data)):
    y[n] = a0*data[n] + a1*xn_1 + a2*xn_2 - b1*yn_1 - b2*yn_2
    xn_2 = xn_1
    xn_1 = data[n]
    yn_2 = yn_1
    yn_1 = y[n]
```

It can be observed from these few lines of code that implementing a filter will be a matter of calculating the corresponding coefficients depending on the filter type (and updating them if, e.g., the filter frequency varies over time), implementing the corresponding difference equation and updating the delayed samples in each iteration. For a real-time implementation we should also consider that the filter loop will be done in chunks (e.g. buffers of samples).

As a final step, we write the output to a file so we can listen to it:

```
wavfile.write("filtered_output.wav", fs, y)
```

6.5 CONCLUSIONS

In this chapter, we reviewed the approaches and steps that can be taken in order to prototype DSP algorithms for our game projects. We used Python along with the Anaconda distribution as a high-level scripting language that allows quick prototyping and iteration of design ideas to show how to examine the properties of a low-pass filter. Python and Anaconda are powerful tools,[15] but this is just the beginning: as you can experience by yourself, the possibilities are endless!

NOTES

1 *DAFX: Digital Audio Effects*, 2nd Edition. Edited by Udo Zolzer. Wiley (2011) www.dafx.de.
2 *Think DSP: Digital Signal Processing in Python*. Allen B. Downey. Green Tea Press (2014) http://greenteapress.com/wp/think-dsp/.
3 http://csound.com/.
4 http://chuck.cs.princeton.edu/.
5 https://supercollider.github.io/.
6 http://faust.grame.fr/.

7 https://cycling74.com/products/max/.

8 https://puredata.info/.

9 www.native-instruments.com/en/products/komplete/synths/reaktor-6/.

10 www.mathworks.com/products/matlab.html.

11 www.anaconda.com/.

12 https://juce.com/.

13 http://audiokit.io/.

14 *The Audio Programming Book*. V. Lazzarini. MIT Press (2011).

15 *Python for Audio Signal Processing*: white paper. J. Glover, V. Lazzarini, and J. Timoney http://eprints.maynoothuniversity.ie/4115/1/40.pdf.

CHAPTER 7

Practical Applications of Simple Filters

Dan Murray

Id Software

CONTENTS

7.1 PRE-EMPHASIS

In this chapter, we will cover how to implement and use a variety of common and useful filter types. We will also cover how to build the sort of equalizer you might find in your digital audio workstation and how to build a crossover that you could use to build a multiband compressor. We will not be covering any of the math or theory behind the design of these filters. Instead, we will just be using the recipes the filter designers created and focusing on how we can use these filters for practical applications. For reference all of the code shown in this chapter and more can be downloaded from the book's website www.crcpress.com.

7.2 BIQUAD

The biquad filter is simple yet versatile. Everything we build in this chapter will be made using only biquads initialized and arranged in different ways. A biquad is simply a few constants and the last two samples of input and output. The input structure might look like this:

```
struct biquad {
  float a0_;
  float a1_;
  float a2_;
  float b1_;
  float b2_;
  float c0_;
  float d0_;
  float x1_;
  float x2_;
  float y1_;
  float y2_;
};
```

Our constants, normally called coefficients, are stored in $a0\_$, $a1\_$, $a2\_$, $b1\_$ and $b2\_$ (more on $c0\_$ and $d0\_$ later). The last two samples of input are stored in $x1\_$ and $x2\_$, where $x1\_$ is the last input sample and $x2\_$ is the input sample before $x1\_$. The last two samples of output are stored in $y1\_$ and $y2\_$, much like the input. It is convention to refer to the input signal as the function $x(n)$, and the output signal, the result of the processing, as the function $y(n)$, where n is the index into a discrete signal. For samples that occur earlier in time, we use typically use negatives $x(n-1)$ and $x(n-2)$ or $y(n-1)$ and $y(n-2)$. $c0\_$ and $d0\_$ are scaling values that some, but not all, of the filter recipes use.

It is important to note here how little state is actually required to represent a biquad. There is no cutoff frequency, sample rate, or quality factor stored here—everything is encoded into the coefficients for our pair of quadratic equations, the scalars, and the stored input and output samples. No matter what the biquad is actually doing to our audio, this data is all we need.

In order to process audio with a biquad, we need to compute the biquad difference equation. This simply works out what the filter's output should be output given the filter's transfer function:

```
float biquad_process_sample(biquad &bq, float sample) {
  float y = (bq.a0_ * sample) + (bq.a1_ * bq.x1_) +
            (bq.a2_ * bq.x2_) - (bq.b1_ * bq.y1_) -
            (bq.b2_ * bq.y2_);
  bq.x2_ = bq.x1_;
  bq.x1_ = sample;
  bq.y2_ = bq.y1_;
  bq.y1_ = y;
  return (y * bq.c0_) + (sample * bq.d0_);
}
```

No matter what the filter's transfer function, we always perform the same operation on each sample. In order for our biquad to actually do some useful filtering of the audio that is passed through it, we need to initialize the coefficients so that the desired transfer function is applied. The following coefficient calculations are copied, practically verbatim, from the book *Designing Audio Effect Plugins* in C++.[1] There are lots of other more complicated and undoubtedly clever ways to compute the coefficients, and many other types of filters that you can create with a biquad. For this chapter, however, we will use the following simple and efficient methods to compute our coefficients so we can start using them right away.
First-order low pass:

```
float x = (2.0f * (float)M_PI * freq) / (float)samplerate;
float y = cosf(x) / (1.0f + sinf(x));
bq.a0_ = (1.0f - y) / 2.0f;
bq.a1_ = bq.a0_;
bq.a2_ = 0.0f;
bq.b1_ = -y;
bq.b2_ = 0.0f;
bq.c0_ = 1.0f;
bq.d0_ = 0.0f;
```

First-order high pass:

```
float x = (2.0f * (float)M_PI * freq) / (float)samplerate;
float y = cosf(x) / (1.0f + sinf(x));
bq.a0_ = (1.0f + y) / 2.0f;
bq.a1_ = -bq.a0_;
bq.a2_ = 0.0f;
bq.b1_ = -y;
bq.b2_ = 0.0f;
bq.c0_ = 1.0f;
bq.d0_ = 0.0f;
```

First-order low shelf:

```
float u = powf(10.0f, gain / 20.0f);
float w = (2.0f * (float)M_PI * freq) / (float)samplerate;
float v = 4.0f / (1.0f + u);
float x = v * tanf(w / 2.0f);
float y = (1.0f - x) / (1.0f + x);
bq.a0_ = (1.0f - y) / 2.0f;
bq.a1_ = bq.a0_;
bq.a2_ = 0.0f;
bq.b1_ = -y;
bq.b2_ = 0.0f;
bq.c0_ = u - 1.0f;
bq.d0_ = 1.0f;
```

First-order high shelf:

```
float u = powf(10.0f, gain / 20.0f);
float w = (2.0f * (float)M_PI * freq) / (float)samplerate;
float v = (1.0f + u) / 4.0f;
float x = v * tanf(w / 2.0f);
float y = (1.0f - x) / (1.0f + x);
bq.a0_ = (1.0f + y) / 2.0f;
bq.a1_ = -bq.a0_;
bq.a2_ = 0.0f;
bq.b1_ = -y;
bq.b2_ = 0.0f;
bq.c0_ = u - 1.0f;
bq.d0_ = 1.0f;
```

Peaking filter:

```
float u = powf(10.0f, gain / 20.0f);
float v = 4.0f / (1.0f + u);
float w = (2.0f * (float)M_PI * freq) / (float)samplerate;
float x = tanf(w / (2.0f * q));
float vx = v * x;
float y = 0.5f * ((1.0f - vx) / (1.0f + vx));
float z = (0.5f + y) * cosf(w);
bq.a0_ = 0.5f - y;
bq.a1_ = 0.0f;
bq.a2_ = -bq.a0_;
bq.b1_ = -2.0f * z;
bq.b2_ = 2.0f * y;
bq.c0_ = u - 1.0f;
bq.d0_ = 1.0f;
```

Linkwitz–Riley low pass:

```
float x = (float)M_PI * freq;
float x2 = x * x;
float y = x / tanf(x / (float)samplerate);
float y2 = y * y;
float z = x2 + y2 + (2.0f * x * y);
bq.a0_ = x2 / z;
bq.a1_ = 2.0f * bq.a0_;
bq.a2_ = bq.a0_;
bq.b1_ = ((-2.0f * y2) + (2.0f * x2)) / z;
bq.b2_ = ((-2.0f * x * y) + x2 + y2) / z;
bq.c0_ = 1.0f;
bq.d0_ = 0.0f;
```

Linkwitz–Riley high pass:

```
float x = (float)M_PI * freq;
float x2 = x * x;
```

```
float y = x / tanf(x / (float)samplerate);
float y2 = y * y;
float z = x2 + y2 + (2.0f * x * y);
bq.a0_ = y2 / z;
bq.a1_ = (-2.0f * y2) / z;
bq.a2_ = bq.a0_;
bq.b1_ = ((-2.0f * y2) + (2.0f * x2)) / z;
bq.b2_ = ((-2.0f * x * y) + x2 + y2) / z;
bq.c0_ = 1.0f;
bq.d0_ = 0.0f;
```

Note that setting the coefficients does not tamper with the delayed input and output state of the biquad. This is important because, not only is this the method by which you initialize a biquad's coefficients for the first time, but it is also the method by which you can change the filter's current effect on an audio signal.

Search engine-friendly terms for this section:

digital filters, transfer function, digital biquad filter, biquadratic, quadractic function, z-transform, network synthesis filters, filter design, butterworth filter, linkwitz–riley filter

7.3 EQUALIZER

In this section, I will outline how you might make a simple five-section parametric equalizer, similar to what you might find in a typical digital audio workstation.

Here is our equalizer structure:

```
struct equalizer {
  float input_gain_;
  float output_gain_;
  biquad low_;
  biquad low_mid_;
  biquad mid_;
  biquad high_mid_;
  biquad high_;
};
```

We have a couple of scalars to apply input and output gain and five biquads. Part of what makes the biquad so versatile is how you can compose them to create more complex filters. For our equalizer, we will run our input signal through each biquad in sequence. Each biquad is responsible for cutting or boosting a different area of the frequency spectrum:

```
float equalizer_process_sample(equalizer &eq, float sample) {
  sample = eq.input_gain_ * sample;
```

```
sample = biquad_process_sample(eq.low_, sample);
sample = biquad_process_sample(eq.low_mid_, sample);
sample = biquad_process_sample(eq.mid_, sample);
sample = biquad_process_sample(eq.high_mid_, sample);
sample = biquad_process_sample(eq.high_, sample);
sample = eq.output_gain_ * sample;
return sample;
}
```

All that remains is to initialize each biquad at the correct cutoff frequency and gain using the peaking and shelf recipes from Section 7.2. Typically, each band of a parametric equalizer will use a peaking filter, but you can also use a low or high shelf just by changing the coefficients of the biquads.

Search engine-friendly terms for this section:

equalization (audio), parametric equalizer (audio), q factor (audio), graphic equalizer

7.4 CROSSOVER

In this section, I will outline how you might make a simple crossover using groups of biquads. A crossover can be used to make a multiband compressor, where the audio is split into multiple bands and compressed separately. The way a crossover works is by combining the outputs of low and high pass filters, each of which is centered on one of the band's crossover frequencies. The lowest band is the output of a low pass filter centered on the high cutoff of the lowest band, and the highest band is the output of a high pass filter centered on the low cutoff of the highest band. The inner bands are formed by combining the outputs of a low and high pass filter so that only the frequencies in the band (between the two filter cutoff frequencies) pass. When making a crossover it's important that we don't change the overall amplitude of the signal as we're splitting it into multiple bands. If we just used a pair of −3 dB/octave first order filters, for example, one low pass and one high pass set to the same center frequency, we'd see a +3 dB boost around our cutoff frequency when we combined the bands again. Instead, we're going to use the Linkwitz–Riley recipes from 7.2 to build our crossovers because they do not suffer from this problem.

Here is the structure for a two-band crossover:

```
struct crossover_2_band {
  biquad biquads_[2];
};
```

A two-band crossover does not have any inner bands and so is simpler to deal with. Each biquad should be centered on the same frequency, i.e. the point at which we crossover, where one is a low pass and the other a high pass.

```
void crossover_2_band_set_band_freqs(
  crossover_2_band &cvr,
  float freq, int samplerate) {
  biquad_set_coef_linkwitz_lpf(cvr.biquads_[0], freq, samplerate);
  biquad_set_coef_linkwitz_hpf(cvr.biquads_[1], freq, samplerate);
}
```

In order to process our input signal, we need to know which band we would like to compute, and then we can use the right biquad to filter the input signal:

```
void crossover_2_band_process_band(
  crossover_2_band &cvr, int band,
  float *input, int samples, float *output) {
  switch (band) {
  case 0: {
    biquad &bq = cvr.biquads_[0];
    for (int i = 0; i < samples; ++i) {
      output[i] = biquad_process_sample(bq, input[i]);
    }
    break;
  }
  case 1: {
    biquad &bq = cvr.biquads_[1];
    for (int i = 0; i < samples; ++i) {
      output[i] = biquad_process_sample(bq, input[i]) * -1.0f;
    }
    break;
  }
  }
}
```

For a three-band crossover we need to compute an inner band in addition to our two outer bands. Because an inner band will require both a low and high pass filter, we will need four biquads:

```
struct crossover_3_band {
  biquad biquads_[4];
};
```

The outer bands, now indices 0 and 3, should be set up as before. Biquads 1 and 2, for our inner band, should be set up to pass the region in the middle:

```
void crossover_3_band_set_band_freqs(
  crossover_3_band &cvr, float low,
```

```
float high, int samplerate) {
   biquad_set_coef_linkwitz_lpf(cvr.biquads_[0], low, samplerate);
   biquad_set_coef_linkwitz_lpf(cvr.biquads_[1], high, samplerate);
   biquad_set_coef_linkwitz_hpf(cvr.biquads_[2], low, samplerate);
   biquad_set_coef_linkwitz_hpf(cvr.biquads_[3], high, samplerate);
}
```

If you have trouble understanding this it helps me to picture the effect each filter would have on the input signal in isolation and then to imagine superimposing each filter output in turn to create each band and to recreate the original input signal. Computing three bands is similar to computing two bands except that, in order to create the inner band, we need to invert the phase of the output of the high pass filter so that the signal is in phase with our outer bands:

```
void crossover_3_band_process_band(
   crossover_3_band &cvr, int band,
   float *input, int samples, float *output) {
   switch (band) {
   case 0: {
      biquad &band0_lpf = cvr.biquads_[0];
      for (int i = 0; i < samples; ++i) {
         output[i] = biquad_process_sample(band0_lpf, input[i]);
      }
      break;
   }
   case 1: {
      biquad &band1_lpf = cvr.biquads_[1];
      biquad &band1_hpf = cvr.biquads_[2];
      for (int i = 0; i < samples; ++i) {
         float lpf_out = biquad_process_sample(band1_lpf, input[i]);
         float hpf_out = biquad_process_sample(band1_hpf, lpf_out);
         output[i] = hpf_out * -1.0f;
      }
      break;
   }
   case 2: {
      biquad &band3_hpf = cvr.biquads_[3];
      for (int i = 0; i < samples; ++i) {
         output[i] = biquad_process_sample(band3_hpf, input[i]);
      }
      break;
   }
   }
}
```

Building a higher N-band crossover just requires that you add more inner bands.

Search engine-friendly terms for this section:

audio crossover, linkwitz–riley filter, LR2 crossover, dynamic range compression, multiband compression

NOTE

1 Will Pirkle (2013). *Designing Audio Effect Plug-ins In C++*. London: Focal Press. pp. 181–196.

SECTION II

Middleware

CHAPTER 8

Advanced FMOD Studio Techniques

Guy Somberg

Echtra Games

CONTENTS

8.1 INTRODUCTION

In Chapter 6 of *Game Audio Programming: Principles and Practices* Volume 1, I covered the fundamentals of using the FMOD Studio low-level and high-level APIs, and touched briefly on some advanced use cases. As I said several times in that chapter, we could only skim the surface of the functionality that is available. In this chapter, we'll dive deeper into more aspects of the API and cover more advanced techniques, secondary classes, and adjunct APIs that are shipped with FMOD. With the fundamentals out of the way in the previous volume, this chapter will take the form of a whole series of short topics with applications, techniques, and source code for each one.

8.2 LIGHTING UP FEATURES

FMOD has a lot of features built in that require a relatively small amount of work to activate, but which can solve certain classes of problems with very little code. Understanding how these features work can help to create the aural experience that certain games require. In general, the default behavior for a particular feature is either to be disabled, or to provide a reasonable default. Turning these features on (or overriding the defaults) is usually fairly easy, and can be extraordinarily powerful, so long as you have a good understanding of the functionality that the feature provides and the way in which it works.

8.2.1 Multiple Listeners

One very common multiplayer mode, especially on console systems, is split-screen multiplayer, where multiple players are experiencing a different viewpoint of the game and controlling an independent character. These viewpoints may be vastly different, or they may be very similar. For example, one player may be on the opposite end of the map from their partner sitting on the couch next to them—or, contrariwise, their characters may be fighting close together, experiencing the same combat from slightly different perspectives.

8.2.1.1 Activating the Feature

All this information must be communicated to the players through a single set of speakers, and this is where FMOD's multiple listener support kicks in. By default, there is only one 3D listener, but you can set up to FMOD_MAX_LISTENERS (which has a value of 8 as of this writing). To control the number of listeners, use either FMOD::System:: set3DNumListeners() or FMOD::Studio::System:: set3DNumListeners(), depending on whether you're using the Studio API or the low-level API.

Once you've set the number of listeners, then you have to tell FMOD which listener to use when assigning listener parameters by passing the appropriate index to the listener parameter to set3DListenerAttributes(). Let's take a look at some example code:

```
void Initialize() {
  // ...
  mSystem->set3DNumListeners(2);
  // ...
}

void Update() {
  // ...
  mSystem->set3DListenerParameters(
    0
    Listener1Position,
    Listener1Velocity,
    Listener1Forward,
    Listener1Up);
  mSystem->set3DListenerParameters(
    1
    Listener2Position,
    Listener2Velocity,
    Listener2Forward,
    Listener2Up);
  // ...
}
```

8.2.1.2 Panning and Attenuation

When using multiple listeners, you don't need to do anything in particular to figure out which sounds are associated with which listener. FMOD, by default, assumes that everything is in one world, and figures out the appropriate panning. Channels or Events that match up to multiple listeners only get played once, so there is no performance penalty or mixing issues.

When figuring out panning and attenuation for multiple listeners, FMOD takes both distance from the source to every listener, and the combination of all listeners panning for that Event. For attenuation, the closest listener is selected; for panning, the resulting speaker matrix for all listeners is combined and the output is distributed accordingly.

8.2.1.3 Listener Weights

There are a few extra features surrounding multiple listeners if you're using the Studio API. The first is a listener weight, which allows you to either set some listeners to be more important than others, or which allow you to crossfade a listener position over time.

Let's take a look at a crossfade. You might want to implement this if your (single) listener is jumping from one location to another that is somewhat distant. Maybe the player teleported, or a cutscene was activated. You can effect a listener position crossfade by creating a new listener and then adjusting the listener weights of both listeners until the crossfade is complete, then setting the listener count back. Let's see this in action.

```
void BeginListenerCrossfade(
  const FMOD_3D_ATTRIBUTES& NewAttributes) {

  // First create a new listener
  mSystem->set3DNumListeners(2);

  // Assign the new listener's attributes to the previous
  // attributes of the old listener
  FMOD_3D_ATTRIBUTES ListenerAttributes;
  mSystem->getListenerAttributes(0, &ListenerAttributes);
  mSystem->setListenerAttributes(1, &ListenerAttributes);

  // Assign the new attributes to the old listener
  mSystem->setListenerAttributes(0, &NewAttributes);

  // Set up the data for the crossfade.  The new
  // listener is at the old position, so it gets a
  // weight of 1.0, and the old listener is at the
  // new position, so it gets a weight of 0.0.  We'll
  // crossfade these values to create a smooth transition.
  mSystem->setListenerWeight(0, 0.0f);
  mSystem->setListenerWeight(1, 1.0f);
}

void UpdateListenerCrossfade(float Amount) {
  mSystem->setListenerWeight(0, Amount);
  mSystem->setListenerWeight(1, 1.0f - Amount);
}

void FinishListenerCrossfade() {
  mSystem->setListenerWeight(0, 1.0f);
  mSystem->set3DNumListeners(1);
}
```

8.2.1.4 Listener Masks

The other feature of multiple listeners that you can light up is listener masks, which allow you to assign a set of listeners to be valid for any given `EventInstance`. You may want to use this if a particular sound should only be audible when a certain player is close to an object in the world; it's a somewhat specialized feature, because everyone sitting on the couch will be able to hear the sound, so it must have some meaningful gameplay functionality to be worth using. To activate this feature, pass in a 32-bit bitmask of the listeners that should be valid for an `EventInstance` to the function `EventInstance::setListenerMask()`. The default mask is `0xFFFFFFFF`, which means to activate all listeners. If you want to turn off listener 1, pass in `0xFFFFFFFE`, and to turn off listener 2, pass in `0xFFFFFFFD`.

8.2.1.5 Interaction with Third-Person Cameras

In Chapter 11 of *Game Audio Programming: Principles and Practices*, Volume 1, we describe a scheme where sounds are relocated to positions relative to the listener in order to create a more correct panning and attenuation scheme. It is worth noting that, without duplicating every Event playback for each listener, this relocation scheme will not work. Any relocation that you pick is not only going to be incorrect for other listeners, it will actually be worse than the original position.

8.2.2 Geometry Processing

Performing occlusion calculations can be tricky. There is no one standard way of implementing occlusion, because every game is different and has different needs. In general, however, a simple occlusion system can be described by two values: how much the direct path is occluded, and how much the indirect path is occluded. With these two values, we can describe occlusion (both direct and indirect occluded), obstruction (only direct path occluded), and exclusion (only indirect path occluded). See Chapter 17 ("Obstruction, Occlusion, and Propagation") and Chapter 18 ("Practical Approaches to Virtual Acoustics") for more in-depth discussions on occlusion techniques.

One option that some games use for occlusion calculation is to run a ray cast through some geometry, which may either be the actual collision geometry or a special set of audio-only shapes. In order to make this easier for those games that go that route, FMOD includes a geometry-processing API that does the ray casts and automatically applies the parameters to the playing sounds.

8.2.2.1 Bootstrapping

Before creating any geometry objects, you must configure the maximum geometry world size using `System::setGeometrySettings()`. This function sets a value that FMOD uses internally for performance and precision reasons. You should select a value that is large enough to include all of your geometry in world space. Any values that are outside of this range will still work, but will have a performance penalty.

Once you have configured the `System` object, you can start to create Geometry objects by using `System::createGeometry()`, which will allocate an empty `Geometry` object that you can fill with polygons using `Geometry::addPolygon()`. You can create as many `Geometry` objects as you want and FMOD will cast rays through them as needed. It is also possible to turn individual `Geometry` objects on or off without having to create and destroy them by calling `Geometry::setActive()`. Do not forget to destroy your `Geometry` objects by calling `Geometry::release()`.

Let's see an example of creating an occlusion cube:

```
// In the initialization. The value of 100 is picked arbitrarily
// to be large enough to fit our geometry without being over-large.
mSystem->setGeometrySettings(100.0f);

// Our vertices, which must all lie on the same plane, and
// be in a correct (counterclockwise) order so that they have
// the correct normal. You can mark polygons as double-sided
// in order to avoid dealing with winding order.
static const FMOD_VECTOR sCubeVertices[] =
{
  // Pane #1
  { -1.0f, -1.0f, -1.0f }, { -1.0f, 1.0f, -1.0f },
  { 1.0f, 1.0f, -1.0f }, { 1.0f, -1.0f, -1.0f },
  // Pane #2
  { -1.0f, -1.0f, 1.0f }, { 1.0f, -1.0f, 1.0f },
  { 1.0f, 1.0f, 1.0f }, { -1.0f, 1.0f, 1.0f },
  // Pane #3
  { 1.0f, -1.0f, -1.0f }, { 1.0f, 1.0f, -1.0f },
  { 1.0f, 1.0f, 1.0f }, { 1.0f, -1.0f, 1.0f },
  // Pane #4
  { -1.0f, -1.0f, -1.0f }, { -1.0f, -1.0f, 1.0f },
  { -1.0f, 1.0f, 1.0f }, { -1.0f, 1.0f, -1.0f },
  // Pane #5
  { -1.0f, 1.0f, -1.0f }, { -1.0f, 1.0f, 1.0f },
  { 1.0f, 1.0f, 1.0f }, { 1.0f, 1.0f, -1.0f },
  // Pane #6
  { -1.0f, -1.0f, -1.0f }, { 1.0f, 1.0f, -1.0f },
  { 1.0f, -1.0f, 1.0f }, { -1.0f, -1.0f, 1.0f },
};

FMOD::Geometry* AudioEngine::CreateCube(
```

```
      float fDirectOcclusion,
      float fReverbOcclusion)
{
   // Create our Geometry object with the given number of
   // maximum polygons and vertices.
   FMOD::Geometry* ReturnValue = nullptr;
   mSystem->createGeometry(6, 24, &ReturnValue);

   for(int i=0; i<6; i++) {
     ReturnValue->addPolygon(
       fDirectOcclusion, fReverbOcclusion, false,
       4, &sCubeVertices[i*4], nullptr);
   }

   return ReturnValue;
}
```

8.2.2.2 Placing Geometry in World Space

When you create a `Geometry` object, all of its vertices are in object space—that is, it's as though the object were centered at the origin. In order to actually use the `Geometry` object, you must place it at the appropriate locations in 3D space using `setPosition()`, `setRotation()`, and `setScale()`. Let's orient our cube in world space:

```
void OrientCube(
   FMOD::Geometry* pGeometry,
   const Vector3& Position,
   const Quaternion& Orientation,
   const Vector3& Scale)
{
   pGeometry->setPosition(VectorToFMOD(Position));
   pGeometry->setRotation(
     VectorToFMOD(Orientation.GetForward()),
     VectorToFMOD(Orientation.GetUp()));
   pGeometry->setScale(VectorToFMOD(Scale));
}
```

8.2.2.3 Saving and Loading

While you can create geometry at runtime as shown, you don't necessarily want to have to do that every single time. Rather, you would want to pre-generate the polygons and load them from a file on disk. To support this workflow, FMOD supports saving and loading geometry from byte streams using `Geometry::save()` and `System::loadGeometry()`.

Let's see these functions in action:

```
std::vector<std::byte> SaveGeometry(
   FMOD::Geometry* pGeometry)
{
```

```
  // First figure out how big the buffer needs to be
  int GeometryDataSize = 0;
  pGeometry->save(nullptr, &GeometryDataSize);
  if(GeometryDataSize == 0)
    return {};

  std::vector<std::byte> OutputBuffer;

  // Resize our buffer to fit the data, then save
  // the data into the buffer.
  OutputBuffer.resize(GeometryDataSize);
  pGeometry->save(
    static_cast<void*>(OutputBuffer.data()),
    &GeometryDataSize);

  return OutputBuffer;
}

FMOD::Geometry* LoadGeometry(const std::vector<std::byte>& Buffer)
{
  FMOD::Geometry* ReturnValue = nullptr;
  mSystem->loadGeometry(
    static_cast<const void*>(Buffer.data()),
    static_cast<int>(Buffer.size()),
    &ReturnValue);
  return ReturnValue;
}
```

8.2.2.4 Initialization Configuration

By default, FMOD will cast a ray from the listener to the sound source, accumulating the attenuation values for each polygon that it intersects. Depending on the density of your polygons, this may be fine, but if you have many polygons, it can cause your sounds to become too occluded.

To resolve these situations, FMOD includes an initialization configuration option FMOD_INIT_GEOMETRY_USECLOSEST, which will only intersect with a single polygon and use the occlusion values for that.

8.2.2.5 Separating Ray-Cast Calculations

By default, FMOD will calculate ray casts for all 3D sounds. If you wish, you can use FMOD to create and manage the Geometry objects, but manage the occlusion calculations yourself. You may wish to do this for performance reasons (to control how frequently the occlusion calculation is run), or because the occlusion calculation uses a different source and destination than the default of listener to sound source.

To accomplish this separation, set the FMOD_3D_IGNOREGEOMETRY mode on your Channels, which will disable automatic occlusion calculation. You can then call `System::getGeometryOcclusion()` and pass the resulting values to `Channel::set3DOcclusion()`. Let's see this in action.

```
void SetIgnoreOcclusion(FMOD::Channel* pChannel)
{
   FMOD_MODE eMode;
   pChannel->getMode(&eMode);

   eMode |= FMOD_3D_IGNOREGEOMETRY;
   pChannel->setMode(eMode);
}

void Update()
{
  // ...
  for(auto& Channel : Channels) {
    float fDirectOcclusion = 0.0f, fReverbOcclusion = 0.0f;
    mSystem->getGeometryOcclusion(
      mListenerPosition,
      Channel.Position,
      &fDirectOcclusion,
      &fReverbOcclusion);

    Channel.FMODChannel->set3DOcclusion(
      fDirectOcclusion, fReverbOcclusion);
  }
  // ...
}
```

8.2.3 Offline Processing

One particularly useful use case for FMOD is offline processing. For example, you may want to batch process sounds by opening them up and performing a particular sequence of filters through them (such as normalization or peak detection), or to record a particularly complex Event and flatten it into a fixed waveform. You may want to examine the waveforms of how a particular DSP or compression format affects a sound. There are any number of reasons to need noninteractive processing of a playback sequence where you do not want to wait for the sounds to play back through the speakers.

FMOD provides two ways to perform offline processing, through the non-real-time (NRT) output modes: FMOD_OUTPUTTYPE_NOSOUND_NRT and FMOD_OUTPUTTYPE_WAVWRITER_NRT. In the NRT output modes, the mixer is run at maximum speed and no audio data is sent to the audio device. For NOSOUND mode, any audio data that is generated by the mixer is dropped and ignored. For WAVWRITER, the audio data is written to a .wav file on disk that you specify.

8.2.3.1 Initialization for Offline Processing

In order to activate FMOD for offline processing, you must set the output type to one of the two modes. For example:

```
mSystem->setOutput(FMOD_OUTPUTTYPE_NOSOUND_NRT);
```

Setting this value is sufficient to activate the mode: once the output type is set, FMOD will begin processing all of its buffers immediately and not output them to the audio device. You can switch to an NRT mode at run time from a non-NRT mode, which may be useful in a tool context where you want to (for example) save an Event to a wave file. A more common use case, however, is to initialize the System in an NRT mode and keep it that way for the lifetime of the object.

When you know that your System object will be living its entire life in an NRT output mode, there are some initialization flags that are useful to set:

- FMOD_INIT_STREAM_FROM_UPDATE—Disables creation of the streaming thread and executes all streaming from within the System::update() function. This is useful in NRT situations because there is no concern about synchronization between the stream thread and the main thread.

- FMOD_INIT_MIX_FROM_UPDATE—Similar to FMOD_INIT_STREAM_FROM_UPDATE, this flag disables creation of the mixer thread. All mixing is done from within System::update(), which means that you can just execute update() in a loop until your stop condition has been reached, then either release the System object, or switch the output more to a real-time output mode.

- FMOD_STUDIO_INIT_SYNCHRONOUS_UPDATE—When using the Studio API, disables the Studio update thread and executes all Event operations in the main thread.

- FMOD_STUDIO_INIT_LOAD_FROM_UPDATE—When using the Studio API, disables creation of threads for bank and resource loading, which are executed on demand in the main thread.

The theme of all of these flags is that they disable various threads from getting created, and perform all of their processing in the System::update()

function. Fewer threads means fewer synchronization problems and less waiting, which is very important in a non-real-time scenario. Let's see how to initialize a Studio `System` object with these flags.

```cpp
FMOD::System* CreateNonRealtimeSystem()
{
  FMOD::Studio::System* pSystem = nullptr;
  FMOD::Studio::System::create(&pSystem);

  FMOD::System* pLowLevelSystem = nullptr;
  pSystem->getLowLevelSystem(&pLowLevelSystem);

  pLowLevelSystem->setOutput(FMOD_OUTPUTTYPE_NOSOUND_NRT);
  pSystem->initialize(
    128, // max channels
    FMOD_STUDIO_INIT_SYNCHRONOUS_UPDATE |
      FMOD_STUDIO_INIT_LOAD_FROM_UPDATE,
    FMOD_INIT_STREAM_FROM_UPDATE | FMOD_INIT_MIX_FROM_UPDATE,
    nullptr // extra driver data
    );
  return pSystem;
}
```

8.2.3.2 Wav Writer Mode

So far, this section has only been demonstrating `FMOD_OUTPUTTYPE_NOSOUND_NRT` mode because it requires less configuration. However, the `WAVWRITER` mode is also very handy because it encompasses one of the very common use cases of NRT modes: writing the data out to a file. The only difference between the two modes is that you must provide an output file in the `extradriverdata` parameter to either `Studio::System::initialize()` or `System::init()`. Let's see how to initialize a `WAVWRITER` output mode:

```cpp
FMOD::System* CreateWavWriterNonRealtimeSystem(
  const std::filesystem::path& WavFilePath)
{
  // The same as CreateNonRealtimeSystem() above
  FMOD::Studio::System::create(&pSystem);

  FMOD::System* pLowLevelSystem = nullptr;
  pSystem->getLowLevelSystem(&pLowLevelSystem);

  pLowLevelSystem->setOutput(FMOD_OUTPUTTYPE_WAVWRITER_NRT);
  pSystem->initialize(
    128, // max channels
    FMOD_STUDIO_INIT_SYNCHRONOUS_UPDATE |
      FMOD_STUDIO_INIT_LOAD_FROM_UPDATE,
    FMOD_INIT_STREAM_FROM_UPDATE | FMOD_INIT_MIX_FROM_UPDATE,
```

```
      WavFilePath.string().c_str() // extra driver data
    );
  return pSystem;
}
```

8.2.3.3 Example NRT Processing

Now that we've seen how to initialize FMOD in non-real-time mode, let's put together an example of writing an `Event` to a wav file.

```cpp
#include "fmod.hpp"
#include <filesystem>

int main()
{
  // Create our system object
  auto pSystem = CreateWavWriterNonRealtimeSystem("test.wav");

  // Load banks.  We'll presume that the Event has been
  // added to the Master Bank.
  FMOD::Bank* MasterBank;
  FMOD::Bank* MasterBankStrings;
  pSystem->loadBankFile(
    "Master Bank.bank",
    FMOD_STUDIO_LOAD_BANK_NORMAL,
    &MasterBank);
  pSystem->loadBankFile(
    "MasterBankStrings.bank",
    FMOD_STUDIO_LOAD_BANK_NORMAL,
    &MasterBankStrings);

  FMOD::EventDescription* pEventDescription = nullptr;
  pSystem->getEvent("event:/TestEvent", &pEventDescription);

  FMOD::EventInstance* pEventInstance = nullptr;
  pEventDescription->createInstance(&pEventInstance);

  pEventInstance->start();

  auto PlayState = FMOD_STUDIO_PLAYBACK_STARTING;
  while(PlayState != FMOD_STUDIO_PLAYBACK_STOPPED)
  {
    pSystem->update();
    pEventInstance->getPlaybackState(&PlayState);
  }

  pSystem->release();
  return 0;
}
```

The thing to note about this program is how unremarkable it is. With the exception of the initial setup (which is encapsulated in the function that we wrote earlier), this program is identical to the one that you would write to play the `Event` out of the audio device.

8.3 THE STUDIO TOOL

There is more to using the FMOD Studio tool than just playing `EventInstances`. Much of the work of integrating the audio middleware is deciding how the game will interact with the `Events` that your sound designers will create, and in creating tools for the sound designers. In this section, we'll explore some of the advanced features of interacting with the tool.

8.3.1 Event Stopping Strategies

Out of the box, FMOD provides two different modes that you can pass to `EventInstance::stop()`:`FMOD_STUDIO_STOP_ALLOWFADEOUT` and `FMOD_STUDIO_STOP_IMMEDIATE`. These operate as you would expect. `ALLOWFADEOUT` will perform any fades, AHDSR releases, or other sorts of finishing touches that your sound designers may have added. `IMMEDIATE` mode stops the `EventInstance` instantly, ignoring any fade times. Under normal circumstances, `ALLOWFADEOUT` is more common, because it allows your sound designers to express their vision.

While a `stop()` call with `ALLOWFADEOUT` will catch most situations, there are a couple of ways in which an Event could require a more complex rule.

8.3.1.1 Sustain Points

Every Event in FMOD Studio has a timeline that constantly moves forward and plays the audio of all of the instruments at that location. A Sustain Point is a way of suspending the motion of the timeline. When the timeline is suspended, any time-locked sounds will stop playing, but any async sounds will continue to play. One great use of this mechanism is to have an Event containing an introduction, followed by a suspension, followed by a tail. In Figure 8.1, we see a scatterer instrument with a sustain point at the very end. This Event will play the scatterer for a minimum of 1.7 seconds (the introduction), then continue to play until the sustain cue is triggered (the suspension), at which point it will finish whichever sounds from the scatterer it played, and then stop the sound (the tail). Another use for sustain points is to suspend a Snapshot instrument at a particular volume. In Figure 8.2, we see an Event containing a single Snapshot, which is to be played when the game pauses. When the Event is played, the snapshot intensity is faded up to 100%, then suspended. When the sustain point is hit, it fades back down to 0% and then stops the Event. While it is

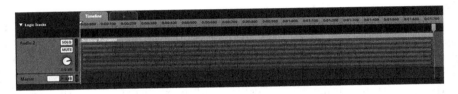

FIGURE 8.1   An Event with a sustain point holding a scatterer sound.

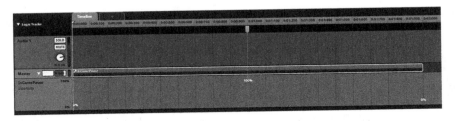

FIGURE 8.2   An Event with a sustain point holding a Snapshot.

possible to add multiple sustain points to an Event to create very complex interactive behaviors, we will not be discussing that use case here.

8.3.1.2 Stop Request

Sometimes an event is sufficiently complex that stopping the timeline at a cue point will not express the behavior that the sound designers require. These situations will happen when you have a time-locked sound that you want to keep playing, or if you have a number of instruments that are triggered over time. One specific example of this would be a music track with an intro, an outro, and a looped section. The music is time-locked, so you can't stop the timeline in order to create a sustain. Furthermore, you want to perform the transition on the next measure, so you may have to wait a moment before moving to the outro.

In these situations, we can implement a pattern called "Stop Request," which allows the timeline to continue running while still enabling tails. With Stop Request, you add a parameter called Stop Request to an Event. Then, in the Event's logic tracks, you add logic and conditions to jump to the end of the Event at the appropriate time. Figure 8.3 shows this setup in action. We have a Stop Request parameter that goes from 0 to 1, and a logic track containing both a Loop Region and a Transition Region quantized to the measure. The Transition Region's target is the End marker that indicates the outro of the music. Figure 8.4 shows the condition for the Transition Region: it's set to transition when the Stop Request parameter gets set to 1.

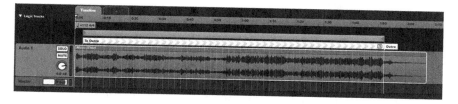

FIGURE 8.3   An Event set up with a Stop Request parameter.

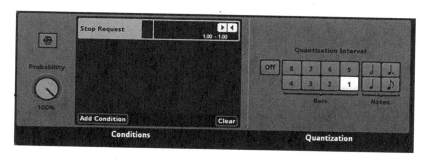

FIGURE 8.4   The Transition Region condition.

We'll see how the code does this in a moment, but the effect of this setup is that the music plays the intro, then loops the music until the game sets the Stop Request to 1. At the next measure after that, the Transition Region will trigger and send the music to the outro, and the Event will finish as normal.

8.3.1.3 Event Stopping Code

With three different ways to stop an Event, what will the code look like, and how do you know which one to trigger? Fortunately, FMOD offers a way to query for the existence of the objects that we've been using, so we can try each one in sequence and trigger it if it exists.

```
void StopEvent(FMOD::EventInstance* pEventInstance)
{
  // Start by releasing the instance so that it will get
  // freed when the sound has stopped playing
  pEventInstance->release();

  // Get the description so that we can query the Event's properties
  FMOD::EventDescription* pEventDescription = nullptr;
  pEventInstance->getDescription(&pEventDescription);

  // First try the sustain point
  bool bHasCue = false;
  pEventDescription->hasCue(&bHasCue);
  if(bHasCue)
```

```
{
  pEventInstance->triggerCue();
  return;
}

// Now check to see if the sound has a Stop Request parameter
FMOD_STUDIO_PARAMETER_DESCRIPTION ParameterDescription;
FMOD_RESULT result = pEventDescription->getParameter(
  "Stop Request", &ParameterDescription);
if(result == FMOD_OK)
{
  pEventInstance->setParameterValueByIndex(
    ParameterDescription.index,
    ParameterDescription.maximum);
  return;
}

// All of our other special stop methods failed, so just do a stop
// with fadeout
pEventInstance->stop(FMOD_STUDIO_STOP_ALLOWFADEOUT);
}
```

This code will work so long as the sound designers follow the rules of the various stopping strategies correctly. For an event with a cue point, it must only have one cue point. For an event with a Stop Request parameter, the logic tracks must be set up correctly. We'll see in Section 8.3.2 how to audit that these events are set up correctly.

8.3.2 Scripting API

The FMOD Studio tool has a built-in scripting engine that uses JavaScript as its language. There are a number of example scripts that are shipped with FMOD which are excellent references for the API, and the Studio Tool documentation includes extensive documentation for how the scripting API works. Because all this documentation exists, we won't delve too deeply into an introduction to the scripting system. Rather, we will just jump right in and demonstrate how to accomplish certain tasks.

8.3.2.1 Exploring Around

In order to get a handle on the scripting API, the best way is to open an existing project and to explore around in it. FMOD provides a Console window (Window->Console, or Ctrl+0) which implements a REPL for the API. Every object in the hierarchy—events, group tracks, logic tracks, mixer buses, VCAs, etc.—is identified by a GUID (object property name: id). You can look up an object by its GUID using the function studio.project.lookup(). One good starting point for experimenting and exploring the object hierarchy is to right-click an Event and select Copy GUID, then execute the following command in the console:

```
var Event = studio.project.lookup("<paste event GUID here>");
```

This creates a variable called `Event` in the global namespace that you can perform operations on. Note that, as you're editing your script, the global context is reset every time you reload the scripts, so you will have to re-execute this command when that happens.

The other useful function for exploring around the object hierarchy is `console.dump()`. This function will output to the log the names and values of all the variables and functions in the object. So, once you've assigned your `Event` variable, you can type into the console window:

```
console.dump(Event);
```

This will output a list of properties and values. A few of them to note:

- `id`—The GUID for this object.

- `entity`—The name of the type of this object.

- `isOfType()` and `isOfExactType()`—Pass in a string containing the entity type (the same value you would see in the entity member) to determine if the object is of that type. `isOfType()` checks the type system, so `Event.masterTrack.isOfType("GroupTrack")` will return `true`, but `Event.masterTrack.isOfExactType("GroupTrack")` will return `false`.

- `masterTrack`—The master track. While it technically has a different type, and lives in a different data member than the rest of the group tracks, you can nevertheless treat it in most ways as an ordinary group track.

- `groupTracks`—An array of tracks, which contain the Event's instruments.

- `returnTracks`—An array containing the return tracks for the Event.

- `markerTracks`—The logic tracks of this Event containing loop regions, transitions, tempo markings, etc.

- `timeline`—The timeline track for this Event.

- `parameters`—The parameters that the sound designer has added to this Event.

- `items`—An array containing this Event's nested Events.

- `banks`—An array containing references to the banks that this Event is assigned to.

There are a number of other properties, and a bunch of functions that you can call to query, playback, and modify the Event. And all of these properties are just for the Event type. Every single entity in the entire project, from tempo markers in Events to profiler sessions to mix buses and VCAs, is accessible, query-able, modifiable, and deletable.

8.3.2.2 Building an Auditing Script

In Section 8.3.1.3, we needed a way to audit our Events and make sure that they're all set up properly with respect to the stop methods. Let's go ahead and build that script now. We'll start at the bottom of our script and work our way upwards. First, we'll add a menu item to perform the audit:

```
studio.menu.addMenuItem({
  name: "Audit",
  isEnabled: true,
  execute: DoAudit
});
```

This snippet will add the menu item and call a function called `DoAudit()` to perform the actual audit. Let's see what `DoAudit()` looks like:

```
function DoAudit() {
  var MasterEventFolder = studio.project.workspace.masterEventFolder;
  AuditFolder(MasterEventFolder);
}
```

The `masterEventFolder` is the root of all of the events in the project; it's type is `MasterEventFolder`, but it inherits from `EventFolder`, so it can be treated the same. The `AuditFolder()` function now recurses down all the `EventFolders`, and visits all of the `Events` in each one.

```
function AuditFolder(Folder) {
  for (var i=0 i<Folder.items.length; i++) {
    var item = Folder.items[i];
    if (item.isOfType("EventFolder")) {
```

```
      AuditFolder(item);
    }
    else if (item.isOfType("Event")) {
      AuditEvent(item);
    }
  }
}
```

We have finally reached the point where we've got an Event to audit.

```
function AuditEvent(Event) {
  // Filter the Event here.  For example, maybe Events with "DNU"
  // in their name are for testing purposes only and shouldn't be
  // audited.

  AuditStopCondition(Event);
  // More audits here...
}
```

The `AuditEvent()` function is a clearing house for all the different sorts of audits that you may have for an Event. In this case, we'll just be demonstrating the one audit, but you can have as many as you can think of for the way in which your project is organized, and the mistakes that your sound designers are likely to make.

Our stop condition tests are actually threefold. We must verify that

- If there is a sustain point, that there is only one.

- If there is a `Stop Request` parameter, that it is used by the condition for a Transition Region with a valid destination.

- We only use one of these two mechanisms.

```
function AuditStopCondition(Event) {
  var HasSustainPoint = AuditSustainPoint(Event);
  var HasStopRequest = AuditStopRequest(Event);

  if(HasSustainPoint && HasStopRequest) {
    OutputAuditMessage(Event,
      "Both sustain point and stop request detected.  This Event will
not stop correctly.  To fix, either remove the sustain point or remove
the Stop Request parameter.");
  }
}
```

We've punted the details of auditing the sustain point and the `Stop Request` parameter to another function, but we have verified that we only have at most one stop method. Note that the audit message contains three pieces of information:

- *The context of the error.* In this case, it will just be the `Event` that is passed in, but other audits may require getting the name of a group track and instrument module, or a parameter name, or various other contexts.

- *A concise description of the problem,* including a reason why this is a problem (if such a reason is not already obvious).

- *Instructions on how to fix the problem.* This is critically important, because a sound designer may not know what to do to fix a problem when they're faced with it. Often there is more than one option to fix a problem, so including all the options is important.

Sometimes an audit may discover something that was done intentionally by a sound designer. For example, you may have an audit that is looking for streaming sounds in situations where they are not expected to be found. In most cases, it would be undesirable to throw a streamed sound into the game willy-nilly for a commonly played sound. However, if a sound designer has consciously decided to place a streamed sound into an Event, you need a way for them to silence the audit message. One good way to do that in the case of the streaming sound module audit is to mark the instrument in the track with the text `Streaming` in its name.

Let's continue our audit by looking for multiple sustain points.

```
function AuditSustainPoint(Event) {
  var FoundSustainPoint = false;

  for (var i=0; i<Event.markerTracks.length; i++) {
    var MarkerTrack = Event.markerTracks[i];

    for (var j=0; j<MarkerTrack.markers.length; j++) {
      var Marker = MarkerTrack[j];

      if (Marker.isOfType("SustainPoint")) {
        if (FoundSustainPoint) {
          // We've already found a sustain point, so output a log
          OutputAuditMessage(Event,
            "Multiple sustain points detected.  This will prevent the
Event from stopping properly.  To fix, remove all but one sustain
point.");
        }
        FoundSustainPoint = true;
      }
    }
  }
}
```

```
    return FoundSustainPoint;
}
```

Here we have to iterate over all of the marker tracks. A marker track is a row of objects in the Logic Tracks area of an Event. We then have to traverse over each row in order to find an entry that matches the `SustainPoint` type. If we find more than one, then we output a message.

Checking for multiple Sustain Points is the easy case. Checking for proper use of a `Stop Request` parameter is a little bit trickier. For this audit, we need to verify that:

- There is a `Stop Request` parameter at all. If not, we can exit early.

- There is exactly one Loop Region.

- There is exactly one Transition Region with the same start and end as the Loop Region.

- The Transition Region has a destination, and that destination is after the region, and there are no Loop Regions or transitions of any sort anywhere after the destination marker.

- The Transition Region has a condition that references the `Stop Request` parameter, and the condition is set to only trigger if the `Stop Request` parameter is set to 1.0.

That's a lot to verify, but we can do it without too much trouble. Note that we are making a number of simplifying assumptions for this audit. For example, we're assuming that this Event will only have a single Loop Region and Transition Region. It is possible to make a valid Event that has multiple regions and exits properly, but auditing that is sufficiently complex that we'll leave it as an exercise for the reader if their sound designers wish to make such complex Events. We're also making a simplifying assumption by enforcing that the start and end of the Loop and Transition regions must be the same, but technically so long as the Transition Region is encompassed by the Loop Region, then it is valid. Finally, it's also possible to use a Transition Marker instead of a Transition Region, but we'll ignore that possibility for this chapter. It is possible to write an auditing check that does not make any of these simplifying assumptions, but its length would be prohibitively long for this chapter.

Once again, we'll split the audit into functions. For brevity from here on out, I will just be writing brief descriptions for each of the audit messages, but you should write proper full-length messages in a real script.

```
function AuditStopRequest(Event) {
  var StopRequestParameter = FindStopRequestParameter(Event);
  if (StopRequestParameter == null) {
    return false;
  }

  var LoopRegion = FindLoopRegion(Event);
  var TransitionRegion = FindTransitionRegion(Event);

  if (CheckRegionsMatch(LoopRegion, TransitionRegion)) {
    OutputAuditMessage(Event, "Regions don't match");
  }

  // We'll output a number of specific errors in these functions
  CheckDestination(Event, TransitionRegion);
  CheckStopRequestCondition(
    Event, StopRequestParameter, TransitionRegion);
}
```

And now we just have to fill in the functions:

```
function FindStopRequestParameter(Event) {
  for (var i=0; i<Event.parameters.length; i++) {
    var Parameter = Event.parameters[i];

    if(Parameter.preset.presetOwner.name == "Stop Request") {
      return Parameter;
    }
  }
  return null;
}

function CheckRegionsMatch(LoopRegion, TransitionRegion) {
  // Loop Regions and Transition Regions both have the same
  // properties, so we can treat them the same in this function.
  if (LoopRegion.position != TransitionRegion.position)
    return false;

  if (LoopRegion.length != TransitionRegion.length)
    return false;

  return true;
}

function CheckDestination(Event, TransitionRegion) {
  if(TransitionRegion.destination == null) {
    OutputAuditMessage(Event, "No destination set");
```

```
    }

    var TransitionRegionEnd =
        TransitionRegion.position + TransitionRegion.length;
    if(TransitionRegion.destination.position < TransitionRegionEnd) {
        OutputAuditMessage(Event, "Marker is not after region");
    }

    for (var i=0; i<Event.markerTracks.length; i++) {
        var MarkerTrack = Event.markerTracks[i];

        for (var j=0; j<MarkerTrack.markers.length; j++) {
            var Marker = MarkerTrack.markers[j];

            if(Marker.position > TransitionRegion.destination.position) {
                OutputAuditMessage(Event,
                    "Marker starts after destination");
            }
        }
    }
}

function CheckStopRequestCondition(
    Event, StopRequestParameter, TransitionRegion) {
    if (TransitionRegion.triggerConditions.length == 0) {
        OutputAuditMessage(Event, "Trigger region has no conditions");
        return;
    }

    var StopRequestTriggerConditionFound = false;
    for (var i=0; i<TransitionRegion.triggerConditions.length; i++) {
        var TriggerCondition = TransitionRegion.triggerConditions[i];

        if (TriggerCondition.parameter == StopRequestParameter) {
            StopRequestTriggerConditionFound = true;

            if (TriggerCondition.minimum != 1 ||
                TriggerCondition.maximum != 1) {
                OutputAuditMessage(Event,
                    "Trigger condition range not set correctly.");
            }
        }
    }
}
```

And now, with all of that code written, we have a menu item that we can trigger that will go through every single Event in the project and output error messages if any part of the Event is not set up properly.

8.3.2.3 Next Steps

There are easy hooks in this script to extend with other audits for individual Events, and for auditing the mixer or any other aspect of the project. But extending the number of audits is just the beginning. The API contains functions to create, modify, and delete every aspect of the project, so it is actually possible to automatically fix the problems as you find them. However, there may be more than one way to fix any given problem that you find, which means that you cannot just blindly apply a fix when you discover an issue. Also, the user interface of this audit is a list of text outputted to the console window, which is not very friendly to the sound designers. Clearly, some more complex tooling is warranted.

In order to facilitate tool implementation, the FMOD Studio tool listens on port 3663 with the same REPL interface that is provided by the console window. By connecting to that port, you can send JavaScript commands and get the results. One good method is not to print out the error messages in the audit script directly, but rather to package up the audit issues discovered into a JavaScript object with an enumeration naming the type of the issue found, and enough context to construct an error string. Then, after the audit is done, write out the JSON representation of the errors. Your tool can read and parse the resulting JSON text, and have full text strings built-in which it displays to the user.

Once you have this tool built, you can actually offer fixes. By having a library of fix functions, each audit can actually include the text of a JavaScript function to call in order to implement the various fixes. The tool can then allow the sound designers to select the appropriate fix, then with the click of a button, the JavaScript is sent over to the tool and the issue is fixed instantly.

8.4 CONCLUSION

There are so many powerful nooks and crannies to the FMOD API, both the low level and the studio API, and we are (once again) only scratching the surface in this chapter. One of the beauties of the FMOD API is the interplay of the low-level and Studio APIs, and how all of the functionality of the low-level API is available to and interacts cleanly with the Studio API. The Studio tool scripting API in particular opens up a whole set of opportunities for tools and improving the lives of the sound designers.

CHAPTER 9

Understanding Wwise Virtual Voices

Nic Taylor

Blizzard Entertainment

CONTENTS

9.1 INTRODUCTION

Virtualizing inaudible or lower priority sounds allows Wwise to track a sound's state without processing the sound's voices through the mix engine in order to save CPU, memory, and in some cases hardware voices. Although these settings are presented to the sound designers or implementers, the programmer's role will require being a source for recommendations on the project and troubleshooting these settings. Handling this communication early in the project will save time later than when the Wwise project becomes large and complex. At a high level, virtual voices are straightforward, so this article aims to cover in detail different use-cases and issues that come up.

There are two reasons a sound goes into a virtual voice mode in Wwise: the voice falls below the volume threshold, or the voice has been pushed out due to playback limits and priority settings.

In Wwise, virtual voices are configured through the "Advanced" Properties section. The settings are:

- Virtual Voice "Below Threshold" Behavior (Continue, Kill, Virtual, Kill if finite else virtual)

- Virtual Voice "Over Limit" Behavior (Kill, Use Virtual Voice)

- When Priority is Equal "Max Reached" Behavior (Discard Oldest, Discard Newest)

- Return from Physical Voice (Play from Beginning, Play from Elapsed Time, Resume)

The last property and its options are the virtual voice modes that will be focused on the most below (Figure 9.1).

9.2 OVERVIEW OF BELOW THRESHOLD BEHAVIORS

The "Virtual voice behavior" property is also called the "Below Threshold Behavior" in XML and code, so the two names are used interchangeably. And although the authoring tool presents this property in the

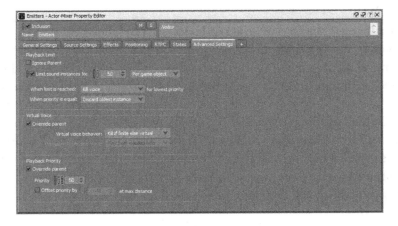

FIGURE 9.1 Wwise "Advanced Settings" where virtual voice behaviors are configured.

"Virtual Voice" group, it is also where the familiar playback settings of "Continue to Play" and "Kill" are assigned. The grouping makes sense when you notice that the playback limit can defer to the "Virtual Voice Settings."

Of the different behaviors, "Kill if finite else virtual" is recommended as the default and hints at the expected use-case for virtual voices covered in detail below. This setting is relatively new to Wwise—it was added in version 2016. Using it as the default is a nice way to cut down on managing virtual voices and aggregating settings across Actor-Mixers. This behavior would be overridden for longer, finite sounds, and loops with specific contexts discussed below.

"Send to virtual voice" is the only setting of the four that lets the sound designer specify the type of virtual voice queue behavior.

9.3 COMPARING VIRTUAL VOICE QUEUE BEHAVIORS

- **Play from Elapsed Time**

   Pros: Audio buffers relating to the voice are flushed so it holds little memory.

   Cons: The voice is still updated every frame. This mode will also require seeking into the audio file and for some audio formats such as ogg, including a seek table for the audio file. Also note that returning from virtual voice is not guaranteed to be sample accurate. As a result, "Play from Elapsed Time" would not be recommended if it were necessary to keep the audio closely synced with another voice or something external to sound like voice animations.

   Applications: Longer one-shot or looping sounds which have sequence, for example, music, or a long conversation or dialog. This mode is also recommended for containers using crossfades which is discussed more in the next section.

- **Play from Beginning**

   Pros: Everything relating to the voice is flushed so it holds no memory. Returning from virtualization does not require a seek.

   Cons: More CPU is expended switching from physical to virtual than "Resume" and similar or less for than "Play from Elapsed." However, this is negligible to processing audio buffers. Events using a random seek or SeekOnEvent will not re-apply the seek action and will still start from the beginning.

Applications: This is ideal for loops which are noisy and do not have recognizable sequences, such as fire loops or water/rain/river loops. A number of ambiences or ambient loops fall in this category. Ambient loops that are comprised of several sounds layered in Blend containers can get quite complex especially if the layers react to real-time game data. In this case, "Play from Beginning" can save CPU used to seek several sounds at once required by using "Play from Elapsed."

• **Resume**

Pros: Voice stops being processed. Minimal (or no) work is done to switch from physical to virtual.

Cons: Internal audio buffers are kept in memory for the voice, which is not ideal for a sound with many layers or many DSPs.

Applications: This would be applicable to ambient loops as well, but in the case that the sound is going from physical to virtual frequently. An example might be a sweetener loop that is on the character or a vehicle which is expected to be pushed below the priority or HDR threshold often when action occurs. This is also useful for streamed sounds which would have to seek. Because the audio buffers are kept in memory this mode is not appropriate for large numbers of voices that are in the world but beyond the attenuation range (Table 9.1).

TABLE 9.1   Summary of the Applications of Below Threshold and Virtual Voice Behaviors

Play from Elapsed	Loops with sequence (such as dialog)
	Music
	Long, finite (or one-shot) sounds
	Looping containers using cross-fades (such as Blend or Random containers)
Play from Beginning	Loops without sequence (such as ambiences)
	3D spatialized loops
Resume	Loops on the listener or loops going in and out of virtual frequently (such as sweeteners or vehicle loops)
	Streamed sources
Kill	Short, finite sounds
Continue to Play	Synced sounds requiring sample accurate playback
	Sounds being metered for other systems (like driving particles with sound)

A note on streaming I/O: "Play from Elapsed Time" and "Resume" flush the corresponding buffer, which can lead to a slight delay before playback can resume. However, all three modes stop using I/O while virtual.

9.4 WHAT DOES BELOW THRESHOLD ACTUALLY MEAN?

In the main project settings of the Wwise project, the per-platform minimum volume threshold is specified. In a given audio frame, a voice's volume in the context of the threshold is the aggregate of mix buses, fading (such as cross-fading within a container or fading out from a Stop action), and attenuation and HDR graphs.

As a result, the audio file or source's loudness does not play a role in the below threshold. For example, if the audio source has a large amount of headroom or long silent sections, it will not impact when or if the sound is virtualized. In addition, the Make-Up Gain property is also not used in the volume calculation making it fundamentally different from the Container's gain.

The side effect of mix buses driving virtualization that might be different from a system written into the game engine is that Real-Time Parameter Controls (RTPCs) on buses or State transition can put most or all sounds below the volume threshold. This is commonly how a volume slider in the in-game audio settings is coupled with Wwise.

9.5 RISKY OR "DANGEROUS" VIRTUAL VOICE SETTINGS

"Play from Beginning" and "Resume" are considered "dangerous" virtual voice settings by Wwise because the voice will not expire based on any time interval, which can behave like a leak in certain setups. The leak is an unintended consequence of virtualized voices being kept in memory. Virtualized voices do not count toward the priority system counts. Therefore, new voices are immediately virtualized when the sound limit is surpassed or the sound is estimated to be under the threshold limit. "Play from Beginning" and "Resume" voices will sit in the virtual voice list waiting to be activated.

For looping sounds this might be the correct and expected behavior, especially if the game engine is tracking the loop's lifetime. However, short sound events may be "trigger and forget" from the game engine, or the game engine may assume that the sound will expire without explicitly being stopped.

In addition, with the virtual voice list growing in an unbounded, leak-like way, virtualized sounds might playback at unexpected times when the volume threshold changes. For example, 3D voices that were started beyond the audible attenuation range may play back long after the sound event's creation when a listener finally moves into range. Imagine bullet impact sounds that were created past the small attenuation range, which start playback when the listener moves into range long after the voice should have expired—perhaps a room in a level that the player came near but entered much later on. Another example is voices being virtualized while the game is in a menu screen state which all de-virtualized when the menu is closed due to a Wwise state change.

In my experience, unintended virtual voice modes are typically introduced by copy/pasting Wwise containers between Actor-Mixers or by a container that is deeply parented where it is not clear that the container is inheriting a "dangerous" virtual voice setting. These are the types of cases where using "Kill if finite else virtual" keeps from introducing bugs but still leverages the virtual voice system.

Keep in mind a sound designer's usual workflow would not require going to the Advanced tab when implementing sounds. And because the settings are on the Advanced tab, it is difficult to know at a glance if there are dangerous virtual voice settings in a project. Even leveraging the Query system, a feature of Wwise authoring tool to search the project for containers with certain properties, could require quite a bit of manual checking in a large project.

9.6 DETECTING "DANGEROUS" VIRTUAL VOICE SETTINGS

As Figure 9.2 demonstrated, it can be clear that there is a bad virtual voice setting by playing the game with Wwise profiler connected. Another run-time solution is to use the `AK_Duration` callback from the `PostEvent` and warn if a sound is lasting longer than its expected time by some amount.

FIGURE 9.2   Example of a sound being virtualized in a way that it behaves like a leak.

Another feature that was added with 2017 can be found in the Project setting "Log" tab where a threshold can be set to generate a warning (Figure 9.3).

When this limit is hit, a message similar to the following will be reported: "Number of Resume and/or Play-From-Beginning virtual voices has reached warning limit (see Project Settings –> Log tab). There may be some infinite, leaked voices."

A better solution would be detecting potential virtual voice leaks when game assets are imported. The import validation should check audio containers for finite sounds with a below threshold property of "Send to Virtual Voice," an integer value of 2 on the property, and a queue behavior of either "Play from Beginning" or "Resume" (integer value of 0 or 2, respectively). There are now two ways to inspect the properties in the Wwise project: parsing the XML work units and the Wwise Authoring API.

Wwise 2017 introduced the Wwise Authoring API (WAAPI) that allows an application to send and receive requests from the running authoring tool with simple json. Through WAAPI, you can request specific properties from containers in full detail. WAAPI is quite powerful with a number of ways to query depending on the specific Wwise integration. A good starting point is to use the `ak.wwise.core.object.get()` function to request properties from the Wwise objects. Specifically, for

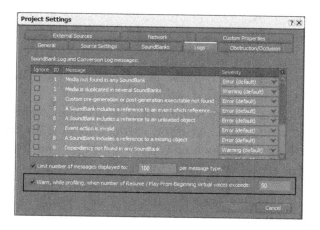

FIGURE 9.3   Configuring the Wwise project to warn about dangerous virtual voices.

the dangerous virtual voice behaviors, the following properties should be queried on each container which can initiate sound:

- `VirtualVoiceQueueBehavior`

- `BelowThresholdBehavior`

- `OverLimitBehavior`

- `IsLoopingEnabled`

- `IsLoopingInfinite`

Using the @@ token in the search will include the source of an inherited property, which is useful in communicating specific containers to address.

Although parsing the Work Unit XML is a similar approach, it is more difficult in that the parser has to reconstruct the Actor-Mixer hierarchy to build a container's set of inherited or overridden properties. Work Units can include other Work Units (and often do in large projects), which means building the hierarchy relationship of a single sound container may require searching across multiple files. But the XML schema for Work Units is clearly documented. Here is an example property list of a container overriding the inherited properties to use the virtual voice mode "Play from Beginning":

```
<PropertyList>
    <Property Name="BelowThresholdBehavior" Type="int16" Value="2"/>
    <Property Name="OverrideVirtualVoice" Type="bool" Value="True"/>
    <Property Name="VirtualVoiceQueueBehavior" Type="int16" Value="0"/>
</PropertyList>
```

If a game project generates Work Units, this would be the XML to interject into the xml to leverage virtual voices.

One more note: similar to warning the sound designer when importing a "dangerous" virtual voice setting on a 3D non-looping (finite) voice, it is also worth calling out 3D looping voices set to "Continue to Play" as this could be a poor allocation of CPU.

9.7 TROUBLESHOOTING ISSUES

Here are some of the virtual voice and below threshold issues that have come up and can be solved from Wwise:

1. **Issue**: Missing sounds after going into a game menu.

   Potential cause: Below threshold is based on the output of the sound source after it has gone through the mix hierarchy. As a result, automated buses from state changes or in-game RTPCs can kill important sounds.

   Solution: Use a virtual voice behavior or continue to play.

2. **Issue**: Blend Container is not playing.

   Potential cause: Cross-fading from Blend or Sequence containers may go below the volume threshold.

   Solution: Check that the virtual voice behavior is "Play from Elapsed Time." A "Resume" behavior could cause the cross-fade to never finish and "Play from Beginning" may have unexpected behavior.

3. **Issue**: Running out of memory in the lower engine pool.

   Potential cause: This might be an indication of a leak in virtual voices.

   Solution: First attempt to repro the out of memory using the Wwise profiler and visually look for obvious leaks. If the issue is difficult to reproduce, use one of the methods from above to look for potential risky virtual voice settings.

4. **Issue**: CPU usage is higher than expected after reorganizing the Master-Mixer bus or Actor-Mixer hierarchies.

   Potential cause: Inaudible 3D sounds may be set to "Continue to play" as a side effect of the default settings being introduced.

   Solution: Attempt to capture the CPU usage with the Wwise profiler connected. Look for containers that should be virtualized.

5. **Issue**: Priority limit behavior of "Discard Newest" or "Discard Oldest" is not working as expected.

   Potential cause: Priority may be distance based through the use of "Use Priority Distance Factor." Since the two properties are not next to each other in the UI, a sound designer may change the priority settings expecting a strict discard when over the max but not notice that it only behaves as expected when the distance factor is disabled.

   Solution: Review priority settings with the sound designer or implementor.

9.8 CULLING SOUNDS AT THE GAME LEVEL OR WITH WWISE

Whether you cull sounds at the game engine level or let Wwise manage all of the game object and/or sound event requests depends on the context of the game. The decision impacts complexity in both maintaining code and debugging issues. Adding redundant functionality should ideally be avoided.

Virtual voices are meant to be rather high bandwidth to support even hundreds of virtual voices where the game may only have 50–100 active voices at a time. If the game does not have a large number of sound sources, having no game engine culling might be viable. If the game engine keeps internal references of every sound event, or there are large numbers of sound events occurring that are known to never be audible, then culling short or all finite sounds based on the max attenuation makes sense. The other main reason to cull at the game engine is custom priority systems. In this case, it would make sense to use a mixture of game engine culling and Wwise virtual voices.

Finally, micromanaging virtual voice settings per container increases the chance of errors and generates unnecessary data. Broad rules should be determined for the project where sound design and engineering both know the role of virtual voices in the project.

SECTION III

Game Integration

CHAPTER 10

Distance-Delayed Sounds

Kory Postma

Offworld Industries

CONTENTS

10.1 INTRODUCTION

In this chapter, we will cover the importance of using distance delays for game audio. We will first look at a common example of lightning and thunder to show the importance and to explain the basics of distance-delayed audio. We will discuss the math and equations behind calculating the speed, distance, and time used to determine distance delays. This will eventually give us the distance delay value in seconds that is required to determine how long to delay sounds to create a realistic sound distance effect. We will then jump into a couple of code samples to demonstrate an example sound scheduler and create a real-world game engine project based upon Unreal Engine 4. Let's get started!

10.2 BASIC THEORY

10.2.1 Lightning

Everyone has seen lightning, followed a few seconds later by a thunderclap. Children grow up learning that every three seconds the sound travels about one kilometer (or about five seconds per mile). They are told to count the number of seconds from the time they see the lightning until they hear the thunderclap, and by using this information they can then determine the distance between themselves and the lightning.

The sound of the thunderclap takes more time to reach us than the flash of light from the lightning does, so we know that sound travels much slower than light. Light also takes time to reach us, but it moves extremely fast (299,792,458 m/s or 186,282 miles/s). In other words, as soon as you see the lightning flash it happened just a few microseconds before you saw it.

Why is sound so slow compared to light? It is because of the medium (air, in this case) that they must travel through to reach us. Scientists have been able to slow down the speed of light to less than 17 m/s by changing the medium that it travels through. Both light and sound travel at different speeds in water compared to air. Light slows down in water, which causes the water to appear shallower than it really is. Sound, on the other hand, travels faster through water because water is much more densely packed than air. Sound traveling through steel is even faster than water because steel is a solid and very densely packed.

The average accepted value for the speed of sound in air is 340 m/s. In reality, the speed of sound in air is dependent upon many factors such as air pressure, temperature, humidity, etc. If you have an underwater game, then sound travels much faster than in air, about four to five times faster (1,400–1,500 m/s). If your game takes place up high in the mountains, then you may want to use 320 m/s. For our purposes, we will design and implement our system around the standard 340 m/s value for the speed of sound through air.

10.2.2 Sound Distance Equation

This section will contain a bit of basic algebra so that we can figure out the amount of time it takes sound to reach us. Speed is defined as distance traveled per time it takes to travel that distance. For instance, if lightning strikes and the thunderclap reaches us 5.2 seconds later, then we can use this information to figure out how far away the lightning was.

$$v = \frac{d}{t}$$

where v is the speed, d is the distance, and t is the time

We know that $v = 340$ m/s and that $t = 5.2$ s, but we do not know what the distance, d, is and that is what we need to find.

Using the equation above and replacing v and t with the values above, we get the following:

$$v = \frac{d}{t}$$

$$\left(340\,\frac{m}{s}\right) = \frac{d}{(5.2\,s)}$$

$$\left(340\,\frac{m}{s}\right) \cdot (5.2\,s) = \left(\frac{d}{(5.2\,s)}\right) \cdot (5.2\,s)$$

The two 5.2 s on the right side cancel out leaving us with the following:

$$\left(340\,\frac{m}{s}\right) \cdot (5.2\,s) = \left(\frac{d}{\cancel{(5.2\,s)}}\right) \cdot \cancel{(5.2\,s)}$$

$$\left(340\,\frac{m}{s}\right) \cdot (5.2\,s) = d$$

Or swapping sides gives us:

$$d = \left(340\frac{m}{s}\right) \cdot (5.2\,s) = (340 \cdot 5.2) \cdot \left(\frac{m}{s}\right) \cdot (s)$$

$$= 1,768\left(\frac{m}{s}\right) \cdot s = 1,768\left(\frac{m}{\cancel{s}}\right) \cdot \cancel{s} = 1,768\,m$$

So, at 340 m/s, lightning that takes 5.2 seconds to reach us is 1,768 meters away.

We can now calculate the time, t, in a similar way if we only know the speed, v, and the distance, d. So, using the same example above but using the time, t, as our unknown:

$$v = \frac{d}{t}$$

$$v \cdot t = \left(\frac{d}{t}\right) \cdot t$$

$$v \cdot t = d$$

This gives us the same equation we had earlier, but we must take it one step farther by dividing both sides by the speed, v:

$$\frac{v \cdot t}{v} = \frac{d}{v}$$

$$\frac{\cancel{v} \cdot t}{\cancel{v}} = \frac{d}{v}$$

$$t = \frac{d}{v}$$

Plugging in our known values from earlier, with the distance, $d = 1,768\,m$, and the speed, $v = 340\,m/s$, we get:

$$t = \frac{1,768\,m}{\left(340\frac{m}{s}\right)} = \frac{1,768}{340} \cdot \frac{m}{\left(\frac{m}{s}\right)} = 5.2 \cdot \frac{m}{\left(\frac{m}{s}\right)} = 5.2 \cdot \frac{\cancel{m}}{\left(\frac{\cancel{m}}{s}\right)} = \frac{5.2}{\left(\frac{1}{s}\right)} = 5.2\,s$$

This last equation, $t = \dfrac{d}{v}$, is the equation we will be using in our game. While we have been using 340 m/s for the value of v, you can substitute a different value if you are using a different speed of sound.

To simulate sounds at a distance, we delay playing the sound to simulate that it took extra time to reach us. We can use the $t = \dfrac{d}{v}$ equation to determine exactly how much time we should delay our sound to simulate the effect of it traveling over distance. This effect is most useful for games that span over great distances and have very loud sounds, such as explosions or gun fire that can be heard at a distance. This effect is not worthwhile for games that have short ranges, quiet sounds at a distance, or for games that do not require the realism afforded by simulating sound travelling over distances. Games that are medium-range (within 100–300 meters) will benefit from this effect because sound is delayed by around one-third of a second at 100 meters or nearly one second at 300 meters.

10.3 DESIGN AND REQUIREMENTS

10.3.1 Requirements

To use distance-delayed sounds, your game audio system must be capable of supporting location-based sounds, must have a mechanism for scheduling sounds, and must be capable of marking some sounds as not participating in the distance delay mechanism.

Location-based sounds require your game audio system to know where a sound was spawned or the location of the actor or object that it is attached to. Most modern game engines have this information and are aware of where sounds spawn, so this is generally not an issue. If you wrote your own game audio engine and if you desire to use distance-delayed sounds, then your system must be aware of where sounds are played or spawned.

The other important consideration for distance-delayed sounds is that your game audio system has a means to schedule sounds or to set a starting time for those sounds. Not all game engines support this and there are some workarounds that you may need to implement in order to support this feature. You may even need to implement your own time-based scheduler before you feed sounds into your game audio engine.

The last requirement is that your game audio system must consider that some sounds should never have distance delays applied to them for things such as music, actor dialogue, UI sounds, and close-range sounds. Some systems may require you to disable delay on close-range sounds because the overhead of calculating the delay and putting it into a queue may be more expensive than just playing the sound.

Think of sounds that play within one meter of the player such as brass bullet shell ejections after firing a full auto weapon. Sounds that occur only one meter from the player have a delay around 3 ms, and most games run at 60 FPS, which is 16 ms per frame. In general, you can safely ignore distance delays within a single frame. With a game running at 60 FPS, and using a standard speed of sound at 340 m/s, that comes to any sound that is about 5 meters from the listener. If you have a real-time audio system and desire the full effect of distance-delayed sounds, then you may choose to still apply distance delays to short-range sounds.

10.3.2 Sound Scheduler and Data Structures

A sound scheduler is essentially a priority queue sorted by ascending start time. This example sound scheduler is good for slow-moving scene actors and players. If the local listening player is moving quickly toward or away from a sound, then calculating the distance and the start time of the sound will not be accurate unless you are constantly checking and updating the distance and calculated start time to accommodate for fast-moving sound listeners or emitters. Basically, if the listening player is moving quickly toward the sound emitter then the sound would play too late according to the distance delay because the listening player would intercept the emitted sound wave before the calculated time. If the listening player is moving quickly away from the sound emitter, then the opposite would occur and the sound would occur too soon. See Figure 10.1 to understand the issue. If your use case requires fast-moving actors and players, and you require highly accurate timing of the sounds, then it is best to check and update the distances and start times of the sounds upon every frame. For this example, we will ignore this particular use case and assume that our actors are moving slowly enough that the time differences will not matter enough and that the distance delay effect will be good enough.

To make the sound scheduler easy to read and understand, I am using a C# `SimplePriorityQueue` available under the MIT License,[1] which includes support for Unity. This code, including the `SimplePriorityQueue` is included as supplementary material for this book. Using a priority queue, we can now create our sound scheduler in C# with the following code:

```
using Priority_Queue;
using System;
using System.Linq;
```

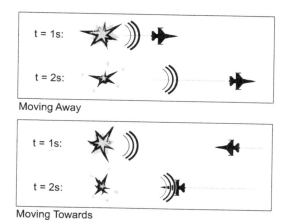

t = 1s:

t = 2s:

Moving Away

t = 1s:

t = 2s:

Moving Towards

FIGURE 10.1   Fast-moving actors affecting when the sound should play. Image by Alastair Sew Hoy.

```
namespace SoundScheduler
{
  class GAPVector
  {
    public double X = 0.0f, Y = 0.0f, Z = 0.0f;

    public GAPVector()
    {
    }

    public GAPVector(Random inRandom, double inMaxDistanceInMeters)
    {
      X = inRandom.NextDouble();
      Y = inRandom.NextDouble();
      Z = inRandom.NextDouble();

      double dist = inRandom.NextDouble() * inMaxDistanceInMeters;

      double distFromOrigin = GetDistanceToOrigin();
      X = X / distFromOrigin * dist;
      Y = Y / distFromOrigin * dist;
      Z = Z / distFromOrigin * dist;
    }

    public double GetDistanceToOrigin()
    {
      return Math.Sqrt(X*X + Y*Y + Z*Z);
    }

    public double GetDistanceToVector(GAPVector inVector)
    {
      double deltaX = (inVector.X - X);
```

```
      double deltaY = (inVector.Y - Y);
      double deltaZ = (inVector.Z - Z);
      return Math.Sqrt(
        deltaX * deltaX + deltaY * deltaY + deltaZ * deltaZ);
    }
}

class Sound
{
  public string SoundFileName;
  public double StartTime;
  public GAPVector Location;

  public Sound(string inSoundFileName, GAPVector inLocation)
  {
    SoundFileName = inSoundFileName;
    Location = inLocation;
    long milliseconds =
      DateTime.Now.Ticks / TimeSpan.TicksPerMillisecond;
    double seconds = milliseconds / 1000.0;
    SetStartTimeBasedOnDistanceDelay(seconds);
  }

  public void SetStartTimeBasedOnDistanceDelay(
    double inCurrentTimeInSeconds)
  {
    SetStartTimeBasedOnDistanceDelay(
      inCurrentTimeInSeconds, new GAPVector());
  }

  public void SetStartTimeBasedOnDistanceDelay(
    double inCurrentTimeInSeconds, GAPVector inListenerLocation)
  {
    double dist =
      Location.GetDistanceToVector(inListenerLocation);
    //340 m/s is the approximate speed of sound on Earth near
    //sea-level
    double speedOfSound = 340.0;
    StartTime = inCurrentTimeInSeconds + dist / speedOfSound;
  }

  public void Play()
  {
    //NOTE: To simulate playing the sound we will just print
    //a string to the console
    long milliseconds =
      DateTime.Now.Ticks / TimeSpan.TicksPerMillisecond;
    double seconds = milliseconds / 1000.0;
    string soundStr =
      string.Format(
      "{0:0.000}: Sound \"{1}\" @ {2:0.000}s with dist: {3:0.00}m",
        seconds, SoundFileName, StartTime,
        Location.GetDistanceToOrigin());
    Console.WriteLine(soundStr);
```

```
    }
}

class Program
{
  static void Main(string[] args)
  {
    //First, we create the priority queue.
    //By default, priority-values are of type 'float'
    SimplePriorityQueue<Sound, double> priorityQueue =
      new SimplePriorityQueue<Sound, double>();
    Random random = new Random();

    //Create the Sounds - this could be done in various ticks,
    //but for simplicity we'll do them all at once
    Sound sound1 = new Sound("Lrg_Exp",
                             new GAPVector(random, 900));
    Sound sound2 = new Sound("Gunshots",
                             new GAPVector(random, 100));
    Sound sound3 = new Sound("Footstep",
                             new GAPVector(random, 50));
    Sound sound4 = new Sound("Med_Exp",
                             new GAPVector(random, 600));
    Sound sound5 = new Sound("Sm_Exp",
                             new GAPVector(random, 300));

    //Enqueue all of the sounds based on when they should
    //start playing
    priorityQueue.Enqueue(sound1, sound1.StartTime);
    priorityQueue.Enqueue(sound2, sound2.StartTime);
    priorityQueue.Enqueue(sound3, sound3.StartTime);
    priorityQueue.Enqueue(sound4, sound4.StartTime);
    priorityQueue.Enqueue(sound5, sound5.StartTime);

    long milliseconds =
      DateTime.Now.Ticks / TimeSpan.TicksPerMillisecond;
    double seconds = milliseconds / 1000.0;
    Console.WriteLine("Scheduler Start Time: " + seconds + "s");

    //Dequeue each Sound from the Priority Queue and print out
    //the relevant Sound information.
    while (priorityQueue.Count != 0)
    {
      milliseconds =
        DateTime.Now.Ticks / TimeSpan.TicksPerMillisecond;
      seconds = milliseconds / 1000.0;
      Sound peekSound = priorityQueue.First();
      if (peekSound.StartTime <= seconds)
      {
        Sound nextSound = priorityQueue.Dequeue();
        //NOTE: This is where you would send the sound to your
        //audio engine and play it
        nextSound.Play();
      }
```

```
    }

  milliseconds =
    DateTime.Now.Ticks / TimeSpan.TicksPerMillisecond;
  seconds = milliseconds / 1000.0;
  Console.WriteLine("Scheduler End Time: " + seconds + "s");

  Console.Write("Please press Enter/Return to exit...");
  Console.ReadLine();
    }
  }
}
```

This simple test program for the sound scheduler checks the time in each frame and then simulates playing the sound by printing a message when a sound would have been played. In this case, all five sounds are being fired off at the same exact time. During gameplay, sounds will fire off at various times, but the Priority Queue is more than capable of accurately and efficiently reordering the sounds based on when they should start playing. The following is the output from one run of test program:

```
Scheduler Start Time: 63648662051.762s
63648662051.860: Sound "Footstep" @ 63648662051.858s with dist: 33.39m
63648662051.958: Sound "Gunshots" @ 63648662051.958s with dist: 67.24m
63648662052.045: Sound "Med_Exp" @ 63648662052.045s with dist: 96.86m
63648662052.516: Sound "Sm_Exp" @ 63648662052.515s with dist: 256.73m
63648662054.254: Sound "Lrg_Exp" @ 63648662054.254s with dist: 849.16m
Scheduler End Time: 63648662054.254s
```

10.4 REAL-WORLD UNREAL ENGINE 4 EXAMPLE

For a real-world example, we will use the Distance Delay Sound Node method as used in Squad from Offworld Industries that utilizes Unreal Engine 4 and the distance delay technology. We will demonstrate how to create this same effect in a real Unreal Engine 4 demo project using a distance delay sound node to delay the start time of a sound cue when it is played anywhere in the game. We will show you how to hook it up into a sound cue with blueprints and how to play it on repeat with a particle effect so that you can experience the distance delay effect and experiment how various settings affect the delay. In this example, we will be using Windows, but you can follow a similar set of procedures for Mac or Linux.

10.4.1 Bootstrapping

First, you will need to obtain Unreal Engine 4, which is freely available at http://unrealengine.com. Open the Epic Games launcher and install a version of the Unreal Engine 4 to your computer. You will also need Visual Studio in order to compile the C++ code. For this example, we used Unreal Engine version 4.18.3 and Visual Studio 2017, which are the latest versions available at the time of writing. Later versions of Unreal Engine 4 may have some API changes, but the concepts should translate fairly directly. Once the install has completed, open the Unreal Engine 4 launcher, as shown in Figure 10.2, and create a new C++ Flying Project, which we will call `DistanceDelayTest`, as shown in Figure 10.3. Make sure you have selected the New Project tab (Step 1) and then the C++ tab (Step 2). Be sure to leave the default to include the Starter Content when creating this project. If you have any issues with the above steps you can seek help via UE4's AnswerHub or via their forums. We are also including this project on the book's website in case you run into any issues duplicating the project on your own.

After creating this new project, the editor will open with a tab called `FlyingExampleMap`. Click on `File -> New C++ Class...` and in that dialog box select the checkbox to `Show All Classes`. Type `SoundNode` in the search box and select it as the parent class, then select Next, as shown in Figure 10.4. Name this class `DistanceDelaySoundNode` and click on `Create Class`, as shown in Figure 10.5. This will create two new files in your project under the Source folder called `DistanceDelaySoundNode.h` and `DistanceDelaySoundNode.cpp`.

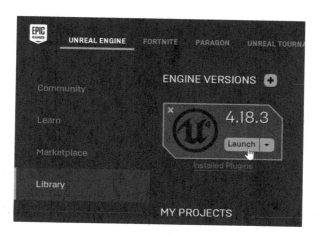

FIGURE 10.2   Start Unreal Engine 4.

FIGURE 10.3   Create a new C++ Flying Project.

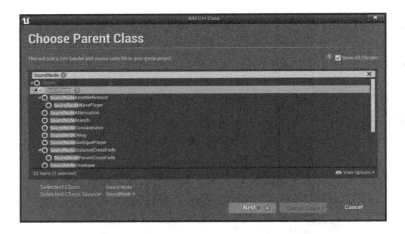

FIGURE 10.4   Use `SoundNode` as the parent class for the new C++ class.

10.4.2 Implementing the Distance Delay Node

In `DistanceDelaySoundNode.h` source file, we will need three `UPROPERTY` variables to control the behavior. The first one is for setting the speed of sound, which we will call `SpeedOfSound`. In this example, we will just have it be a configurable property, but you can hard code this value, pull it from physics volumes, or data-drive it via any other method. The second property is for the maximum delay allowed by this node, which we will call `DelayMax`. The last property is useful with testing the

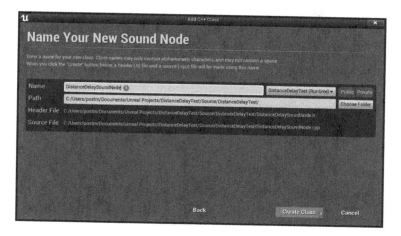

FIGURE 10.5 Naming and creating the new C++ class.

distance delay feature in the editor, which we will call `TestDistance`. We will also need to add a constructor, a couple of function overrides required for `USoundNodes`, and finally our custom `GetSoundDelay()` function that accepts two location-based vectors to calculate the amount of the delay. Your header file should now look like the following:

```
#pragma once

#include "CoreMinimal.h"
#include "Sound/SoundNode.h"
#include "DistanceDelaySoundNode.generated.h"

/**
 * Defines a delay for sounds that contain this based upon the
 * distance to the listener.
 */
UCLASS()
class DISTANCEDELAYTEST_API UDistanceDelaySoundNode :
  public USoundNode
{
  GENERATED_BODY()

protected:
  /** This is the speed of sound in meters per second (m/s) to use
      for this delay. */
  UPROPERTY(EditAnywhere, Category = Physics)
  float SpeedOfSound;

  /** The upper bound of delay time in seconds, used in GetDuration
      calculation and as an upper bounds for sound effects, 3.0 is
      probably a good setting for this. */
  UPROPERTY(EditAnywhere, Category = Delay)
```

```
    float DelayMax;

    /** Used to test distance in the editor (in meters). */
    UPROPERTY(EditAnywhere, Category = Testing)
    float TestDistance;

public:
    UDistanceDelaySoundNode(
        const FObjectInitializer& ObjectInitializer);

    // Begin USoundNode interface.
    virtual void ParseNodes(
        FAudioDevice* AudioDevice,
        const UPTRINT NodeWaveInstanceHash,
        FActiveSound& ActiveSound,
        const FSoundParseParameters& ParseParams,
        TArray<FWaveInstance*>& WaveInstances) override;
    virtual float GetDuration() override;
    // End USoundNode interface.

    virtual float GetSoundDelay(
        const FVector& ListenerLocation, const FVector& Location,
        const float SpeedOfSoundInUU) const;
};
```

Now, we need to implement these functions in `DistanceDelay`
`SoundNode.cpp`. The code in the following listing is heavily com-
mented, but I do want to call special attention to the `ParseNodes()`
function, an overridden function from `USoundNode`. This function is
called every tick while the sound cue instance is active. The first time
this function is called we will initialize the distance delay, and then prevent the children of this node from playing until the delay time has been
reached. Once that time has been reached we will call the parent function
to continue parsing the children nodes. The `GetSoundDelay()` function is used to determine how long we should delay this sound based upon
the location of the sound emitter, the sound listener, and various other
parameters such as the speed of sound.

```
#include "DistanceDelaySoundNode.h"

// Required for FActiveSound, FAudioDevice, FSoundParseParameters,
// etc.
#include "SoundDefinitions.h"

/*------------------------------------------------------------------
UDistanceDelaySoundNode implementation.
------------------------------------------------------------------*/
// Constructor used to set the SpeedOfSound to 340 m/s and the
```

```
// DelayMax to 3 seconds, or about 1 km.
UDistanceDelaySoundNode::UDistanceDelaySoundNode(
  const FObjectInitializer& ObjectInitializer)
  : Super(ObjectInitializer)
{
  SpeedOfSound = 340.0f;
  DelayMax = 3.0f;
}


// ParseNodes is used to initialize and update the sound per tick.
// Other effects like pitch bending can be applied here as well.
// Initial call to this function per instance will have
// RequiresInitialization set to true, subsequent calls will be
// false.
void UDistanceDelaySoundNode::ParseNodes(
  FAudioDevice* AudioDevice, const UPTRINT NodeWaveInstanceHash,
  FActiveSound& ActiveSound,
  const FSoundParseParameters& ParseParams,
  TArray<FWaveInstance*>& WaveInstances)
{
  // Define the data that is stored with this instance as the size
  // of a single float value.
  RETRIEVE_SOUNDNODE_PAYLOAD(sizeof(float));
  // Declare the data that is stored with this instance as the
  // EndOfDelay, this is the time when the sound should start playing.
  DECLARE_SOUNDNODE_ELEMENT(float, EndOfDelay);

  // Check to see if this is the first time through.
  if (*RequiresInitialization)
  {
    // Make sure we do not go through this initialization more
    // than once.
    // NOTE: for actors that are fast moving you may consider
    // updating EndOfDelay more often, but here we only do it the
    // first time.
    *RequiresInitialization = false;

    // Get the default unreal unit conversion and store it
    // statically in this class, this value will not change during
    // gameplay
    static const float WorldToMeters =
      (ActiveSound.GetWorld() != nullptr) ?
        (IsValid(ActiveSound.GetWorld()->GetWorldSettings()) ?
          ActiveSound.GetWorld()->GetWorldSettings()->WorldToMeters :
          100.0f) :
      100.0f;

    // The WITH_EDITOR tag is used to only compile this section for
    // editor builds, the else clause is for live/shipping builds.
#if WITH_EDITOR
    // This is where we determine the actual delay of the sound
    // based upon sound emitter and sound listener locations.
    // The transform stores location, rotation, and scaling
    // information but this function only requires the
```

```
      // location / translation.
      float ActualDelay =
        GetSoundDelay(AudioDevice->GetListeners()[0].
                      Transform.GetTranslation(),
                      ParseParams.Transform.GetTranslation(),
                      SpeedOfSound * WorldToMeters);
      // If we are testing this sound inside of the editor's SoundCue
      // window then the World will be nullptr and we will use our
      // TestDistance value defined for this node instead of the
      // in-game calculated distance.
      // This is very useful for testing that the delay is working
      // according to your design.
      if (ActiveSound.GetWorld() == nullptr)
      {
        ActualDelay = GetSoundDelay(
          FVector(),
          FVector(TestDistance * WorldToMeters, 0.0f, 0.0f),
          SpeedOfSound * WorldToMeters);
      }
#else
      // This is the calculation used for shipping and other
      // non-editor builds.
      const float ActualDelay =
        GetSoundDelay(AudioDevice->GetListeners()[0].
                      Transform.GetTranslation(),
                      ParseParams.Transform.GetTranslation(),
                      SpeedOfSound * WorldToMeters);
#endif
      // Check if there is any need to delay this sound, if not
      // then just start playing it.
      if (ParseParams.StartTime > ActualDelay)
      {
        FSoundParseParameters UpdatedParams = ParseParams;
        UpdatedParams.StartTime -= ActualDelay;
        EndOfDelay = -1.0f;

        Super::ParseNodes(AudioDevice, NodeWaveInstanceHash,
          ActiveSound, UpdatedParams, WaveInstances);

        return;
      }
      // Set the EndOfDelay value to the offset time when this sound
      // should start playing.
      else
      {
        EndOfDelay =
          ActiveSound.PlaybackTime + ActualDelay
            - ParseParams.StartTime;
      }
    }

    // If we have not waited long enough then just keep waiting.
    if (EndOfDelay > ActiveSound.PlaybackTime)
    {
```

```
    // We're not finished even though we might not have any wave
    // instances in flight.
    ActiveSound.bFinished = false;
  }
  // Go ahead and play the sound.
  else
  {
    Super::ParseNodes(AudioDevice, NodeWaveInstanceHash,
      ActiveSound, ParseParams, WaveInstances);
  }
}

// This is used in the editor and engine to determine maximum
// duration for this sound cue.  This is used for culling out sounds
// when too many are playing at once and for other engine purposes.
float UDistanceDelaySoundNode::GetDuration()
{
  // Get length of child node, if it exists.
  float ChildDuration = 0.0f;
  if (ChildNodes[0])
  {
    ChildDuration = ChildNodes[0]->GetDuration();
  }

  // And return the two together.
  return (ChildDuration + DelayMax);
}

// This is the bread and butter of the distance delay custom sound
// node.  Pass in both the listener location and the sound emitter
// location along with the speed of sound (in unreal units (cm)) to
// get the amount of delay to use.
float UDistanceDelaySoundNode::GetSoundDelay(
  const FVector& ListenerLocation, const FVector& Location,
  const float SpeedOfSoundInUU) const
{
  // Calculate the distance from the listener to the emitter and
  // get the size of the vector, which is the length / distance.
  const float DistanceToSource =
    (ListenerLocation - Location).Size();
  // Calculate the amount of delay required to simulate the sound
  // traveling over the distance to reach the listener.
  const float TimeDelayFromSoundSource =
    DistanceToSource / SpeedOfSoundInUU;
  // Useful to verify the values during testing and development,
  // should be commented out during production.
  UE_LOG(LogAudio, Log,
      TEXT("UDistanceDelaySoundNode::GetSoundDelay: %f cm => %f s"),
      DistanceToSource, TimeDelayFromSoundSource);

  // Returns the distance delay after making sure it is between 0
  // and the maximum delay.
  return FMath::Clamp(TimeDelayFromSoundSource, 0.0f, DelayMax);
}
```

10.4.3 Building the Sound Cue

With the code written, go back to the UE4 Editor and click on `Compile`, as shown in Figure 10.6. If everything was successful you will then be able to create a new sound cue that utilizes this new node, if you had issues it may be best to close the editor and compile the code in Visual Studio and then reopen the editor.

To create a new Sound Cue, navigate to the Content Browser tab and click on the folder icon next to the `C++ Classes`, then select the folder called `Content`, as shown in Figure 10.7. In the Content Browser click on `+Add New` and under the `Create Advanced Asset` header hover

FIGURE 10.6   Compiling the new C++ code.

FIGURE 10.7   How to go to the Content Browser to create new assets.

over the `Sounds` menu and click on `Sound Cue`, as shown in Figure 10.8. Give it a name, such as `DistanceDelayedExplosion` and then open it by double-clicking on it.

You should now be able to see the `Distance Delay Sound Node` on the right-hand side under the Palette tab in the `Sound Node` category. To use your new sound node, just drag it off and hook it up next to the output speaker and then drag off a `Wave Player` node and hook that into the `Distance Delay Sound Node`. In the `Wave Player` node, select the `Explosion01` sound as the `Sound Wave` variable. Click on the `Distance Delay Sound Node` and adjust the parameters to your liking, then press the `Play Cue` button to test the implementation, see Figure 10.9. Click on the `Save` button to save your work.

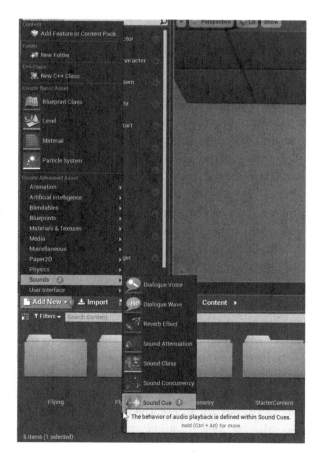

FIGURE 10.8 Create a new Sound Cue.

FIGURE 10.9 The complete `DistanceDelayedExplosion` **Sound Cue** blueprint.

10.4.4 Creating an Actor Blueprint

Back in the Content Browser, click on +Add New again to create a new Blueprint Class under the Create Basic Asset header. Select the Actor button as the parent for this class, and call it `DistanceDelayActor`. Double-click on your new actor to open up the blueprint editor.

Under the Components tab click on the green +Add Component button and add two components: one Audio and one Particle System. Click on the Audio component and set the Sound variable in the Sound category of the Details tab to `DistanceDelayedExplosion`.

Now that the audio is set up, we need to set up a particle system so that we have a visual effect to tell when the delay is starting. Click on the ParticleSystem component and set the Template variable in the Particles category of the Details tab to P_Explosion. The first time you select this you may need to wait for the shaders to compile, but after those have been compiled you should now be able to see the explosion particle effect when you click on the Simulation button, but you will not be able to hear the sound. To continue editing your blueprint you will need to make sure the Simulation button is not activated.

The last piece of the puzzle is to set up the Blueprint script. Go to the Event Graph tab to access the Blueprint code for this actor. You can delete the Event ActorBeginOverlap and Event Tick nodes. Click on the execution pin of the Event Begin Play node and drag off to create a new Set Timer by Event node. Set the

Time on that node to 5 for a five second delay and check the `Looping` checkbox. Drag off the `Event` pin and under the `Add Event` category there is an `Add Custom Event...` menu item. Select that and name this new custom event `Explode`.

For the `Explode` custom event drag off of the execution pin and type `Play (Audio)`. This node will play the sound associated with our Audio component we added earlier. Drag off of the execution pin of the `Play` node and select `Activate (ParticleSystem)`. You may also want to include a `Print String` when the Explode custom event is triggered node for testing purposes. Your complete blueprint graph should look like Figure 10.10. Click on the `Compile` and then on the `Save` buttons to save your work.

10.4.5 Testing the Distance Delay Actor

Every time `DistanceDelayActor` is spawned in the world it will play the explosion particle system and the explosion sound with the distance delay effect on a looping timer that will trigger every five seconds. You can disable automatic triggering of the particle and sound effects the first time the actor spawns by unchecking the `Auto Activate` variable on the `Audio` and `Particle System` components. Similarly, if you don't want this actor to loop every five seconds and you want to spawn in the actor yourself during gameplay events, then you can modify the blueprint by hooking up the `Event Begin Play` directly to the `Play`

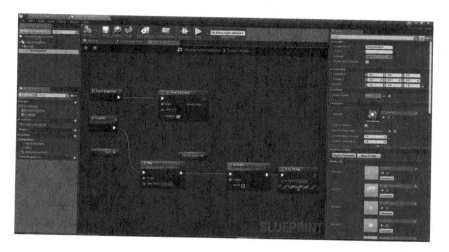

FIGURE 10.10 The `DistanceDelayActor` Blueprint Event Graph.

and `Activate` nodes and remove the `Set Timer by Event` and `Explode` custom event nodes.

Now that everything is set up, close the `DistanceDelayActor` blueprint and go back to the Content Browser and then drag your new `DistanceDelayActor` into the world, then click on the `Play` button to test out the explosion in the editor. You will see the particle effect and then later hear the sound based upon how far away you are from the actor and your speed of sound settings (try setting the speed of sound in your Sound Cue's `Distance Delay Sound Node` to 34 m/s to experience the effect more readily).

You can drag the actor around to different locations, have more than one throughout the world, have the level blueprint randomly spawn them on timers, or setup missiles to fire from your flying ship and when they impact spawn this actor. Regardless of how you use them, the distance delay will always be respected as long as you use the `Distance Delay Sound Node` in your `Sound Cues`.

10.5 ISSUES AND CONSIDERATIONS

There are a few issues and considerations that should be taken into account when using distance delayed sounds.

10.5.1 Fast-Moving Actors or Players Require Updated Delayed Start Times

Actors or objects that travel fast enough to significantly affect the delay caused by distance, either making it shorter or longer, should be updated more often. The delay should be shortened if the two are moving quickly toward each other, or lengthened if they are moving quickly away from one another. There are many ways to handle this situation, but it is something to consider for games that require this use case.

10.5.2 Looping Audio Requires Time-Delayed Parameters

Sounds that loop their audio will not work well with only delaying their start times. You will need to think of other ways of handling looping sounds, especially with moving actors or actors that have particle effects that are coordinated with sounds. For instance, if you have a sound with control parameters, you will have to delay setting those parameters, but not delay them to the particle system. One example where this might occur is a vehicle moving up a hill in the distance: you will see extra exhaust particle effects when the engine is working hard to get up the hill. The sound parameters affecting the engine's RPM should be distance delayed corresponding to the distance between the vehicle and the listener and with the particle effects from the exhaust.

10.5.3 Platform Latency

Some audio systems have very high audio latency, upwards of 200–500 ms for some mobile devices. These latency delays should be considered when delaying distance sounds based upon the platform. You may need to subtract this time from your delay to offset the effect for more accurate timing. For instance, if your distance delay is calculated as 150 ms, but you have a platform latency of 200 ms, then you should just play the sound immediately without any delay because the latency is higher than the distance delay. If your distance delay is 300 ms and your platform latency is 200 ms, then you could set the distance delay offset to 100 ms and will come in on time at the 300 ms mark.

10.6 CONCLUSION

In this chapter, we covered the importance of using distance delays for game audio. We showed how to determine how long it takes sound to reach a listener based on their distance. This gave us the distance delay value in seconds that is required to determine how long to delay sounds to create a realistic sound distance effect. Finally, we learned how to apply this to an example sound scheduler, as well as to a real-world game engine project based upon Unreal Engine 4 and provided sample code for both.

NOTE

1 https://github.com/BlueRaja/High-Speed-Priority-Queue-for-C-Sharp.

CHAPTER 11

Designs for Ambiences in Open-World Games

Matthieu Dirrenberger

Ubisoft

CONTENTS

11.1 INTRODUCTION

There are many ways to manage sound ambiences in games. In this chapter, I will present some of the tools we are using in open-world games at Ubisoft. While all the examples represent real systems, they are simplified from what may actually be implemented in a game engine. The purpose of this chapter is to provide a high-level survey of the sorts of tools for ambiences in open-world games that developers can customize for their own purposes.

The first important thing to think about is that, as is usual in open-world games, we use a loading ring around the player for loading game objects (entities), and as sound objects are loaded, some of them may send play events as soon as they are loaded. The second important general point is to think about ambience as comprising a variety of sounds. We don't use one very complex system for everything, but rather a set of simple tools. Throughout it all, we try to minimize the memory and CPU cost.

11.2 SOUND REGION

The most fundamental concept for ambiences is to split your game into sound regions. The regions represent areas where you expect to hear different ambience sounds. These areas contain data and sound pads (wind, bugs, room tone), weather (rain, snow storm), a reverb, and distinct gun/explosion tails. These elements define the audio immersion of the player for a specific area. Imagine the map of your world as a two-dimensional grid that you can paint. The map is divided into little squares two meters across which we call Sound Region Units. By assigning each unit a color, you will be able to save your data using a texture-like format that will be easy to edit/load/unload, etc.

11.2.1 Sound Region Painting Tool

The main tool in our ambience arsenal is the sound region painter, which allows the designer to paint the world map. You can set a brush size, then choose a sound region and paint it over the ground. In Dunia2 (our game engine), the only rule is one sound region painted for one two meter square ground unit. There is no overlapping using the painting tool. After computation (see Section 11.2.2), each sound region will have a ratio value used to define the current audio volume. The ratio sets the weight between the different painted sound regions. 100% means there is only one sound region painted around the player. 50% means there are two different sound regions painted around the player with equal proportions and the player sits exactly in the middle.

11.2.2 Sound Region Computation

Computing the sound regions playing is fairly simple:

- Define a struct SSoundRegion having these parameters and function:

```
struct SSoundRegion
{
  U8 region; // Region unique ID
  U32 refCount; // Ref count of the region
  F32 ratio; // Volume ratio

  void IncRefCount(); //function which increases ref counter
};
```

- Create a static vector of SSoundRegion named m_region-Weights.

- Define an integer #define SOUNDREGION_MAX_ALLOWED 3 which is how many sound regions can play simultaneously.

- Define an integer proxRange around the player to use for the computation. Starting from the player position you will know the discrete map coordinates you are parsing.

- Parse the sound region's cells to collect your data, then add them to your vector m_regionWeights by increasing their reference counter using their unique id as a key.

- Create a vector of SSoundRegion named m_current-PlayingSoundRegions containing SOUNDREGION_MAX_ALLOWED entries, which contains the most ref-counted (most weighted) sound regions. We must first sort the vector and compute the ratio factor at the same time.

- Iterate on m_currentPlayingSoundRegions, then divide by the number of units parsed, so you get a percentage factor per sound region and play the most weighted sound regions.

```
// Make an evaluation of the surrounding ambiences
m_regionCount = 0;

//radius in meters checked around the player
U16 proxRange = m_manager->m_effectRange;
```

```
// Do not process position outside of the world
const S32 xMin = Max(xref - proxRange, 0);
const S32 xMax = Min(xref + proxRange,
                     m_sectorSizeX*m_sectorCountX);
const S32 yMin = Max(yref - proxRange, 0);
const S32 yMax = Min(yref + proxRange,
                     m_sectorSizeY*m_sectorCountY);

U16 sectorX;
U16 sectorY;
U16 xloc;
U16 yloc;
U8 value;
U8 region;

CSparseByteGrid* sectorData;

for (ndS32 x = xMin; x < xMax; x++)
{
  for (ndS32 y = yMin; y < yMax; y++)
  {
    sectorX = U16(x) / m_sectorSizeX;
    sectorY = U16(y) / m_sectorSizeY;

    xloc = U16(x) % m_sectorSizeX;
    yloc = U16(y) % m_sectorSizeY;

    // Support missing data, in case of late dynamic loading
    sectorData =
      GetSectorData<CSoundRegionLayer>(sectorX, sectorY);
    if (sectorData != nullptr)
    {
      value = sectorData->GetFromCoordinate(yloc, xloc);

      // Used here as a way of extracting multiple info
      // from one value
      region = value & SOUNDREGION_ID_MASK;

      // Here we use a predefine static tab containing all
      // the sound regions for performance purpose
      m_regionWeights[region] += 1.0f;
      m_regionCount++;
    }
  }
}
```

11.3 SOUND SHAPE TOOL

The sound shape tool is used to define ambience zones. It allows the user to define shapes by placing points on the floor, then giving a height to the shape. In the end, it creates a volume that is used to trigger different types of ambient sounds. As the player moves into this volume, it triggers the playback of the user-defined ambience sounds. Each ambience zone can define two types of sounds: Random FX (described in Section 11.4) and Ambiance Follower (described in Section 11.5). The main advantage of the sound shapes compared to the classic painting tool is that sound shapes are game entities that can be loaded optionally depending on a gameplay context. As a result, you can use mission layers to decide to load a sound shape at a precise moment. We use this kind of approach for outposts before and after we liberate them, in order to change the ambiance from a more oppressive feeling to a more open feel.

11.4 RANDOM FX

Random FX are mainly used for improving the immersive aspect of the game by triggering sounds according to a defined polyphony, min/max radius around the player, and a frequency added to a random factor. These sounds are usually sounds such as leaf rustles, tree shakes, insect chirps, animal calls, and wind sounds. Given the player's current position and orientation, the system plays random one-shot sounds in a defined radius or box around the player. Randomized parameters such as min/max height and distance from the player further control the resulting sound. Random FX are very simple to code and use, but they increase the immersive aspect by playing iconic one-shot sounds at places where the player needs to identify a specific context (Figures 11.1 and 11.2).

11.4.1 Dynamic Loading of Variations

One of the main problems with randomized effects is to keep enough aural variation so that players do not notice repetition, while keeping the memory footprint as low as possible. One good approach is to use a set of containers with multiple variations. Then, on some data-driven interval (usually on the order of a small number of minutes), the code will unload the current loaded set and load the next one. This way, there will be enough variety in the sounds to mask any repetition, without putting an undue burden on the memory. In general, players won't notice a sound being repeated after more than 2 minutes if other variations were played in between. This kind of optimization is not necessary in games with a smaller scope, but we can easily hit memory limits on large open-world games, especially if there are limits on the number of sound streams. For the game Far Cry 5 we had a budget of around 380 MB, which we exceeded easily before we optimized both data and dynamic loading systems.

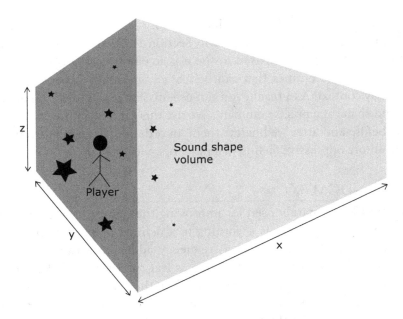

FIGURE 11.1   Random FX played in a sound volume.

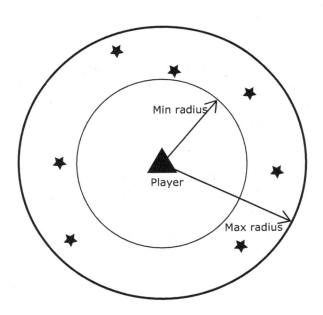

FIGURE 11.2   Sound placement with a minimum and a maximum radius.

11.4.2 Custom Random Containers

Many audio middleware libraries contain functionality to implement randomized triggers of sounds. However, when a game becomes large enough, it can become worthwhile to implement your own randomized trigger system. Doing so becomes particularly useful for restricting memory usage. By hooking a customized random container directly to a dynamic loading system, you can make far more efficient use of memory resources.

11.5 AMBIANCE FOLLOWER

The Ambiance Follower is a system that plays one or more 3D-positioned ambiance loops that follow the player. For each loop, the sound designers can set a distance from the player, an angle at which followers must be distributed, and optionally a movement latency that permits making the sound drift for some specific cases. Additionally, there is a latency factor between 0 and 1 that controls a delay that the follower will use when following the player. The sound designers can also control whether the followers follow the orientation of the listener. When true, the follower will rotate with the listener, when false, the followers keep constant orientation. By placing the sound in 3D and having it move with the player, the sound designers can create more immersive environments, and provides them with a way to easily simulate environments cheaply, since there is no complex computation behind it.

11.6 SOUND LINE TOOL

Sound line is a system where the sound designer can place a minimum of three points on the floor. These points will be connected to generate line segments. We then drive a virtual speaker (sound emitter) along the connected lines, playing a looping sound or a sequence of randomized sounds. This virtual speaker will follow the player's movement by finding the two closest points on the line, and placing the emitted sound at the projection of the player's position onto the line segment.

There are two different approaches to implement this feature. The simplest option is to keep a single emitter following the player as it passes through every line segment. This first version is okay for simple lines, but can cause problems if your lines have angles that make the sound jump from one segment to another. To alleviate this problem, an alternative technique is to create one emitter per line segment. Under this second scheme, you add to the algorithm a max number of active segments and compute all the N closest segments—not just the one related to the two closest points. In a system with multiple emitters, it is a good idea to have a minimum of three in order to avoid artifacts when the segments are angles into curves.

11.7 MULTIPLE SPEAKERS WITH SOUND LINE

A variation on sound lines can be used for specific places needing a system that plays multiple sounds at the same time. We used this kind of systems for rivers by placing the line at the center of the river bed, then following the river path. The idea is to use multiple sets of virtual speakers.

A set contains

- Two virtual speakers equidistant from the line. In our example, one set for the river flow and one set for the river sides.

- The speakers will share a set of parameters: minimum and maximum distance from the line, speaker orientations, and minimum and maximum distance from the next/previous segment.

These speaker sets will follow the player by moving along the segment and with a rectilinear movement from the line according to the limits set, as described in Section 11.6.

It is important to use sounds that are very different between speakers to avoid phasing issues. If the sounds are too similar they will overlap each other and create digital phasing, which is not very pleasing to the ear. For more details on curve-following ambiences, see Chapter 12 "Approximate Position of Ambient Sounds of Multiple Sources".

11.8 SOUND POINT TOOL

The sound point is probably the most common object used in open-world games. It exists in two different forms: as an independent object or as a sound component from an existing game object.

The purpose of the object is only to provide a position and optionally an actual entity to load into the game. Once the sound has played, it can accept input from the gameplay data in order to control playback rules, change its behavior, or set RTPCs.

The sound points can be registered on game objects having gameplay states permitting us to control the play/stop of the sound point.

Here are some examples of options used with sound points:

- Auto start—Whether the sound should be playing automatically.

- Stop on state change—Stops the sound automatically when there is a gameplay state change.

- Update position—Whether the sound should update its position every frame.

- Fade out curve type—The shape of the fadeout curve.

- Fade out duration—How long the fadeout should be.

- Stop event—Optional. Whether to stop the event instantly instead of fading out.

11.9 DUPLICATED SOUND POINT AND OFFSETS

When a sound point is attached to an actual object, you can think about it as a sound decorator. One example is a big building with different air conditioner fan sounds hooked on every wall of the building. The best way to make this happen is to have one sound point attached to the building itself. By default, it will be placed at the center of the building, but it will contain a list of duplicated sound points, each one having a different offset. The system then selects the best position or positions to play the sound based on the proximity to the player. This system allows the sound designers to set up as many triggers as they want, while still only playing a single sound.

11.10 VIRTUAL SOUND POINT MANAGER

When you have a situation with lots of identical sounds—for example, a forest where each tree has a wind rustling sound attached to it—it can become very expensive to play all the sounds at once. A virtual sound point manager system examines the sound points near the player and limits the number of instances playing at the same time up to a data-driven maximum by selecting the closest sounds and only playing those. This system is effective in managing the ambient sounds for forests, vegetation, and some random ambiance sounds. By default, this system will use a "discard new" behavior, wherein newly played sounds are discarded if the count is above the limit. New sounds can play once the number of sounds has gone below the limit. Most of these sounds are not meant to play all the times, and it is good to have a certain randomness. Also, they usually have a short roll-off distance so it works pretty well.

11.11 SOUND ROOM

Sound rooms are a simplified version of a portals system used to define a shape where a sound region ambience is set. This is similar to the Sound Regions from Section 11.2, but it overrides the regions that are painted with the Sound Region Painting Tool. As the listener enters a room, the ambience is changed to match the ambience in the room. Each room has a priority, which enables multiple rooms to be created within each other. One example where you might want to use nested sound rooms is a building with an office or meeting room. The open space outside the meeting room will have one ambience, and the meeting room (inside of the office) contains another. Outside of the building, the ambience painting system takes effect.

When the player goes into or out of a room the system has to manage the transition between the overridden room ambiance and the standard outdoor painted ambiance.

While there are many approaches to implement this transition, one good option is to use a "leaving distance" for each room in the game. The leaving distance is used as an automatic fade-out distance when the player is leaving a room for an outdoor ambience. It works the same the other way when the player is moving into a room. For example, if you have a big room like a cave entrance, you will use a big value like twenty meters in order to create a smooth transition. An opposite example is a bunker door which will use a very short leaving distance, because the bunker muffles the outdoor sound.

In our specific game, the room to room transitions are always set to one meter because we added new dynamic doors/openings permitting some occlusion effects based on these values.

11.12 WEATHER SYSTEM

Weather systems can be very tricky, but if you think about weather as a single system, it can simplify the implementation. A weather system should integrate all the interesting variables from the game and the sound regions and trigger the appropriate sound based on those inputs. Some inputs can switch out which sound is played (snow vs rain, for example), and the rest are passed in as RTPCs to control the weather system. In order to reduce resource consumption, switching out weather types should hook into the dynamic loading system, and perform a smooth cross-fade as the player transitions weather types.

Here are some of the parameters used by the weather system in our game:

- Player relative height from the ground

- Player absolute height

- Player speed

- Player/camera pitch/tilt orientation

- Wind strength

- Wind type

- Snow strength

- Snow type

- Rain strength

- Rain type

11.13 CONCLUSION

All these little tools and design ideas presented here give a general overview of sound ambience systems in a game such as Far Cry. The systems described here are only scratching the surface of what is possible, and what an open-world game will need. As your game evolves, and as you release multiple iterations year after year, you will end up with far more complex systems. The shapes those systems take will depend upon your specific game, but you can use these concepts as a starting point.

CHAPTER 12

Approximate Position of Ambient Sounds of Multiple Sources

Nic Taylor

Blizzard Entertainment

CONTENTS

12.1 INTRODUCTION

This chapter covers fundamental point projection operations on 3D geometry to approximate the 3D spatialization of ambient sounds using a single-sound event or input. The operations covered first are generic and most game engines provide utilities to do these operations without a custom solution. So, instead of reviewing the underlying math, which is effectively summarized entirely by understanding the dot product, the aim is to show how these operations can be applied or extended in the context of audio. The first part will summarize the following:

1. Closest point to a line segment

2. Closest point to a linear spline path

3. Closest point to a rectangular volume

4. Closest point to a capsule

5. The Doppler effect

The second part will go into detail in solving unwanted jumps in panning by returning to point projection along a linear spline path. Using the derived technique, the last part will then go into a broader discussion of using the average direction of a set to points to represent common game audio features such as ambient sound being tied to regions on a 2D grid or sounds representing area effects.

In this chapter, the term "input" will refer to the audio/sound event provided by the sound designer. The term "source" refers to a single point emitting sound waves, and the term "geometry" refers to the 2D or 3D shapes approximating the volume in space that would enclose all of the sources represented by the input.

12.2 CONTEXT

Nearby sound sources are modeled as point emitters and, in games, point emitters are perfect for most cases. It is simple to use a point source for distance checks and obstruction/occlusion systems. But for ambient sources, where sound designers create loops or randomly firing sounds abstracting a volume of space, point emitters may not represent the audio input well.

One example is a river loop. At a micro level, the sound of a river is made up of millions of individual monopole sources (bubbles) which resonate when they burst at the surface of the water. At a larger scale, the river sound is predominantly composed of point sources where the water is most turbulent and loud relative to the listener's position. What the sound designer has authored includes a region of a river with many complex point sources represented in the loop. Another example is rainfall where each individual rain drop is the micro level, and points where the rain is loudest relative to the listener represent the larger scale. Again, the sound designer provides an input that may represent several locations. In both cases, as the listener moves away from the sources, natural audio attenuation is desirable. As the audio programmer, the goal is to approximate the river or rainfall's location in an expected way with the sound designer's single audio input.

12.3 POINT PROJECTION

Using the river example, imagine the sound designer has created an ambient bed loop that should play back uniformly when observed anywhere near a small stream. Since the stream is narrow, it could be represented by a linear spline path, or a set of connected line segments. The source should be the closest point along the spline relative to the listener. Naturally, the closest point is the closest point of the set of the points found by projecting the listener to each line segment.

Starting from the basics, a line segment is specified by two end points. To find the closest point along the segment from another point, the listener in this example, the listener location must be projected to the line that the line segment belongs. The solution is the point along the line formed by the segment which when making a line connecting the solution to the listener is perpendicular with the original line. If the projected point is not on the line segment, then the closest point is the closest end of the line segment (Figure 12.1).

This projection will be the basis of most of the ideas in this chapter. More generally, the problem of point projection can be thought of as finding the closest point from all points for which the line connecting the point and the geometry is orthogonal to a tangent at that point.

In the case of a point to line projection, it is found by taking the magnitude of the vector starting at one end of the line segment to the listener multiplied by the cosine of the angle between the connecting line and the line segment. This is quite simple using the dot product. Organizing your math as follows, you can avoid a square root operation:

FIGURE 12.1 *Left*: Example of a listener's position being projected to a new source location. *Right*: The same but the projection is beyond the range of the line segment.

```
Vector ProjectToLineSegment(
  const LineSegment& line_segment,
  const Vector& position)
{
  Vector projected = position - line_segment.start;
  const Vector translated = line_segment.end - line_segment.start;
  const double proportion = Dot(projected, translated);
  if (proportion <= 0.0)
  {
    return line_segment.start;
  }
  const double length_sq = LengthSquared(translated);
  if (proportion >= length_sq)
  {
    return line_segment.end;
  }

  return
    ((proportion / length_sq) * translated) + line_segment.start;
}
```

This approximation of the stream does have a flaw. As the source moves, the projected point following along the path will attenuate with distance properly. However, the direction of the source is not guaranteed to be continuous, which means the panning can jump from one speaker to another quite noticeably. We will cover approaches to solve these discontinuities later.

(Aside: Modern game engines almost universally have some sort of cubic spline path tool. Point projection to cubic splines becomes quite an involved problem. As mentioned above, one must find points along the spline where the tangent is perpendicular to the line connecting the listener and that point. This turns out to be a fifth degree polynomial. Approximating the cubic spline with linear spline paths is probably preferred (Figure 12.2). There are a number of approaches to do this approximation but they are beyond the scope of this chapter.)

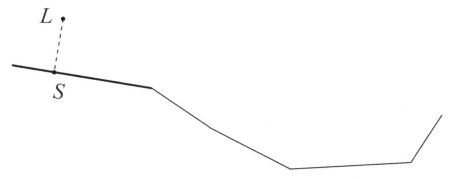

FIGURE 12.2 Projecting a listener's position to a new source position on the closest line segment from a set of line segments.

12.4 PROJECTION—RECTANGULAR VOLUME

Going back to the river example, assume the stream widens out into an area of loud rapids. The sound designer has supplied a separate audio loop to capture this area. The linear path no longer represents the area well. However, the area of rapids is enclosed by a non-axis-aligned rectangular volume (Figure 12.3).

Rectangular volumes can be represented in data in many forms. The form I will use is four vectors stored in a 4×4 transform matrix. The first three vectors store the rotation (or axes) as the half-extents of the rectangular volume and one vector for the translation representing the center of the rectangular volume. (Another common representation using about half the memory would be a quaternion plus translation vector. Whichever form, it can be transformed into a form which will work in the code below.)

The projection to the surface of a rectangular volume from outside the volume is the sum of the listener projected to each of the axes. First, the listener is translated such that the volume's center is the origin. Since the axes are stored as half extents, each line segment to be projected onto starts at the positive value of the extent and ends at the negative extent.

```
Vector ClosestPointToRectangleEx(
   const RectVolume& rect,
   const Vector& position,
   bool& position_inside)
{
   const Vector pos_relative = position - rect.Position();
   Vector projected = rect.Position();
   bool projected_on_segment;
```

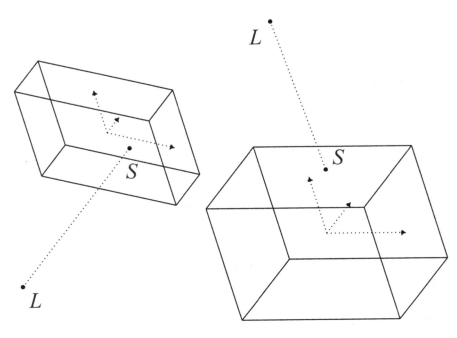

FIGURE 12.3 Examples of projecting a listener's position to a new source position on the surface of a rectangular volume.

```
position_inside = true;
for (int axis_id = 0; axis_id < 3; ++axis_id)
{
  const LineSegment relative_axis =
    { rect.HalfExtent(axis_id), -1.0 * rect.HalfExtent(axis_id) };
  projected +=
    ProjectToLineSegment(relative_axis, pos_relative,
                         projected_on_segment);
  position_inside &= projected_on_segment;
}
  return projected;
}
```

When the listener is on the interior of the volume, we would rather play the sound in 2D and not project it back out to the surface. We handle this case with a slight tweak to `ProjectToLineSegment()` to include a boolean value indicating if the projection was on the line segment.

```
Vector ProjectToLineSegment(const LineSegment& line_segment,
  const Vector& position,
  bool& projected_on_segment)
{
  Vector projected = position - line_segment.start;
```

```
  const Vector translated = line_segment.end - line_segment.start;
  const double proportion = Dot(projected, translated);
  if (proportion < 0.0)
  {
    projected_on_segment = false;
    return line_segment.start;
  }
  const double length_sq = LengthSquared(translated);
  if (proportion > length_sq)
  {
    projected_on_segment = false;
    return line_segment.end;
  }

  projected_on_segment = true;
  return
    ((proportion / length_sq) * translated) + line_segment.start;
}
```

12.5 PROJECTION—CAPSULE

Our stream continues on and then plunges over a cliff making an even louder waterfall. A line segment fits nicely at the base of the waterfall, but the sound designer wants a uniform loudness some distance away without authoring it into the attenuation curves. Here another common primitive, the capsule, would enclose the area.

The capsule can be represented as one axis, a radius, and a translation. Just like with the spline and rectangular volume, projection onto the capsule begins with a point to line projection onto the axis of the capsule. Again, the end points are the positive and negative of the extent.

If the point returned is less than the radius, the listener is inside the volume and we can return to the original listener position. Otherwise, the point on the surface is the point which is the distance of the radius along the vector from the point on the line segment back to the listener (Figure 12.4).

```
Vector ClosestPointToCapsule(
  const Capsule& capsule,
  const Vector& position,
  bool& position_inside)
{
  // Project position along the line segment formed by the
  // capsule's axis.
  const LineSegment axis =
    { capsule.Position() + capsule.HalfExtent(),
      capsule.Position() + (-1.0 * capsule.HalfExtent()) };
  const Vector projected = ProjectToLineSegment(axis, position);

  // use coordinate space of the projected point
  const Vector position_relative = position - projected;
```

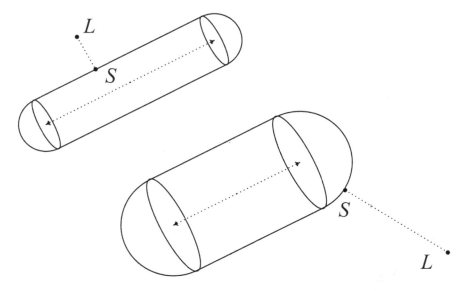

FIGURE 12.4 *Top left*: A listener's position projected to a new source on the cylindrical portion of a capsule. *Bottom right*: On a cap portion of the capsule.

```
const double project_dist_sq = LengthSquared(position_relative);

if (project_dist_sq < (capsule.Radius() * capsule.Radius()))
{
  position_inside = true;
  return position;
}
else
{
  position_inside = false;
  const Vector position_along_radius =
    (capsule.Radius() / sqrt(project_dist_sq)) * position_relative;
  return position_along_radius + projected;
}
}
```

12.6 PROJECTION—DOPPLER EFFECT RATIO

We now take a short departure from strictly ambient sounds to demonstrate one last example using point projection. Past the waterfall, the stream opens up into a lake. On the lake, a boat is driving at a fast speed. The engine sound of the boat feels a bit static from the listener, so the sound designer would like to add a Doppler effect such that the engine pitches up when approaching and pitches down when moving away from the listener.

The equation for the Doppler effect ratio is

$$\text{Frequency ratio} = \frac{c + \text{relative listener velocity}}{c + \text{relative source velocity}}$$

where c is the speed of sound in the medium. For air, this is about 340 m/s.

It is unlikely in your game that the source and listener are always moving in the same direction, so the relative velocity is found using point to line projection (Figure 12.5).

To find the velocity of the listener with respect to the source and the source with respect to the listener means only using the component of the vectors which are collinear with the line connecting the listener and source. (The orthogonal component is neither moving toward nor away from the listener.) The first step is to project each velocity vector with the line formed by the source and listener. Some simple algebra can be used to reduce the number of calculations required to calculate the formula as seen by the variable constant below.

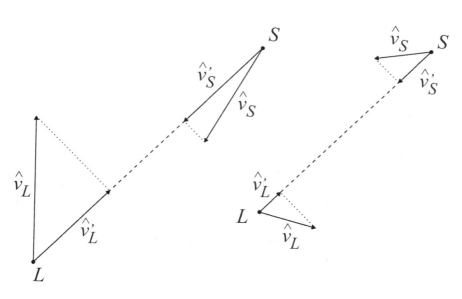

FIGURE 12.5 Two examples of listener and source velocity vectors being projected along the line connecting the listener and source to be used in calculating the Doppler effect ratio.

```
double DopplerRatio(const Vector& listener,
  const Vector& listener_velocity,
  const Vector& source,
  const Vector& source_velocity,
  const double speed_of_sound = 340.0)
{
  const Vector direction = source - listener;
  const double length = Length(direction);

  if (length > DBL_EPSILON)
  {
    const double listener_component =
      Dot(direction, listener_velocity);
    const double source_component = Dot(direction, source_velocity);
    const double constant = speed_of_sound * length;
    assert(abs(listener_component) + DBL_EPSILON < constant
          && abs(source_component) + DBL_EPSILON < constant);
    const double doppler_ratio =
      (constant + listener_component)
      / (constant + source_component);
    return doppler_ratio;
  }

  return 1.0;
}
```

Finally, if the audio engine is expecting the frequency ratio in cents, we can perform a simple conversion.

```
double FrequencyRatioToCents(const double frequency_ratio)
{
  return 1200.0 * log2(frequency_ratio);
}
```

12.7 IMPROVED PROJECTION

We now return to the first example where a linear spline path was used to represent the geometry of a narrow stream. The problem with projecting the listener to the closest point on the set of line segments is that on interior angles, the panning direction of the source can jump. Not only does the jump sound disorienting, but the single source does not represent that the stream is now on more than one side (Figure 12.6).

Section 12.8 will briefly discuss a multiple-emitter approach to solving this problem, but we will not delve deeply into that solution. Instead, we will derive an approach that still uses point projection, but splits the source into three variables (direction, magnitude, and spread), each of which is solved separately. This direction, magnitude, and spread approach is then applied to two more scenarios.

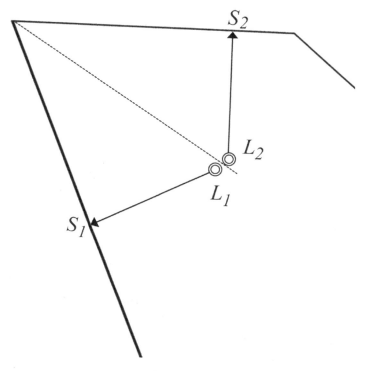

FIGURE 12.6   Although the change in magnitude is small when moving the listener position from one location to another, the change in direction can be quite large.

12.8 MULTIPLE EMITTERS

Using multiple emitters abandons the goal of having one source to represent the area of the sound, and instead divides the spline into sections each assigned an unmoving emitter. For something such as a river input, each emitter could be playing back in perfect time sync or on random start points. Certain considerations need to be made, such as how much space should be between each emitter. The drawback is that there is no longer a uniform output and there will be multiple sources to manage. This approach does work nicely if the spline needs to be broken into pieces for loading purposes anyway, and obstruction/occlusion can be handled the same as other sound sources. In a way, having a nonuniform sound may reflect reality better. For example, in Figure 12.6 hearing different audio in the left channel and the right channel could represent the scene well.

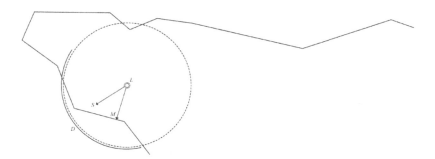

FIGURE 12.7 Dotted line represents the maximum distance or attenuation of the input relative to the listener. Vector M is used to find magnitude, which in previous examples was also the final location of the source. The arc, D, represents the spread distribution.

12.9 ANALYTICAL SOLUTION—OVERVIEW

The single source approach is more mathematically involved and requires some definitions. The idea starts by using the typical method of culling sound sources: only the intersection of the geometry and a sphere around the listener with radius equal to the attenuation range of the input sound needs to be evaluated (Figure 12.7).

More generally only the subset of points—in this case any points on the line segments forming the spline path—should contribute to the solution. This time instead of finding a position for the source through projection, we will break the source into three variables: magnitude, direction, and spread. Spread is the amount of sound that bleeds into other speakers from the sound's true direction. Ranging from 0 to 1, 0 represents no dispersion and 1 represents uniformly spread across all speakers. Spread can also be used as a measure of deviation from a direction where 0 is a single point on a sphere and 1 is the entire sphere.

Each point evaluated inside the sphere should contribute with the following goals:

1. Direction should be impacted less the farther a point is from the listener.

2. Similarly, spread should be impacted less the farther a point is from the listener.

3. The spread of two parallel lines with the listener equidistant from the lines should be 1.

4. The spread of a line segment that is collinear with the center (but not passing through the center) should be 0 regardless of the magnitude of the line.

5. Small changes in position of the listener should result in small changes in direction, magnitude, and spread.

6. Subdividing a line segment should not alter the direction, magnitude, or spread.

We discussed earlier that the magnitude of the vector projected to the closest point on the linear spline is smooth, which we will continue to use. The magnitude is found by iterating each line segment along the path, projecting the center of the sphere (the listener) to each line segment, and identifying the closest of all projected points.

For direction and spread, goal 6 (being able to subdivide line segments) guides us to one possible solution. The average direction of a set of vectors is the normalized sum of those vectors. To find the total sum of every point as a vector along a line segment, the line segment must be subdivided into smaller and smaller pieces. Taking the limit of this process, as the subdivision size goes to 0, can be represented as a line integral. The specific integral I will show breaks down into a line integral of a few irrational functions and turns out to be solvable on paper. Using the criteria for spread and thinking of it as a measure of deviation, spread can be solved in a similar way.

(Aside: Although this was developed to solve a specific issue with interior angles of multiple line segments, this approach is also an improvement over projection to a single line segment. As shown in Figure 12.8, using a standard point projection on a line segment which clearly has more power on the left-hand side would put equal power in the right and left channels.)

12.10 ANALYTICAL SOLUTION—WEIGHT FUNCTIONS

To address the goal that points farther away contribute less to direction and spread, a weighting function needs to be introduced to give a weighted average of the evaluated points. The weighting function should also enforce the goal that points outside the sphere do not need to be evaluated. This led to choosing a linear scale from one to zero moving from the center to the boundary:

$$W(\hat{v}) = \begin{cases} 1 - \dfrac{\|\hat{v}\|}{\alpha} & \text{if } \|\hat{v}\| < \alpha, \\ 0 & \text{if } \|\hat{v}\| \geq \alpha. \end{cases} \qquad (12.1)$$

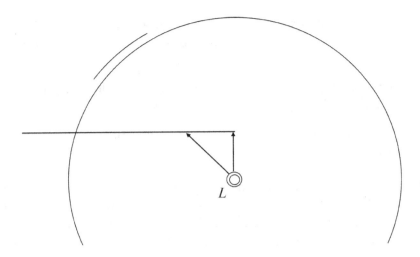

FIGURE 12.8 Average weighted distance used for single-line segments can be preferable over point projection as well. In this example, the vertical vector is the solution for point projection and does not capture that more of the sound pressure would be arriving from the left.

where α is the radius of the sphere, or the attenuation range of the sound source, $\hat{v}$ is any vector relative to the center of the sphere, and $\|\hat{v}\|$ indicates magnitude. While we will be using this particular formula in this chapter, in fact any weighting function converging to zero at the boundary of the sphere could be an option. This formula works well for audio purposes because the linear scale resembles sound falloff as a gain factor, and also because it has an easy to find analytical solution under integration. Later on, I'll give an example that breaks away from the constraint of being integrable.

Because spread is a value from 0 to 1 and direction has no magnitude, neither spread or direction are dependent on the attenuation range of the input. To simplify both the math and the algorithm, the sphere and each line segment can be scaled such that the sphere becomes the unit sphere. Then the weight function simplifies to

$$W(\hat{v}) = \begin{cases} 1 - \|\hat{v}\| & \text{if } \|\hat{v}\| < 1, \\ 0 & \text{if } \|\hat{v}\| \geq 1. \end{cases} \tag{12.2}$$

One important detail is that our weight function is only continuous inside the sphere, so line segments intersecting the sphere need to be clipped by finding the intersection point(s) with the sphere (Figure 12.9).

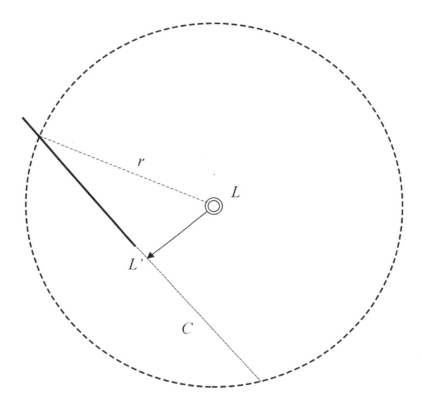

FIGURE 12.9   Line segment clipped by circle.

To clip a line segment by a sphere, project the sphere's center L onto the line created by the line segment. The projected point L' is half way along the chord C formed by the two intersecting points of the line. If either end point of the line segment is farther than the sphere's radius, replace the end point by the chord's end point in that direction. The chord's endpoints are a distance of $\pm\sqrt{r^2 - \|L'\|^2}$.

```
// Assumes LineSegment is valid with two distinct end points.
// Returns false if the line segment is outside the bounds of
// the sphere.
bool ClipLineWithSphere(
  const Sphere& sphere,
  LineSegment& input)
{
  const Vector closest_to_line =
    ClosestPointToLine(input, sphere.center); // 1
  const double distance_to_line_sq =
    LengthSquared(closest_to_line - sphere.center);
  const double radius_sq = sphere.radius * sphere.radius;
```

```
if (distance_to_line_sq + DBL_EPSILON >= radius_sq) return false;

const Vector direction = input.end - input.start;
const double segment_length_sq = LengthSquared(direction);
const double half_chord_length_sq =
  radius_sq - distance_to_line_sq;
const double length_to_intersect =
  sqrt(half_chord_length_sq / segment_length_sq);

const Vector intersect = length_to_intersect * direction;
if (LengthSquared(input.start - sphere.center) > radius_sq)
{
  input.start = closest_to_line - intersect;
}
if (LengthSquared(input.end - sphere.center) > radius_sq)
{
  input.end = closest_to_line + intersect;
}

return true;
}
```

Note that line 1 of the above code is projecting the sphere's center to the line formed by the line segment input and can fall outside the bounds of the line segment.

12.11 ANALYTICAL SOLUTION—DETAILS (OR THE MATH)

The total weighted direction is the sum of the normalized direction of each point along the line segment multiplied by the weight function:

$$\hat{\sigma} = \lim_{\Delta s_i \to 0} \sum_{i=1}^{n} \frac{\hat{v}}{\|\hat{v}\|} W(\hat{v}) \Delta s_i = \int_{C} \frac{\hat{v}}{\|\hat{v}\|} W(\hat{v}) \Delta s \qquad (12.3)$$

To solve the line integral, the line segment is parameterized as $\hat{A} + \hat{B}t$, where $\hat{A}$ is the start point and $\hat{B}$ is the direction of the line segment. Or as vector components:

$$v_x(t) = A_x + B_x t$$

$$v_y(t) = A_y + B_y t$$

$$v_z(t) = A_z + B_z t$$

which forms the definite integral using the definition of the line integral:

$$\hat{\sigma} = \langle \sigma_x, \sigma_y, \sigma_z \rangle = \int_c \frac{\hat{v}}{\|\hat{v}\|} W(\hat{v}) \Delta s$$

$$= \int_0^1 \frac{\hat{A} + \hat{B}t}{\|\hat{v}\|} W(\hat{v}) \sqrt{x'(t)^2 + y'(t)^2 + z'(t)^2} \, \Delta t$$

The length of the curve of integration is the length of line segment and we can make this substitution:

$$\sqrt{x'(t)^2 + y'(t)^2 + z'(t)^2} = \sqrt{v_x'(t)^2 + v_y'(t)^2 + v_z'(t)^2}$$

$$= \sqrt{B_x^2 + B_y^2 + B_z^2}$$

$$= \|L\|$$

Another substitution which simplifies integration is to arrange the parametric form of the magnitude of the vector into the square root of a quadratic:

$$\|\hat{v}\| \rightarrow \sqrt{ax^2 + bx + c}$$

where a, b, and c are dot products (denoted by angle brackets) of the start, A, and direction, B, of the line segment. This is done by expanding the vector and collecting the terms around the parametric term t.

$$\|\hat{v}\| = \sqrt{(A_x + B_x t)^2 + (A_y + B_y t)^2 + (A_z + B_z t)^2}$$

$$= \sqrt{\langle \hat{B}, \hat{B} \rangle t^2 + 2 \langle \hat{A}, \hat{B} \rangle t + \langle \hat{A}, \hat{A} \rangle} \qquad (12.4a)$$

Note that $\langle \hat{B}, \hat{B} \rangle$ is also the squared magnitude of the line segment and is guaranteed to be positive. This is also used to simplify the integration.

Now the integral can be separated into parts that each has well-defined solutions for each x, y, and z. For the x component, it would look like:

$$\sigma_x = \int_0^1 \frac{A_x + B_x t}{\|\hat{v}\|} W(\hat{v}) \|L\| \Delta t$$

$$= \|L\| \int_0^1 \frac{A_x + B_x t}{\|\hat{v}\|} (1 - \|\hat{v}\|) \Delta t \qquad (12.4b)$$

$$= \|L\| \left(A_x \int_0^1 \frac{1}{\|\hat{v}\|} \Delta t + B_x \int_0^1 \frac{t}{\|\hat{v}\|} \Delta t - \int_0^1 A_x + B_x t \Delta t \right)$$

By combining Eqs. 12.4a and 12.4b, the first two integrals, which are of the form of the square root of a quadratic equation, can be calculated directly by looking up the integrals from a list:

$$\int_0^1 \frac{1}{\|\hat{v}\|}\Delta t \rightarrow \int \frac{\Delta t}{\|\hat{v}\|} = \frac{1}{\sqrt{a}}\log\left|2\sqrt{a}\|\hat{v}\| + 2at + b\right|$$

and

$$\int_0^1 \frac{t}{\|\hat{v}\|}\Delta t \rightarrow \int \frac{t\Delta t}{\|\hat{v}\|} = \frac{\|\hat{v}\|}{a} - \frac{b}{2a}\int \frac{\Delta t}{\|\hat{v}\|}$$

where log is the natural logarithm.

Spread can be found in a similar way to total distance. Instead of integrating each weighted distance, the cosine of the angle from the total or average direction to each point is integrated. The other difference is that to normalize spread between 0 and 1, the limit needs to be normalized by the sum of all the weights:

$$\mu_\theta = \frac{\displaystyle\lim_{\Delta s_i \to 0}\sum_{i=1}^n \cos\left(\theta_{\hat{\sigma}}^{\hat{v}}\right)W(\hat{v})\Delta s_i}{\displaystyle\lim_{\Delta s_i \to 0}\sum_{i=1}^n W(\hat{v})\Delta s_i}$$

$$= \frac{\displaystyle\int_0^1 \cos\left(\theta_{\hat{\sigma}}^{\hat{v}}\right)W(\hat{v})\|L\|\Delta t}{\displaystyle\|L\|\int_0^1 1 - \|\hat{v}\|\Delta t} \qquad (12.5)$$

The denominator, or total of all weights, again involves an integral of the square root of a quadratic which has the following direct solution:

$$\int \|\hat{v}\|\Delta t = \frac{2at+b}{4a}\|\hat{v}\| + \frac{4ac - b^2}{8a}\int \frac{\Delta t}{\|\hat{v}\|}$$

Notice the magnitude of the line segment, $\|L\|$, was not canceled out of the equation. This allows the numerator to be replaced with a value we have already solved for. Start by replacing the cosine with its equivalent dot product:

$$\cos\left(\theta_{\hat{\sigma}}^{\hat{v}}\right) = \frac{\langle\hat{\sigma}, \hat{v}\rangle}{\|\hat{\sigma}\|\|\hat{v}\|} \tag{12.6}$$

Substituting Eq. 12.6 back into the numerator and expanding out the dot product simplifies as follows:

$$\text{numerator}\left(\mu_\theta\right) = \int_0^1 \cos\left(\theta_{\hat{\sigma}}^{\hat{v}}\right) W\left(\hat{v}\right)\|L\|\Delta t$$

$$= \frac{1}{\|\hat{\sigma}\|}\int_0^1 \frac{\langle\hat{\sigma}, \hat{v}\rangle}{\|\hat{v}\|} W\left(\hat{v}\right)\|L\|\Delta t$$

$$= \frac{1}{\|\hat{\sigma}\|}\int_0^1 \frac{\sigma_x v_x + \sigma_y v_y + \sigma_z v_z}{\|\hat{v}\|} W\left(\hat{v}\right)\|L\|\Delta t$$

$$= \frac{1}{\hat{\sigma}}\left(\sigma_x \int_0^1 \frac{A_x + B_x t}{\|\hat{v}\|} W\left(\hat{v}\right)\|L\|\Delta t\right.$$

$$+ \sigma_y \int_0^1 \frac{A_y + B_y t}{\|\hat{v}\|} W\left(\hat{v}\right)\|L\|\Delta t$$

$$\left. + \sigma_z \int_0^1 \frac{A_z + B_z t}{\|\hat{v}\|} W\left(\hat{v}\right)\|L\|\Delta t\right)$$

$$= \frac{\langle\hat{\sigma}, \hat{\sigma}\rangle}{\|\hat{\sigma}\|}$$

$$= \|\hat{\sigma}\|$$

The numerator turns out to be the magnitude of the total distance.

One more adjustment needs to be made. Spread near 0 should represent a distribution concentrated around the average direction and values near 1 to represent a distribution equally spread across the sphere. The calculation of spread should be

$$1 - \mu_\theta = 1 - \frac{\|\hat{\sigma}\|}{\text{total weight}} \tag{12.7}$$

12.12 ANALYTICAL SOLUTION—THE IMPLEMENTATION

Calculating the spread distribution and total direction of a single line segment:

```
// Analytical solution for the total average, weighted direction a
// line segment.
Vector TotalAttenuatedDirection(
  const Sphere& sphere,
  const LineSegment& line,
  double& out_spread)
{
  LineSegment clipped_line(line);
  if (ClipLineWithSphere(sphere, clipped_line))
  {
    const double inv_radius = 1.0 / sphere.radius;
    // Convert line segment into a scaled coordinate system where
    // the sphere is centered on the origin and has a radius of 1.
    const Vector start =
      inv_radius * (clipped_line.start - sphere.center);
    const Vector direction =
      inv_radius * (clipped_line.end - clipped_line.start);

    // Solve the line integral over the parametric form of the
    // line segment, start + direction * t, for the function:
    // f = (v * Weight(v)) / magnitude(v)
    // where Weight(v) = 1 - magnitude(v).
    // This reduces to two integrals involving a form of
    // sqrt(ax^2 + bx + c)
    // in which and a, b, and c can be expressed as dot products
    // of the line segment being integrated.

    const double dot_end = LengthSquared(direction); // a
    const double dot_start = LengthSquared(start); // b
    const double dot2 = 2 * Dot(start, direction); // c

    // distance at t = 1
    const double param1 = sqrt(dot_end + dot2 + dot_start);
    // distance at t = 0
    const double param0 = sqrt(dot_start);

    const double length = sqrt(dot_end);

    // integral of the inverse distance
    const double int_inv_root1 =
      log(Max(DBL_EPSILON,
              2 * length * param1 + 2 * dot_end + dot2)) / length;
    const double int_inv_root0 =
      log(Max(DBL_EPSILON, 2 * length * param0 + dot2)) / length;

    // integral of the normalized vector length
    const double int_t_inv_root1 =
      (param1 / dot_end) - (dot2 * int_inv_root1) / (2 * dot_end);
    const double int_t_inv_root0 =
```

```
          (param0 / dot_end) - (dot2 * int_inv_root0) / (2 * dot_end);

      // Spread
      {
          // Arc length is the dot product of the normalized average
          // direction and the vector to the point.
          // Taking the limit of the dot product to find the total arc
          // length simplifies to the length of the total direction.
          // To find the average spread needs to be normalized by the
          // total weight. This is the line integral of the form:
          // integrate (W(v))dt or integrate (1 - magnitude(v))dt,
          // where v is expressed parametrically with t.
          const double discriminent =
              4 * dot_end * dot_start - dot2 * dot2;
          const double total_weighting1 =
              1 - ((2 * dot_end + dot2) * param1) / (4 * dot_end) -
                  (discriminent * int_inv_root1) / (8 * dot_end);
          const double total_weighting0 =
              -(dot2 * param0) / (4 * dot_end) -
                  (discriminent * int_inv_root0) / (8 * dot_end);

          out_spread = length * (total_weighting1 - total_weighting0);
      }

      // definite integrals
      const double definite_start = int_inv_root1 - int_inv_root0;
      const double definite_end = int_t_inv_root1 - int_t_inv_root0;

      // Apply constants factored out.
      const double x =
          start.x * definite_start + direction.x * definite_end -
              start.x - direction.x / 2.0;
      const double y =
          start.y * definite_start + direction.y * definite_end -
              start.y - direction.y / 2.0;
      const double z =
          start.z * definite_start + direction.z * definite_end -
              start.z - direction.z / 2.0;

      const Vector total_direction = { x, y, z };
      return length * total_direction; // apply last constant factor
  }
  return { 0.0, 0.0, 0.0 };
}

// Helper struct to store return values:
// Stores the result of finding the average attenuated direction.
struct AverageAttenuatedDirection
{
  Vector closest_point;
  Vector avg_direction;
  double closest_distance;
  double avg_spread;
};
```

Calculating the spread distribution, average direction, and closest magnitude of a set of line segments:

```cpp
// Returns true if at least one line segment was inside the sphere.
template<class LineSegmentContainer>
bool SolveAverageAttenuatedDirection(
  const Sphere& sphere,
  const LineSegmentContainer& lines,
  AverageAttenuatedDirection& result)
{
  static_assert(
    std::is_same<LineSegment,
      LineSegmentContainer::value_type>::value,
    "LineSegmentContainer must iterate over LineSegment.");

  Vector total_direction = { 0.0, 0.0, 0.0 };
  double total_weighting = 0.0;

  double closest_distance_sq = DBL_MAX;
  bool within_range = false;
  const double radius_sq = sphere.radius * sphere.radius;

  for (const LineSegment& line : lines)
  {
    const Vector closest_point =
      ClosestPointToLineSegment(line, sphere.center);
    const double distance_sq =
      LengthSquared(closest_point - sphere.center);

    if (distance_sq < closest_distance_sq)
    {
      closest_distance_sq = distance_sq;
      result.closest_point = closest_point;
    }

    if (distance_sq + DBL_EPSILON < radius_sq) // audible
    {
      double weighting = 0;
      total_direction +=
        TotalAttenuatedDirection(sphere, line, weighting);
      total_weighting += weighting;
      within_range = true;
    }
  }

  const double total_length = sqrt(LengthSquared(total_direction));
  result.closest_distance = sqrt(closest_distance_sq);

  if (total_length > DBL_EPSILON)
  {
    result.avg_spread = 1.0 - total_length / total_weighting;
    result.avg_direction = total_direction / total_length;
  }
  // If length went to zero, the distribution of lines cancelled out.
```

```
// For example, if the input were two parallel lines.
else if (closest_distance_sq < radius_sq)
{
  result.avg_spread = 1.0f;
  result.avg_direction = result.closest_point;
}
else
{
  result.avg_spread = 0.0f;
  result.avg_direction = result.closest_point;
}

return within_range;
}
```

12.13 NEAR FIELD

Even though the analytical solution is nearly continuous, the direction can change rapidly as the listener and the source become very close. In the real world a sound emitter and listener would not be in an identical position. The inverse distance rule is only valid for some distance away from the sound source. Within the distance, the volume is called the near field. A suitable approximation is to set a near field distance and to scale spread to 100% once in the interior of the near field. We need to keep in mind that time is discrete in video games and so this near-field distance might be up to one meter.

12.14 AVERAGE DIRECTION AND SPREAD OF RECTANGLES

We now limit ourselves to just two dimensions. This next example uses the same reasoning from a set of line segment but applied to axis-aligned rectangles. The 2D rectangle also has an analytical solution that is still practical to solve. A set of 2D rectangles could approximate regions of rainfall or broadly defined ambient areas on a grid. The somewhat complex scenario in Figure 12.10a and b could be represented by one emitter.

The problem can be stated as the solution to the following integral aggregated for all rectangles:

$$\hat{\sigma} = \iint_R \frac{\langle x, y \rangle}{\sqrt{x^2 + y^2}} \left(1 - \sqrt{x^2 + y^2}\right) \Delta x \Delta y$$

and

$$\mu_\theta = \frac{\|\hat{\sigma}\|}{\iint_R \left(1 - \sqrt{x^2 + y^2}\right) \Delta x \Delta y}$$

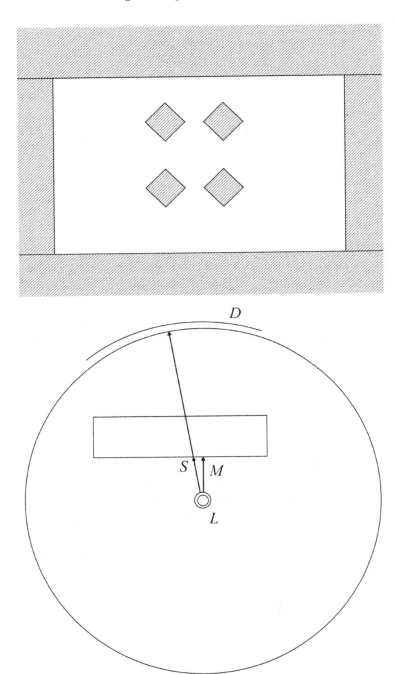

FIGURE 12.10 *Top:* Approximating the location of rain with rectangles (shaded areas). *Bottom:* Rectangle problem formulated.

And as with a set of line segments, spread will simplify to the magnitude of the total direction divided by the sum of weights. Although the solution to the integral for the sum of weights exists, it certainly is not a succinct solution in code. For a small number of rectangles, this still seems reasonable to compute. However, continuing to expand in this analytical manner for more complex areas or in 3D would likely be a dead end. There is much written on the topic of numerical methods for solving these kinds of problems which is out of the scope of this chapter.

```
// Assumes Rectangle is inside the circle
Vector TotalAttenuatedDirectionRect2D(
  const Circle& circle,
  const Rect& rect,
  double& out_spread)
{
  Vector total_dir = { 0.0, 0.0 };
  const double inv_radius = 1.0 / circle.radius;
  const double x1 = (rect.coords[0].x - circle.center.x) * inv_radius;
  const double x2 = (rect.coords[1].x - circle.center.x) * inv_radius;
  const double y1 = (rect.coords[0].y - circle.center.y) * inv_radius;
  const double y2 = (rect.coords[1].y - circle.center.y) * inv_radius;

  // Because this uses a double integral, the inner
  // integration introduces two parts which becomes four when
  // solving the definite integral of the outer integration.
  // The x coordinate and the y coordinate are solved independently.
  // The lambda functions are meant to cut down on the repetition
  // although they introduce some redundant work.

  // Returns twice the integration of inverse magnitude along the
  // line specified by constant.
  auto two_integrate_sqrt =
    [](const float constant, const double var) -> double
    {
      const double constant_sq = constant*constant;
      const double mag = sqrtf(var*var + constant_sq);
      return
        var * mag + constant_sq * log(Max(var + mag, DBL_EPSILON));
    };

  // x
  {
    double total_x =
      two_integrate_sqrt(x2, y2) - two_integrate_sqrt(x1, y2);
    total_x -=
      two_integrate_sqrt(x2, y1) - two_integrate_sqrt(x1, y1);

    total_dir.x = 0.5 * (total_x - (y2 - y1) * (x2 * x2 - x1 * x1));
  }
```

```
// y
{
  double total_y =
    two_integrate_sqrt(y2, x2) - two_integrate_sqrt(y1, x2);
  total_y -=
    two_integrate_sqrt(y2, x1) - two_integrate_sqrt(y1, x1);

  total_dir.y = 0.5 * (total_y - (x2 - x1) * (y2 * y2 - y1 * y1));
}

// Spread
{
  const double int_1 = (x2 - x1)*(y2 - y1);

  const double int_r_x2y2 = x2 * 0.5 * two_integrate_sqrt(x2, y2);
  const double int_r_x2y1 = x2 * 0.5 * two_integrate_sqrt(x2, y1);

  const double int_r_x1y2 = x1 * 0.5 * two_integrate_sqrt(x1, y2);
  const double int_r_x1y1 = x1 * 0.5 * two_integrate_sqrt(x1, y1);

  auto int_sq_log_sqrt =
    [](const float constant, const double var) -> double
    {
      const double constant_sq = constant * constant;
      const double var_cub = var * var * var;
      const double mag = sqrtf(var*var + constant_sq);
      const double sum[4] =
      {
        3.0 * constant * var * mag,
        6.0 * var_cub * log(Max(DBL_EPSILON, mag + constant)),
        -3.0 * constant_sq * constant *
          log(Max(DBL_EPSILON, mag + var)),
        -2 * var_cub
      };
      const double inv_eighteen = 1.0 / 18.0;
      return (sum[0] + sum[1] + sum[2] + sum[3]) * inv_eighteen;
    };

  const double int_sq_log_x2y2 = int_sq_log_sqrt(x2, y2);
  const double int_sq_log_x2y1 = int_sq_log_sqrt(x2, y1);

  const double int_sq_log_x1y2 = int_sq_log_sqrt(x1, y2);
  const double int_sq_log_x1y1 = int_sq_log_sqrt(x1, y1);

  const double total_weight = int_1 - 0.5 *
    ((int_r_x2y2 - int_r_x2y1) - (int_r_x1y2 - int_r_x1y1) +
    (int_sq_log_x2y2 - int_sq_log_x2y1) -
    (int_sq_log_x1y2 - int_sq_log_x1y1));

  out_spread = 1.0 - Length(total_dir) / total_weight;
}

return total_dir;
}
```

There are a couple more details to mention on rectangles. Being constrained to axis-aligned rectangles might defeat the versatility of this approach in certain applications. Since the algorithm handles each rectangle individually, a non-axis-aligned rectangle can be converted into an axis-aligned problem by rotating the rectangle around the listener until it is axis aligned. One approach would be to build a 2D rotation matrix. To find the angle to rotate by, notice that given any extent or edge of the rectangle, the rotation will either minimize the delta between x or y to 0. Working this out will lead to the following equation.

```
const double angle = atan2(v1.x - v2.x, v1.y - v2.y);
```

With the angle, the rotation matrix can be applied to solve the rotated average direction which will then need to be rotated back to the original coordinate system.

The other detail is how to clip a rectangle with a sphere. Doing this adds many different cases to solve. Instead, a rectangle not fully inside or outside the sphere can be subdivided and each subdivision either subdivided further or solved as an independent rectangle. The process can be repeated within some error tolerance (Figure 12.11).

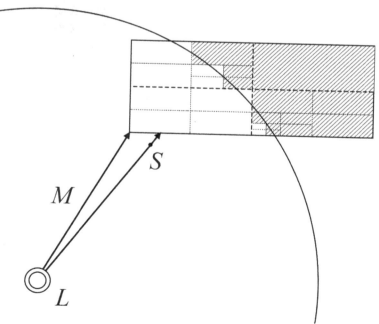

FIGURE 12.11   Subdividing rectangles.

However, by subdividing the rectangle, the algorithm is no longer an analytical solution and the process introduces a numerical component. The complexity to accuracy tradeoff is also quite high which leads us to the final example in this chapter.

12.15 AVERAGE DIRECTION AND SPREAD USING A UNIFORM GRID OR SET OF POINTS

The last example, although yielding interesting results, is fairly constrictive in its uses. However, it was what brought me to the next algorithm which is possibly the most useful of all the ideas presented so far.

I have worked on more than one game where regions of the game world are marked up by a 2D grid broadly labeling spaces. For audio, entering this region would kick off an ambient loop. It would be much nicer if this was a 3D sound which transitioned to 2D when the listener entered the space and eliminate any time-based component or fade-ins (Figure 12.12).

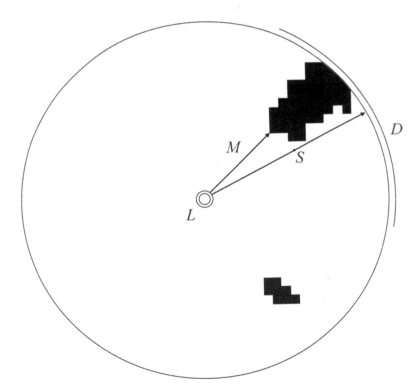

FIGURE 12.12 Average weighted direction and spread of grid cells where each cell is treated as a single point.

Notice from the analytical solution of a rectangle that, as a rectangle is subdivided more, the area, the delta x, and the delta y become less significant in the integration. If the rectangles become sufficiently small compared to the circle represented by the attenuation range, they can be approximated by discrete points. This does something nice to the equation: integration becomes summation over a set of points.

Here is one possible implementation:

```cpp
template<class PointContainer>
Vector TotalAttenuatedDirectionPoints(
  const Sphere& sphere,
  const PointContainer& points,
  const double grid_cell_size, // 0 is valid
  double& out_spread)
{
  static_assert(
    std::is_same<Vector, PointContainer::value_type>::value,
    "PointContainer must iterate over Vectors.");
  // Assumes point is the center of a grid cell.
  const double minimum_distance = grid_cell_size / 2.0;

  double total_weight = 0.0;
  Vector total_dir = { 0.0, 0.0, 0.0 };

  for (const Vector& point : points)
  {
    const Vector direction = point - sphere.center;
    if (grid_cell_size > 0.0 &&
        fabs(direction.x) < minimum_distance &&
        fabs(direction.y) < minimum_distance &&
        fabs(direction.z) < minimum_distance)
    {
      // Inside the a grid cell and should treat the sound as 2D.
      out_spread = 1.0;
      return{ 1.0, 0.0, 0.0 };
    }
    const double distance = Length(direction);
    if (distance < sphere.radius)
    {
      const double weight = sphere.radius - distance;

      total_dir += (weight / distance) * direction;
      total_weight += weight;
    }
  }

  out_spread = 1 - Length(total_dir) / total_weight;
  return total_dir;
}
```

In this implementation, the details of the order in which points are iterated is purposely left out. How this code is integrated in game heavily depends on the context. For example, if the geometry is a set of distinct objects in the world, such as a large number of torches bordering a room, the container might be a vector or array. On the other hand, if the points being iterated is a search space around a listener, as would happen with 2D grid in the world, the container might iterate more efficiently starting at the listener and fill out until a maximum number of points have been found. Another example of a custom container is one that only processes as many points for some given limited amount of time or spreads the processing over multiple frames variable on how much other audio activity is happening.

12.16 CONCLUSION

The last example is a starting point for a huge amount of flexibility and creativity. Even the geometry mentioned early in this chapter (line segments, rectangular volumes, spheres) can be discretized or voxelized and solved as the average of a set of 3D points. Obstruction and occlusion that would have been difficult to rationalize about can be handled by testing each point or a subset of them.

The focus of this chapter was on ambient sounds, but as hinted at earlier, this approach can also be applied to effects, weapons, or spells which cover an area. Examples for line segments might be a beam weapon or a spell where the caster leaves a trail of fire with clear start and end points. Examples for a grid could be an explosion or skill that creates a large number of randomly placed events. Another extension I have used is that time can be an additional parameter in the weighting function. Using time, points can fade out of the equation, for example, damage over time effects such as a poison pool or fire which burns out.

CHAPTER 13

Techniques for Improving Data Drivability of Gameplay Audio Code

Jon Mitchell

Blackbird Interactive

CONTENTS

13.1 PROBLEMS WITH EMBEDDING AUDIO BEHAVIOR IN GAMEPLAY CODE

On many games I've worked on, even larger scale ones making use of well-developed middleware, the audio-related behaviors have become gradually and unpleasantly intertwined with the gameplay code. This is a fairly natural consequence of the game audio behaviors starting off very simple—usually no more than "play sound x when y happens"—and evolving from there.

There is nothing wrong with this, of course. It probably covers a large percentage of all the game sounds since game audio began, and even in more complex games is still a sizable percentage, especially in simpler and smaller scale games.

However, it doesn't scale well as the complexity of the audio behaviors we require grows, and has at least three major problems. First, it's fragile: When coders restructure the gameplay code there's a good chance the audio hooks and associated logic will be made obsolete, refactored out of existence, or, in the best-case scenario, made more complicated to refactor. Second, it's often repetitive: Whether the audio behavior is for a crowd system, a model of vehicle audio, or weapons firing, there are core aspects that are often the same for each. Third, embedding audio behavior in gameplay code requires a programmer. It must be done either by the gameplay coder or by an audio programmer. The less programmer time required to get the desired audio behavior, the happier the designers will be, and (usually) the happier the programmers are.

In an ideal world, the audio designers would have tools that empower them to create their own audio control logic in a way that scales well as the game grows, is validatable and solid, and is powerful enough to support some fairly complex behaviors.

13.2 MODEL-VIEW-VIEWMODEL

Dealing with the first problem, fragility, is really just a matter of applying good software engineering practices. In general, gameplay code is hard to keep tidy. It often has to pull together and drive AI, rendering, physics, and UI code, in addition to audio, and the more these various aspects of the game code can be cleanly separated the more robust the code will be.

Gameplay audio code is actually quite similar in many ways to the code to drive UI elements. Both are representations of game entity state, need to monitor game entity state (while usually leaving it unaffected), respond

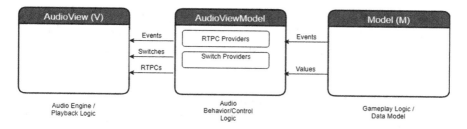

FIGURE 13.1   Model-View-ViewModel

rapidly to changes, and often require transitional behaviors and lifetimes that don't correspond exactly to those of the underlying game objects.

The *Model-View-ViewModel* pattern used by Microsoft for their WPF tools is their approach to decoupling application logic from UI behavior logic, and those concepts map very neatly to the challenges we have as audio behavior logic becomes more complex.

In a game audio context, the *Model* is solely responsible for providing methods to query the current state of properties of our game objects, whereas the *View* solely manages submission of state to the presentation layer of the audio. The *ViewModel* binds the two together, providing a way to translate game events and changing gameplay values into the control parameters understood by the game audio engine.

Figure 13.1 illustrates the Model-View-ViewModel pattern in the context of an audio engine.

13.3 CREATING AUDIOVIEWMODELS FROM DATA

At a minimum, the `AudioViewModel` for a specific type of game object can be broken out in a separate class or structure, to be controlled by the gameplay code. While this still requires dedicated programmer time, it reduces the coupling to the gameplay code. When common patterns in the `AudioViewModel` code are identified, they can be extracted and reused. Better still, they can be exposed to the designers, enabling them to create their own view model behaviors.

13.4 REMAPPING AND MANIPULATING GAME VALUES

Often, we want to use a game parameter value (velocity, time in a certain state, health, etc.) to drive one of our audio parameters. In the simplest case, all our *ViewModel* needs to do is read from the *Model* (usually a property on the game entity) and pass that value to the *AudioView*. More often than not, though, it's more convenient for the designer to work with a modified version. Some manipulation, such as scaling and clamping, can be done in the RTPC response curves in most audio middleware authoring tools, but it's often cleaner to modify them *before* they're sent to the audio engine.

13.5 BLENDING GAME VALUES

Much like remapping, you can perform basic combinations of game parameters by adding multiple RTPCs to your objects and using your audio engine to add them together—but there are lots of other useful blend operations that aren't often supported, and trying to do it in the playback tool will often just complicate the designers' lives.

13.6 RTPC BLEND TREE

One very flexible method I've used for allowing designers to manipulate RTPC values is a blend tree. Each leaf node in the tree provides an RTPC value, and the parent nodes apply a blend operation and pass the results to their parent nodes, until the final value is reached at the root, and can be sent to the desired parameter on the AudioView.

Figure 13.2 shows an evaluator that takes the larger of two game parameters, then scales the result by 2.5.

Conceptually, this is very similar to a simple programming language's expression tree. While it's probably not a good idea to perform any heavyweight calculations this way for the sake of both your game's performance and your designers' sanity, it does work well for performing a lot of commonly needed operations.

Here are the core of the node types we use in the project I'm working on at the moment:

- **Constant**: Provides a constant floating-point value.

- **Blend**: Combines the values of one or more child nodes, using the blend types *add, min, max, multiply, clamp, and average.*

- **Select**: Selects between two child nodes, depending on if a given condition is true or false. Our game engine has the concept of a *Requirement*, which is a predicate base class that returns true or false when evaluated on a given game entity. We have conditions which take other conditions such as *OrRequirement* and *AndRequirement*, so in combination with the **Blend** node, the fairly simple tree structure does give us a lot of flexibility.

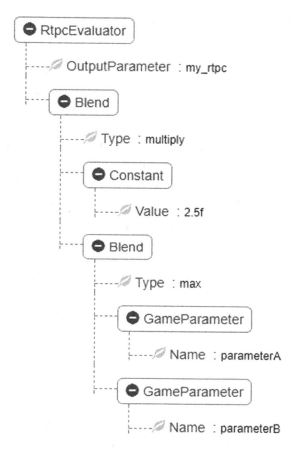

FIGURE 13.2   An evaluator that takes the larger of two game parameters, then scales the result

- **GameParameter**: Retrieves an *int* or *float* parameter by name from the game entity the audio view is attached to.

- **GameParameterMap**: Using a dictionary-like key/value collection, this is used to retrieve non-numeric game entity data such as strings or enum values before mapping them to a floating-point parameter.

- **GameParameterGraph**: Much like **GameParameter**, this retrieves a floating-point value by name from the game entity but, before returning it to the blend tree, applies a piecewise linear function—much like the RTPC curves in Wwise.

- **ActiveTagCount**: Each of the audio objects and active audio events in the game can be tagged with a set of 32-bit hashed IDs, used for grouping sounds into collections of sounds that share certain properties. This node returns the number of active objects or events containing the passed-in tag. This might seem a little abstract but has turned out to be useful for all sorts of things. For example, in my current project, this node is used to drive a `nearby_combat_intensity` parameter by counting all the events within a given radius that contain the `combat` tag. Any sound event triggered by one of our **WeaponView** objects will have this applied.

- **ControlSourceReceiver**: Similar to **ActiveTagCount**, this node is a way for audio objects' parameters to be driven not by their own internal state, but by the state of objects around them. These read values from **ControlSourceEmitters,** which can be used to route parameters from one object to another, or to provider values for object-to-object parameters such as distance between objects. I'll go into more detail about Control Sources in Sections 13.8–13.10.

13.7 HEAVY

While I've found it's best to roll your own parameter manipulation code, Enzien Audio's *Heavy*[1] tool can be very useful as a quick-and-dirty method of allowing designers to do their own manipulation of game parameters. It takes Pure Data (PD) patches and compiles them into plugins for most popular audio engines. It was quick to use to create plugins to blend multiple parameters by taking the min, max, average, and so on, as I later implemented in our game engine as part of our parameter blend tree. Figure 13.3 shows an example PD patch which can be compiled with Heavy, which takes two input parameters, and outputs the maximum to a third parameter.

13.8 CONTROL SOURCES

The core idea behind control sources is allowing audio entities to broadcast and/or receive control parameter values from other audio entities, giving the designers the power to build interesting interactions between them. A little like patch cords on modular synths—if the programmers concentrate on building boxes that do interesting and useful things, then hopefully the designers can connect them together in ways the programmers hadn't originally even dreamed of. Although, admittedly, there's an equally good chance that they'll use them in ways that may give the programmers nightmares.

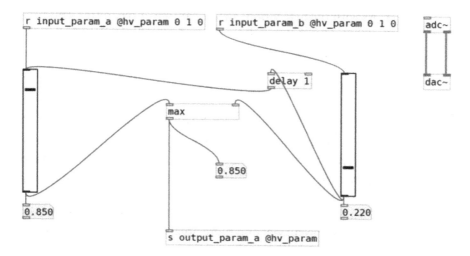

FIGURE 13.3 A PD patch which takes two input parameters and outputs the maximum to a third parameter

13.9 CONTROL EMITTERS

Much like an audio emitter, a control source has a position and an area of effect. But instead of being a source of sound, they're a source of something that controls the sound, like an RTPC. An audio emitter is only audible when within range of a listener object, and a control source only does anything when queried by a *Control Receiver.*

13.10 CONTROL RECEIVERS

Like an audio listener, a control receiver's job is to determine which control emitter objects are within range and apply those parameters. Not all emitters are of interest to all receivers, so each emitter and receiver has a *channel* ID they broadcast/receive on.

Unlike a listener, there are a variety of ways to do this beyond just summing. We have the following types in our system:

- **Sum**: Adds the values of any emitters with range and broadcasting on the receiver's channel.

- **Average**: The same as **Sum,** but the total value is divided by the number of active emitters.

- **Nearest**: Only the value of the nearest in-range emitter is received.

- **Select**: As with the **Select** node in the parameter blend tree, this uses our requirement system to filter out what would otherwise be candidate control emitters.

13.11 USES OF CONTROL SOURCES

13.11.1 Volumetric Control Emitters for Reverb Zones

One of the first uses of control emitters in our game was as a basic implementation of reverb zones. Since each emitter is essentially just a sphere controlling a game parameter, the distance from the center of the sphere can be used to control the send level of a reverb effect. Overlapping control emitters with carefully tuned radii and falloff parameters let us approximate some of the curvier and more organic areas where we needed reverb, such as a riverbed. It's worth noting that this was more of a case of the designers doing something because it was the only way they had at the time, rather than a way I would particularly recommend, but one of the nice things about giving your designers flexible tools is that even what you might consider misuse of a system can point to areas to improve or serve as requirements for entirely new subsystems.

13.11.2 Mixing

The first version of control sources in the game was initially written to perform a sort of dynamic mixing. Our game is RTS-like, and like any RTS, one of the big challenges for audio is dealing with closely packed units. If we have 50 vehicle units in an area, and they are all playing a loud engine sound, the game will start to sound loud and unpleasant pretty quickly. My first impulse was to simply limit the number of vehicle voices and put a limiter on the buss, but this meant that large groups of units would steal from small groups or single units, when often they were just as important to hear. Similarly, just using the limiter meant that single units were drowned out, as large groups activated the limiter. What we needed was some way of reducing the volume of the engines, depending on how many other loud sounds were nearby. With this approach, dense groups of units would all reduce each other's volume substantially, but sparse groups and single units would be less affected. Figure 13.4 shows an example of this in action.

13.11.3 Controlling a 2D Layered Background Ambience

Initially, background ambience in our game was handled by simply placing a large number of positional 3D emitters and allowing the voices to be

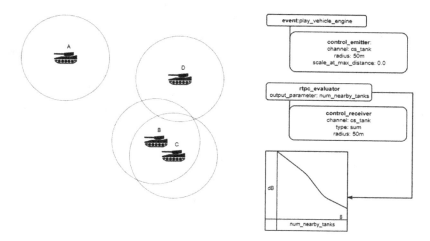

FIGURE 13.4   Control Surface mixing in action

blended and culled by our audio middleware. While this sounded great, the large number of audio objects and simultaneously active streams was a performance issue, as well as cluttering up our audio profiler logs. To keep things to a constant number of streams and active audio objects, the audio emitters were replaced with control source emitters, with one control source channel for each ambience layer. The N ambience layers were instead triggered as a 2D sound on a single audio object, and the final volume of each layer controlled by a control receiver placed at the listener's position, calculating the sum of the active control emitters within range of the receiver. I've implemented similar systems on previous games to control things such as the volume of crowd audio layers, in response to the number of nearby pedestrians, but those have usually been bespoke code—in this case, the designers were able to implement a similar system without coder intervention (occasional advice and discussion aside).

13.12 SPEEDING UP CONTROL SOURCES

My first naive implementation of control sources worked well but performed a distance check for every receiver against every emitter, every frame. Our game can have thousands of active objects, so running $O(N^2)$ tests like this meant endangering our frame budget pretty badly.

13.12.1 Spatial Hashing

Using spatial hashing improved the speed of the implementation dramatically. Rather than performing a distance check against every existing emitter, I was able to loop through the grid cells known to be within the radius of each receiver and build a collection of candidate emitters from their contents. This worked especially well when the majority of the emitters were offscreen, although didn't help too much when multiple dense clusters of objects were within range. One problem I'm still looking for the solution for is finding a good way to trivially accept when an emitter should be active, as well as trivially reject.

13.12.2 Reducing the Update Rate

Another big improvement was reducing the rate at which the `control_receiver` values were calculated. A quick A/B with our designers confirmed that we couldn't tell the difference between calculating the control values every frame (~30 fps) or once every 8 frames (~4 fps), especially with parameter rate limiting and interpolation enabled in Wwise. Having a calculation spike every 8 frames isn't substantially better than having it continually, so I added code to split the receivers into N buckets and updated only one bucket per frame. Amortizing update costs across multiple frames is a simple but effective technique I've used in many audio subsystems, so much so that it's often worth thinking about your likely required update rate when you start implementing one and finding a consistent way to decouple from the graphical frame rate.

13.13 CONCLUSIONS

As well as giving the designers more power, making an effort to keep our gameplay audio code modular and extensible, with as few underlying assumptions about the type of game we're making as possible is paying dividends in making it reusable across multiple projects—both in terms of code reuse, and providing a somewhat consistent cross-project interface for audio designers, who at many companies will work on more than one project, or have periods of helping out when one project is particularly busy.

While much of this chapter describes work we've done for our custom game engine, a similar system should be easily applicable in most Entity Component System style engines, including commercially available ones such as Unity and Unreal.

NOTE

1 Downloadable from https://enzienaudio.com/.

CHAPTER 14

Data-Driven Sound Limitation System

Akihiro Minami and Yuichi Nishimatsu

Square Enix

CONTENTS

14.1 INTRODUCTION

Looking back into the history of video game audio, the number of sounds that could be played was very limited due to hardware constraints. When *Dragon Quest* and *Final Fantasy* first appeared, their hardware platform was strictly restricted to five channels of audio output. But today, after 30 years of advancement in technology, we do not need to worry about those hardware audio channel restrictions. The only factor that limits the number of sounds being played simultaneously is CPU, and even considering the fact that we must share that with other sections, we have abundant power to play sounds beyond human cognition. But even if we went further and could play an arbitrarily large number of sounds—that is, playing sounds in every possible occasion—should we do it in video games? The idea of sound limitation begins from this question.

There are all sorts of hooks for sound effects in a game context: character motion, collision, VFX, HUD, landscape, etc. Although firing off the sound effects at all those occasions may be correct from a physical perspective, it may not always correctly reflect the sound designers' aesthetics. Even without taking psychoacoustics into account, sound effects for the player-controlled protagonist are much more important compared to those for a random NPC just passing by. This differentiation can be seen in graphics as well: non-player characters are intentionally authored and rendered to be much more inconspicuous compared to the protagonists.

And of course, that is not the only situation where there is a mismatch between the game world and the real world. Consider a situation where an enemy is about to attack the player-controlled character. A sound effect can be an effective warning of the oncoming attack, especially if the enemy is out of sight. When the attack would be fatal for the player character, that sound effect could be the most important aspect of the game at the moment. These decisions of choosing what to play, what not to play, and what to emphasize are an important part of video game audio design. We can see that our answer to the aforementioned question "should we play sounds in every possible occasion?" is "clearly not."

With that said, now we need to figure out how we are going to limit the sounds that are playing. One basic approach is to have a priority for each and every sound. That is, when the number of sounds exceeds a threshold, the one with the lowest priority will be stopped. Although this will work to a certain extent, it is not always something that will satisfy the sound designers' aesthetics. Some of the things they will say are the following:

- "I don't want two of the same sound effect to be played simultaneously"

- "When there are too many sounds playing, I want the one with multiple instances to be stopped before others"

- "I don't want sound effect A to play when sound effect B is playing"

- "I want to duck other sounds down while this sound effect is playing"

A basic priority-based limitation system is not able to handle these requests. But building and debugging a new system every time a sound designer comes up with a new limitation rule can become burdensome. In order to solve this problem in a generic fashion, we built a system called the Sound Limitation Macro System or simply "Macro."

14.2 SYSTEM DESIGN

In designing the Macro system, there were four key concepts: data driven, flexibility, simplicity, and extensibility.

14.2.1 Data Driven

The task of sound limitation design must be in the sound designers' hands. Our system must be data driven in order to accomplish this goal: the data that the sound designers create is the main variable controlling the sound limitation. Also, this will decrease the cost of repetition because the sound designers only need to replace the data instead of waiting for the programmers to fix the code. Note that even if the code modification was just a couple of lines, the sound designers may have to wait for hours to compile if this were done in code. This way of working is extremely powerful when adjusting audio scenes, where it can take copious amounts of trial and error to get it sounding right.

14.2.2 Flexibility

There are a variety of situations where sound limitation will come into play, and thus it must be extremely flexible to accommodate any conditions that may happen in the game scene. One sound designer may wish to limit sound based on characters, and another may wish to do it using sound category, such as music, UI, or footsteps. Even going further, a very special sound limitation could become necessary in certain occasions such as "do not play this sound if this and that are playing" or even "stop all sounds belonging to a certain category when this sound is played."

14.2.3 Simplicity

Given the above two requirements, we should never create a system that is incomprehensible for the sound designers, who are not programmers and therefore do not have strong backgrounds of algorithm design. If the system is too complicated, sound designers may have to go ask the programmers every time to review if they are doing the right thing. That interaction would be a failure of a system designed for sound designers to use. We also believe it is important to keep the system itself simple so that users new to Macro can quickly pick up on it.

But being simple does not constrain the sound designers to simple use-cases, it also enables the users to easily construct a complex Macro once they achieve mastery.

14.2.4 Extensibility

Lastly, we need to always be mindful of the future. In video game development, it is not unusual to extend the system out of unpredictable necessity. Therefore, we must avoid as much as possible the case of those unseen implementations being impossible due to system limitations.

14.2.5 Macro

To meet the above requirements, we decided to implement a command-based system. The series of commands is packaged with the sound effect data to be triggered upon start, stop, or even every frame of its life. It is flexible due to the variety of commands that are available. It is a simple structure where a series of simple commands are executed one by one from top to bottom. New features can be added easily by implementing a new command. In designing, or scripting, the sound limitation, the macro instruction of commands is what the system revolves around, which led us to the name "Macro."

14.3 IMPLEMENTATION

Now that the design of the system is set, let's go to the actual code implementation. There are two types of commands in our Macro system: Filter commands and Execute commands. Filter commands are in charge of extracting the desired sounds from the mass of sounds that are currently in play at the moment. Once the search is done by the Filter commands, Execute commands will execute the sound limitation given certain conditions. Below are some of the commonly used Filter and Execute commands.

Filter Commands:

```
Filter: Clear
Filter: Same Sound
Filter: Same Category
Filter: Same Macro
Filter: Sound ID [parameter: Sound ID]
Filter: Category [parameter: Category Number]
Filter: Priority [parameter: Priority]
Filter: Priority Difference [parameter: Difference]
Filter: Panning [parameter: Panning]
Filter: Panning Difference [parameter: Difference]
```

Execute Commands:

```
Exec: Cancel Play
Exec: Stop Oldest
Exec: Stop Furthest
Exec: Set Own Sound Volume [parameter: Volume, Fade Time]
Exec: Set Sound Volume [parameter: Sound ID, Volume, Fade Time]
Exec: Set Category Volume [parameter: Category, Volume, Fade Time]
```

Note that some of the commands take parameter arguments. For an example, Exec: Set Own Sound Volume command takes Volume and Fade Time as its arguments. Using these parameters, sound designers are able to make adjustments to the volume of the sound that triggered the Macro. Also, Execute commands all have a common, extremely important parameter: count. This is the count of the sounds left in the list after the Filter commands. The variable enables the Execute commands to be executed only when the number of sounds matches a certain condition. Taking Exec: Set Own Sound Volume command once again, it will be used as below.

```
Exec: Set Own Sound Volume if (count >= 2) [Volume = 0.5, Fade time =
1.0 sec]
```

Another useful type of command is the Difference Filter commands. Other Filter commands take an immediate value and find sounds with matching values, but Difference Filter commands are more complex. Let's look at Filter: Priority Difference as an example. This command takes Difference as its parameter and performs a subtraction between the priority of sound that triggered the Macro and the priority of every other sound in play. With this command, sound designers are able to not just eliminate sounds with lower priority, but keep the sounds with close priority and kill all others with lower priority.

Taking the command design pattern, we believe the class structure is nothing difficult. Each `Filter` command and `Execute` command are command classes, and a static manager class that receives the Macro (a series of commands) from the sound at an arbitrary timing will execute the commands in order. There is absolutely no need to go back to what has already been done, so unlike the advanced implementations of command pattern, only the execute function is implemented. That is all there is to it: simplicity is the ultimate sophistication.

14.4 CASE STUDY

Now, let's look at few examples of the Macros that have been actually written by our sound designers.

14.4.1 Case 1

Macro on play:

```
Filter: Same Sound
Exec: Stop Oldest if (count >= 1)
```

Let us start with a simple but frequently used Macro. This one is set as "on play Macro," meaning that it is triggered when the sound is about to be played. To walk through the commands, `Filter: Same Sound` will search for all the instances of the sound that triggered the Macro. Then `Exec: Stop Oldest` comes into action. Because the `count` parameter is set to 1, the Execute command will not do anything if the sound effect instance that triggered the Macro is the only one alive. However, when another instance of the same sound is about to be created, this Macro will stop the older sound instance. Although the `count` may vary depending on the sound effect, this is used to prevent the same sound from accumulating to the point where the mix gets too crowded. This can be applied to all different combinations of `Filter` commands and `count` parameters to be the most useful Macro when it comes to limiting the number of sounds to be played at once.

14.4.2 Case 2

Macro on play:

```
Filter: Same Sound
Exec: Cancel Play if (count >= 1)
```

This one seems to be very similar to the first one, but its outcome and usage are very different. The change we made from the first example is the second command: `Exec:  Stop  Oldest` has turned into `Exec:  Cancel  Play`. So, instead of stopping the older sound, we now will cancel the new sound instance to be played. This is commonly used in character voices, because it is extremely unnatural for a character to suddenly stop in middle of a sentence and start a new one.

14.4.3 Case 3

Macro on play:

```
Filter: Same Sound
Filter: Elapsed Time [Elapsed < 0.5 sec]
Exec: Cancel Play if (count >= 1)
```

Again, working from the previous case, this one adds another `Filter` command before the `Execute` command. `Filter: Elapsed Time` takes a time parameter as its argument and filters out the sounds that had been played for more than the given time (one half second in this example). So, translated into English, this Macro states "do not play this sound if the same sound has been played within the last half second." This is the type of Macro used to avoid repetition in a short amount of time.

This macro is also sometimes used to avoid bugs due to the game behavior. For example, when footsteps are triggered from collision, a complex form of collision may result in awkward audio bugs such as triggering multiple footstep sounds in a single frame or several frames in row. Near the end of development phase, programmers and level designers are often reluctant to fix these bugs if their impact is confined to audio, because the changes may cause yet another bug while time is running out. With the power of Macros, sound designers can solve these problems on their own.

14.4.4 Case 4

Macro on play:

```
Filter: Same Sound
Filter: Panning Difference [abs(Difference) < 15 degrees]
Exec: Set Volume if (count >= 1) [Volume = 0.5, Fade time = 0.1 sec]
```

Let's try something different now. In this example, the `Filter:  Same Sound` command comes with a `Filter:  Panning  Difference` command. As we saw earlier, `Difference  Filter` commands will compute the difference between the sound that triggered the Macro and the sounds in play. This one works for panning, seeing if the direction of sound is within the range of ±15°. So, with this combination of `Filter` commands, the instances of the same sound effect that exists in the same general direction are collected. Then, `Exec: Set Volume` command will change the volume of the sounds that were captured by the Filter commands; in this case, the volume is halved.

This type of Macro is sometimes used in a scene where the player is surrounded by a crowd of enemy characters of the same type. The sound designers do not want to play every single sound of the enemies at full level, but at the same time, they want to be tricky and want to keep the surroundedness. Looking only at the numbers does not help maintain spatialization, so they had to find the difference between the panning vectors. This way, older sounds coming from the same direction will be ducked down while the fresh ones are clear on their attack.

14.4.5 Case 5

Macro on play:

```
Exec: Set Category Volume if (count >= 0) [Category = BGM, Volume =
0.3, Fade time = 1.0 sec]
```

Macro on stop:

```
Exec: Set Category Volume if (count >= 0) [Category = BGM, Volume =
1.0, Fade time = 1.0 sec]
```

Macros can be worked in combination as well. All sounds that are started must stop at some point, so making a pair of Macros on play and on stop can be useful in making changes back and forth. In this case, the Macro works as a ducking process to turn down the background music volume. This is commonly used for music to avoid a dissonant mixture of two musical chords.

14.4.6 More Complex Usages

The examples above only contain one `Execute` command per Macro, but of course, multiple `Execute` commands are allowed in a single Macro. Not only that, the user may use another `Filter` command after the first `Execute` command to narrow down the target sounds of the second `Execute` command. If the sound designer wishes to put two totally different processes in a single Macro, that is possible as well. `Filter:`

`Clear` command will clear the current result of the `Filter` commands and gets the user ready to start a whole new process.

14.5 GUI DESIGN

We have implemented the Macro system, but we still have some work left to do: creating a user-friendly tool to write the Macro. Again, the users who write the Macro are not programmers, and we definitely should not tell the sound designers to write the script like above on text editors. There is absolutely no need for typing every single command word for word to find themselves stuck in syntax errors. What we implemented is a spreadsheet-like GUI where the first column contains the command name, and proceeding columns contain the numerical parameters. Command names are inputted from the list that appears upon clicking the add command button, and the rest are simple numerical text input. By using a list of commands, we can avoid a variety of human errors such as misspelling, misremembering, and making up commands that do not even exist. This user interface has a huge advantage in the rest of the system, as we can save the data in a structured format, and do not have to write a text analysis algorithm. We can replace the command to an enumerated command ID at tool time and simply save and load the numbers.

14.6 CONCLUSION

Using a data-based script-like sound limitation system, sound designers are able to control the psychoacoustics of the game and emphasize on what is important in the audio scene. With the power of the system, sound designers are much more capable of supporting the gameplay, enlivening the narrative, and even alleviating (or heightening) the players' stress. There is great merit for programmers as well. The computation resource freed by limiting the number of sounds can be used for other audio algorithms such as audio propagation, signal processing, and procedural audio synthesis to enhance the audio quality. We believe the Sound Limitation Macro System is one of the most versatile solutions to "level up" our games.

CHAPTER 15

Realtime Audio Mixing

Tomas Neumann

Blizzard Entertainment

CONTENTS

15.1 INTRODUCTION

In-game mixing is a very broad topic and nothing new conceptually. The first primitive forms of dynamic volume change or sound swapping in video games history happened, I am sure, several decades ago. Since then, the industry understood that creating great sounding audio assets is only one part of the game's audio. The other part is to make them sound great together. Video games continue to sound better and better over the past several years, and that is to a large extent because the quality of the in-game mixing is continually improving. There also have been some excellent articles written about this topic, as well as presentations at conferences [1–3]. New technologies were invented and integrated into game engines and audio middleware. You can find links to some of them at the end of this chapter. You might think this should be a settled case by now.

So, given the amount of content already out there about this subject, why should we address it in a dedicated chapter in an audio programming book?

Even after many years and fantastic advances in great games, real-time mixing is still an open field with new technical approaches yet to be discovered by all of us. That's why I think it is valuable to write this chapter specifically for a programming audience, and hopefully bring you up to speed in an informative and entertaining way on the following pages.

There are many tools at our disposal already, and so we need to establish first what we mean, when we talk about real-time mixing. I will clarify the terminology of all the different ways, how a mix can be manipulated efficiently. You will understand how and why it evolved, and where it might be heading to, so your contribution will advance this field even further. What you will not find in this chapter are very detailed and explicit implementation examples for each method we discuss. Each of those deserves their own chapter in a future book. I hope you will gain some insight into what to keep in mind when you implement your feature set for real-time mixing.

15.2 CLARIFYING TERMINOLOGY

We need to take a quick moment to agree on basic terms and interpretations. This will make it easier to follow this chapter, but also when you are talking to other people in the game audio field like sound designers, other programmers, or middleware representatives.

15.2.1 Mixing

In short, mixing for a video game is the act of bringing all audio assets of different disciplines, such as music, voice, ambiance, SFX, or UI together in a way that listening to the result is enjoyable, not fatiguing, and supports the gameplay.

15.2.2 Offline Mixing

Mixing offline describes the process of defining the volume and frequencies of audio assets in a separate program (usually a DAW), so that the result is statically saved out and then used in the game as they were authored. This definition of mixing is pretty much identical to the mixing for TV or movies.

15.2.3 Realtime Mixing

In this chapter, we will focus on mixing in real time so that properties such as volume or frequencies of the audio assets are being changed while the game is running. This requires additional computational effort. There are two different types of real-time mixing: passive and active.

Passive Realtime Mixing

Passive mixing occurs when the meta-data and behavior of the audio was authored in a static way (for example, routing and ducking of busses), so that the audio signal itself changes dynamically by being routed through a DSP effect. One example would be a compressor on the master bus, or a sidechain ducking of the music bus by the voice bus.

Active Realtime Mixing

We speak of Active mixing when events in the gameplay manipulate the mix dynamically, and the authored audio assets are being changed on the fly. A classic example would be the simulation of a tinnitus effect when the game detects that an explosion occurred very close to the player, by ducking the SFX bus for a short time and playing a ringing sound.

15.3 THE PURPOSE OF REALTIME MIXING

Many reasons come to mind when you ask yourself why offline mixing would not be enough for a video game. Affecting the audio dynamically to enhance the player's experience is desirable because it allows us to decide what this experience should invoke. Similar to choosing different music for certain gameplay moments, realtime mixing is used to influence the state of the player in a way that deepens the engagement with the game [4].

It is very important to understand that different games need different mixing. There is no single best way. A sports game requires different techniques and results than a horror game or a procedural open-world game. I encourage you to experiment with what techniques your game needs and discuss the features with the sound designers so that everyone works toward the same goal.

15.4 REALTIME MIXING TECHNIQUES

Now that we understand what realtime mixing means and what it is for, we can look at how different techniques affect a certain part toward the broader concept.

15.4.1 Playback Limit

Since the beginning, every gaming platform had a limitation on how many sounds could be played simultaneously. Depending on the hardware and terminology this can also be called channel or voice limit. The first PlayStation, for example, had an impressive 24 channels. But often the game could request more sounds at one time than the hardware supports. So, you want to choose which are the sounds to play physically and which should be rejected or virtually simulated, so they can be easily swapped back in when a slot opens up again.

One of the first techniques to achieve this was to assign a **priority** number to each sound, sort by it, and then play the n first instances which the hardware supported. This way a gunshot sound could win over a reload sound. The problem with only using this approach in a 3D game is that the gunshot could be very far away and the other sound much closer and louder. It is rather common now to define a basic priority value, and additionally change the value up or down depending on the listener's distance to the sound.

You can achieve a very similar effect by using the audio signal strength or **volume** to cull the sounds which are simply quieter than the n louder sounds. The problem with this approach is that now a bee sound which got authored pretty loud, could win over a gunshot sound. As a result, we lost the meaning of the sounds. Combining both techniques is a great start to work toward the hardware limitation of your platform.

Powerful modern hardware allows hundreds of sounds, and the challenge is to make the result sound clear and not muddy. That's why instead of a global playback limit we use scoped limits on busses, categories, or objects. If your game does not need unlimited gunshot sounds, then this bus could be limited to, for example, 30 instances, so other sounds still have a chance to appear. This creates a more diverse spectral audio signal, and keeps the gunshots which do play a bit clearer.

15.4.2 HDR Audio

Another technique that can push other sounds from being physically played is called high dynamic range (HDR) audio, which simulates the ear's impressive ability to hear quiet and loud sounds, but not necessarily at the same time. There are a few different methods, all with their own pros and cons. At its core, HDR audio is implemented by creating a distinction between the volume of a sound file and its loudness.

Without HDR, a sound designer would author the loudness into the file using a DAW. If we represent volume as a float from 0.0 to 1.0, then a quiet sound would peak somewhere around 0.2, while a loud sound would be around 0.9. The same result can be achieved with normalized sounds so both files peak at 1.0, but some volume metadata is attached to the sounds so that at runtime they get scaled to 0.2 and 0.9, respectively. The limitation of this system is that we cannot effectively represent a volume difference of 10 or 20 times because the quiet sound would not be audible, and we cannot peak higher than 1.0 without introducing clipping.

HDR solves this problem by using normalized audio files, and instead of defining volume we add a loudness value to the files. As an example, the gunshot could be 130 dB and the bee sound could be 20 dB. Then we define the height of a moving decibel window, which can vary for a given output system, such as a TV or high-quality speaker. In our example, we'll say that it is 100 dB tall. When the bee sound plays with a loudness of 20 dB, it will fit through the window and is audible. Once the gunshot starts, however, the upper edge of the window is pushed toward 130 dB, and everything under the lower edge of 30 dB will be culled. This creates the impression that the gunshot is so loud that it completely covers quieter sounds. Once the gunshot rings out, the window starts to shift down again toward the now loudest sound (Figure 15.1).

HDR is very effective for keeping the mix clear in different loudness scenarios, but it also has limitations. If the loudness values are authored statically, then HDR cannot differentiate between important and less important loud sounds. For example, the same gunshot aiming straight at you or slightly besides you are treated identically.

15.4.3 Importance

I recently contributed to a mixing technique we simply called Importance [5]. Our game analyses how important an opponent is in regard to you by looking at the damage dealt, your size on their screen, their distance and view direction, or if they have you in the center of their sniper scope. All the values are weighted and combined, and then we sort the opponents into buckets of different sizes. The most important bucket holds the opponent that is most relevant to the player. The other buckets hold opponents

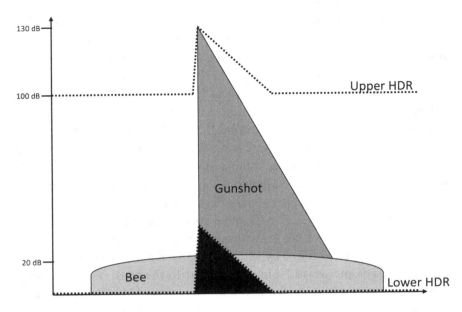

FIGURE 15.1 The gunshot sound pushes the lower edge of the HDR window up and effectively cuts out the bee sound for a while.

who are less relevant or can be safely ignored. Each bucket drives most of the mixing techniques mentioned above on all the sounds related to the opponents in it. We change the priority of the most important opponent dynamically to make sure the most valuable sounds are reliably heard on the platform. We change the volume and pitch to simulate an HDR effect, where non-important sounds are pushed out of the audible window. But what was most important to us was that we don't statically author loudness by category, such as footsteps or gunshots, because depending on the gameplay situation both could be critically important to help you hear your opponent's approach and learn to listen to the game to become a better player [6]. This allows us to solve the dilemma that the footsteps of someone sneaking up behind you with a loaded shotgun should be much louder than the gunshots of some firing at you from a distance.

15.4.4 Player Perspective

I want to write about an example in which sound asset authoring itself can be interpreted as realtime mixing. It is easy to imagine how one sound can be used in different contexts. For example, a boot footstep on a stone surface can be used on the player, an enemy, or an NPC. I like to look at this scenario and ask myself: should that sound be different when perceived through the player's perspective?

If I play in first person view, then my footsteps could sound less spatialized and give me a good understanding what surface I am walking on. If an NPC is walking by, then maybe I do not really care about hearing her footsteps at all, unless no other sounds are around. But when an enemy is walking around, I want to really quickly understand there is a potential threat over a larger distance [7].

We could use this sound in different perspectives. 1P stands for first-person of the player, 3P is third-person view of the player, and 3PR stands for third-person of a remote entity (Table 15.1).

We can achieve the different 3PR entries either by authoring different sounds with different radii, or we can combine the player perspective with the Importance technique. Then the fact that a friendly unit is less important would result in a steeper falloff curve of 30 m and we can make the sound quieter and even use different sound layers, compared to the important enemy version.

Another example we used a lot was to have different bullet impacts for player-generated shots than bullet impacts for impacts triggered by other players. Authoring different sound assets gives the sound designers the freedom to define large falloff radii for the player, so she can hear her glass shatter from far away, but then the same window is shot by someone else, the player might not be interested in this at all.

15.4.5 Busses and DSP Chain

The sound designers will creatively decide the layout of the busses. Modern games can easily have up to a hundred busses, with unique needs for DSP effects and reverb properties, or audio signal routing. As mentioned above, the bus on which critical dialog is played on could be side-chained to drive a compressor effect on the music bus. The more that sound designers inflate these structures and exercise control, the more computational

TABLE 15.1 Example of How Differently Authored Audio Assets Affect the Mix

Perspective	Spatialization	Radius (m)
1P	2D	—
3P	3D	10
3PR (enemy)	3D	70
3PR (friendly)	3D	30

cost is needed. It is very valuable to develop CPU budgets in addition to the decoding of audio files, so that the additional signal mixing stays under control.

15.4.6 Mix States

Imagine a modern mixer console with different channels and all their knobs for volume and pitch. Years ago, someone in the studio would need to write down every single value, so a band could play the same song identically. Mix states are essentially snapshots of audio properties of a bus hierarchy, which we can restore, blend in and out, and discard dynamically at runtime. A decade ago, games such as *Heavenly Sword* and *Hellgate: London* used techniques like that.

I also programmed a mix state system for *CryEngine* called "SoundMoods," which was able to blend multiple mix states together across different properties such as volume, low pass, and pitch, and then apply it to different busses. That way we could create a specific mix for complex gameplay situations, for example, being low on health, and driving a tank after crashing into a lake.

Since then, most audio middleware engines have integrated and improved this technique and now it is much easier for a programmer to add a mix state feature for sound designers for all different use cases. Mix states can be activated by different areas in a map, by changing player stats such as health, or by any player actions such as firing a gun. It is a powerful tool of realtime mixing, and it is not hard to imagine a great use case for your game.

When you design a feature like this, think about which states are mutually exclusive, or if you need to have multiple states active at the same time. Just like looping sounds, you never want to leak a sound state. It can be useful to organize states in independent groups, for instance, UI and gameplay. The UI group could have states such as "main menu," "options," team roster," and "score flash." The gameplay group could have states such as "isShooting," "isDiving," "usesUltimate," and "isDead." Both groups can be active independently and be reset at specific times.

15.5 MONITORING

Sound designers are most interested in two analytic audio values: volume and frequency. The volume of a sound or a bus is usually represented with a VU meter, which drives colored bars and indicates the most recent peak.

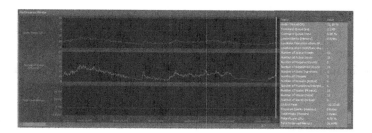

FIGURE 15.2 Performance graphs in WWise.

The unit is usually displayed as dB and most middleware presents this information when connected to the game. But, depending on the needs of your game, you can think about other areas to display this information. If your game has an in-game overlay, for example, it can be invaluable to enable a debug mode that displays a VU meter on the screen.

The second piece of information that sound designers are interested in is a spectral view of the frequency distribution of a sound, a bus, or a game object. This allows sound designers to see where a sound sits spectrally and how they combine with other sounds. A mix that reduces the overlap of sounds in the frequency domain is easier to listen to and can hold more information for the player.

In addition to volume and frequency spectrum, the CPU and memory consumption can be very important values to monitor. For example, the audio middleware WWise by Audiokinetic allows connecting their authoring tool to the running game in order to monitor various statistics, and other audio middleware solutions provide similar tools. This capability provides visibility for sound designers to stay within budget with their DSP and mixing costs (Figure 15.2).

15.6 OTHER MIX-RELATED AUDIO FEATURES

If you define mixing very broadly, then every falloff curve, compression setting, or reverb setting would be counted as a mixing technique. They do affect the outcome of the audio signal, but their main purpose is to create a specific effect. Falloff curves simulate distance, compression settings control data sizes and decoding load, and reverb simulates environmental dimension and changes. But they can have a noticeable effect on the overall mix.

Another example is how you compute obstruction and occlusion in a game to simulate sound propagation. Newer approaches with voxel-based data sets and path data can be used to create impulse responses, which strongly manipulate how a player hears a sound, and in which situation or location.

The basic functionality of the human hearing relies only on three core abilities:

- Analyzing changes in the frequency domain due to distance, obstruction, or the incoming angle affected by your ear flap

- Detecting time delay and volume differences of incoming sound waves between the two ears due to the extra distance to reach around your head

- Filtering of repetitions in the audio signal caused by early and late reflections

When we use DSP effects, we try to replicate these signal changes to trick the ear into "believing" our virtual sound world. If we apply a low-pass filter to convey that the player has low health, we run the risk that the ear might also mistakenly process this as sounds being further away. In that sense, certain mixing effects can be combined in a counterproductive way that influences the psycho-acoustic experience negatively. This can be a risky pitfall, and it is good practice to be aware of harming the player experience by applying all kinds of DSP effects onto the sound signal.

Another application which might get negatively affected by filtering is *Spatial Audio*, the process of enhancing the virtual positioning of sounds in AR/VR by using head-related transfer functions. Depending on the incoming angle of a spatialized sound, the signal gets filters with high and low passes. If your obstruction and mixing techniques already apply those, then the quality of the perceived positioning can be harmed.

15.7 IT IS MIXING TIME

It is very common in the industry for the sound designers to dedicate some time shortly before shipping the game to do a final mix, often in a different room or facility. There is great information available how to start up such a session from a creative point of view and to avoid fatigue. I want to add some thoughts specifically for programmers, who should try to prepare, participate, and support these efforts.

Here are a few features to allow sound designers to be most efficient during a mix session:

- **Mobility**: The game can be moved and transported to different rooms or external facilities potentially without connection to game servers or databases.

- **Security**: To avoid data breaches and leaks all game data should be encrypted and securely stored overnight and during breaks.

- **Connectivity**: Changes to the mix are locally stored and can be easily synced with the game data at the studio, or transported in any other form, while avoiding merge conflicts with changes made at the studio. One brute-force solution is to exclusively keep all audio data checked out while the mix session is ongoing.

- **Independence**: Changes to the game data can be applied on the spot, without the need to wait for a sync or an overnight build from the studio.

- **Iteration**: Allow sound designers to listen, change, and verify their work as fast as possible. Often games allow runtime connection to the game to audition changes on the fly.

- **Information**: Sound designers can detect quickly which sound is currently playing in game and how to find it in your tool set. Also, they can easily visualize sound properties in the game, such as 3D max radius.

- **Monitoring**: Loudness and frequency values can be easily observed and tested.

- **Filter**: Sounds can be filtered/muted/soloed by category, mix, bus, or discipline so these sounds can be easily mixed in a consistent way.

- **Efficiency**: Any part of the game can be easily reached by cheats and repeated instead of the need to reach this by actually playing.

There is one potential pitfall to a dedicated mix session, especially if no game designer is present. The core game play could be mixed more toward sounding cinematic than supporting the game, but this is clearly in the responsibility of the design experts. However, if most of the features above are available to the sound designers during the development of the game, they can react and apply feedback from testers and designers efficiently so that the game's mix is already in great shape. Essentially, the game is mixed as we go. This is also valuable when showcasing the game internally or externally to publishers. Then the final mix session might be very short, less costly, or even unnecessary altogether.

15.8 FUTURE TECHNIQUES

We can talk about where realtime mixing techniques will go next by asking two questions:

- What mixing will the games need which we will be making in the future?
- What technology will become available by increased resources to mix games which are similar to the current ones?

I think we might see more AR/VR games on mobile devices, at home, or as spectators of larger (eSports) events. These games would require extra attention of mixing through low-quality speakers or headphones, or due to loud background noise. Maybe we will see noise cancellation technology appear in AR audio mixes. AR and VR typically require more explicit 3D sounds, because 2D sound beds do not work well with head movement. These games could use their understanding of the real or virtual world around the player to actively affect not only the reverb, but the mix itself. Cameras and microphones could be driving forces of adapting the mix for each player.

More powerful hardware will allow us to compute more of what we already know. We can author more complex sounds, and turn on and off more layers depending on the mixing requirements. It is very likely that machine learning will be integrated into the audio process to assist sound designers finding the best mix. If thousands of players do not react to a critical sound, these algorithms can detect that and either change the mix accordingly, or bubble this information up to someone who can. Maybe it is AI itself, which can listen to a mix and tell us if it was able to play the game better with it.

Regardless of what technology is at your disposal or you are able to develop, I encourage you to always question whether the game actually needs it. Does the player get an advantage out of a mixing technique? Avoid using something just because everyone else is doing it. Defining and solving your unique needs could lead you to an innovative discovery we currently cannot imagine.

15.9 CONCLUSION

By now, I hope you have a good insight into the complexity of realtime mixing and which great techniques are already available for you to be used. It is clear that we have not reached the perfect solution yet, because all games are different. Not only do our mixing techniques get better, but they can also interfere with each other and there are plenty of technical challenges for you to discover and solve.

REFERENCES

1. Garry Taylor, Blessed are the Noisemakers, http://gameaudionoise.blogspot.com/p/all-in-mix-importance-of-real-time.html.
2. Rob Bridgett, The Game Audio Mixing Revolution, www.gamasutra.com/view/feature/132446/the_game_audio_mixing_revolution.php.
3. Rob Bridgett, The Future of Game Audio—Is Interactive Mixing the Key, www.gamasutra.com/view/feature/132416/the_future_of_game_audio__is_.php.
4. Etelle Shur, Remixing Overwatch: A Case Study in Fan Interactions with Video Game Sound, http://scholarship.claremont.edu/cgi/viewcontent.cgi?article=2019&context=scripps_theses.
5. Steven Messner, How Overwatch Uses Sound to Pinpoint Threats You Can't See, www.pcgamer.com/how-overwatch-uses-sound-to-pinpoint-threats-you-cant-see/.
6. Marshall McGee, Is Overwatch the Best Sounding Shooter Ever? www.youtube.com/watch?v=MbV_wKScrHA.
7. Scott Lawlor, Tomas Neumann, GDC 2016 Overwatch—The Elusive Goal: Play by Sound, www.youtube.com/watch?v=zF_jcrTCMsA.

CHAPTER 16

Using Orientation to Add Emphasis to a Mix

Robert Bantin

Massive Entertainment - An Ubisoft Studio

CONTENTS

16.1 A BASIS OF REALITY

When we think about designing sound placement in 3D games, we tend to start out with a basis of reality and build our bespoke systems on top of that: attenuation is based on distance to the listener; the loudspeaker matrix is based on orientation to the listener. With the exception of 3rd-person player cameras (a special topic handled in Chapter 11 of *Game Audio Programming: Principles and Practices*, Volume 1), it should be pretty straightforward, and for a low number of sound-emitting actors, it usually is. However, with the technological advances we've had over the last few console generations, the number of sound emitters we've been allowed to use has increased dramatically. Add to that the merit of being able to use ambient processing in multiple zones to create an ever more detailed environment, and we should be getting ever nearer to our understanding of what "reality" should be.

And yet with all that, the audio mix can end up sounding muddled and undesirably chaotic—much like a documentary film of a gun battle with location sound. If this is happening to you, you should not feel bad. After all, it is exactly what you designed in the first place! If it's not what you wanted, then perhaps consider that what you were looking for was not "reality," but rather "heightened reality."

16.2 A PRACTICAL EXAMPLE OF
HEIGHTENED REALITY MIXING

In film postproduction (and let's face it, for most of us that is the "gold standard"), the dubbing stage mixer will be very selective in what they bring into focus in the mix and what they'll allow to be masked, and this will change from moment to moment. Consider the government lobby scene from the first Matrix movie. It is constantly isolating some sounds while blurring out others: single bullets leaving the chamber of a single gun when the film cuts to the close up of that gun and wall tiles cracking to bullet impacts when the film cuts to the close up of a wall. Meanwhile, every other sound is noticeably attenuated or low-pass filtered for that moment. I've picked this movie because it is an extreme example of the concept I'm trying to illustrate, but in lesser forms is rather commonplace in film mixing. It brings emphasis to the mix so that the viewer can be drawn to what's important.

16.3 HOW CAN WE MODEL THE DUB MIXER'S
BEHAVIOR IN A NON-SCRIPTED ENVIRONMENT?

Normally we can't do the creative mix of a human in games unless it's a cutscene. In the more typical scenarios, the player has agency over the point of view, NPCs will have complex behaviors, and then there's all that rigid-body physics triggering sound effects to boot. It all makes for a highly emergent (and therefore unpredictable) system—essentially the exact opposite of a movie, in fact. What we can do, though, is define certain mixing behaviors that we can apply to some of our sound emitting actors. We just need to decide what those rules are and what to apply them to.

16.4 MICROPHONE POLAR PATTERN MODELING

When you think about it, a listener whose sensitivity has no preference over its orientation to an emitter is rather like using an omnidirectional mic on a film set and then simply throwing the result at the audience. For reasons that should now be apparent, that isn't always useful, which is why on-set sound recordists and Foley artists will usually exploit the discriminatory nature of directional mics to control what gets captured. We can't change how our sound assets were recorded after the fact, but what we can do is apply a similar emphasis rule (attenuation and/or filtering) to some of the emitters based on their orientation to listener (i.e., prioritize the perceptual loudness of some sound-emitting actors to the player camera according to how central they are to the player's view) (Figure 16.1).

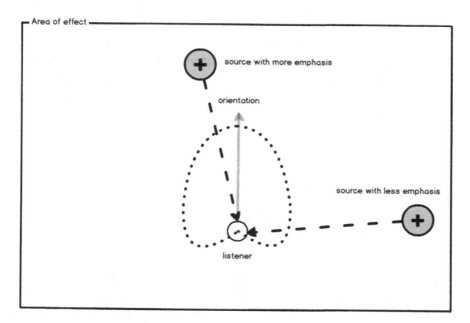

FIGURE 16.1   How emitter positions could be emphasized as if the listener was like a single cardioid-pattern mic.

So first of all, we need an algorithm that can

i. Control a level based on angle like a microphone: Let's say omnidirectional to hyper-cardioid. Let's not specify what kind of emphasis that is yet as we'll want to allow the sound designer to try different things, not just attenuate. The control level should be used as a real-time parameter to drive something else.

ii. Vary the polar pattern smoothly from one extreme to the other so we can adjust it whenever we need to.

iii. Orient off the result of a dot product of two normalized direction vectors in the range of $\{-1 \leq d \leq +1\}$, so that the game-side programmer can use a unit of measure they are familiar with. This can work for both azimuth and zenith planes, but for now we'll assume we're only interested in the azimuth plane.

16.4.1 The Polar Pattern Function

We can address the first requirement with a little bit of mathematics if we first consider how multi-pattern microphones work. Normally, this is achieved with two capsules and a preamplifier circuit that allows their signals to interact (Figure 16.2).

If we define our virtual microphone in the same way (and we ignore the fact that the real-world polar pattern would be almost always omnidirectional at very high frequencies), we just need to describe the effect of the pressure zone and the pressure gradient of the two opposing capsules and add them together.

$$g(\theta) = \frac{P_{ZF} + P_{GF}\cos\theta - P_{ZB} + P_{GB}\cos\theta}{2}$$

θ	Azimuth or zenith angle (the response is the same on either plane)
P_{ZF}	Pressure zone (front capsule)
P_{GF}	Pressure gradient (front capsule)
P_{ZB}	Pressure zone (back capsule)
P_{GB}	Pressure gradient back capsule

Using θ in the typical range of $\{0 \leq \theta \leq 2\pi\}$ or $\{-\pi \leq \theta \leq \pi\}$ radians, we then get a linear gain value in the range of $\{-1 \leq g \leq 1\}$. The only question is what to set for P_{ZF}, P_{GF}, P_{ZB}, and P_{GB}, and an interesting aspect of this equation is that there are multiple answers to the same solution. For example, Table 16.1 and Figure 16.3 show one solution for the typical polar patterns:

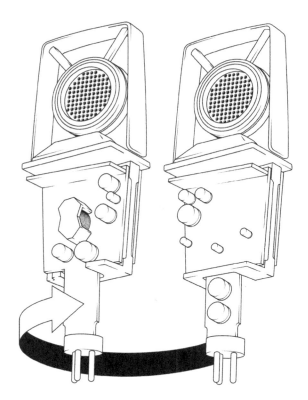

FIGURE 16.2   Multi-pattern microphones normally contain two capsules back to back.

Source: Dan Tyler www.mephworks.co.uk.

TABLE 16.1   Coefficients That Can Produce the Standard Polar Patterns - This is Just One of Multiple Solutions

Polar Pattern	P_{ZF}	P_{GF}	P_{ZB}	P_{GB}
Omnidirectional	2	0	0	0
Sub-cardioid	1.31	0.69	0	0
Cardioid	1	1	0	0
Super-cardioid	0.67	0.67	0	0.67
Hyper-cardioid	1/2	1/2	0	1

16.4.2 Morphing Between Polar Patterns

To address the second requirement, we need to discover a combination of P_{ZF}, P_{GF}, P_{ZB}, and P_{GB} that have a distinct progression from one extreme (omnidirectional) to the other (hyper-cardioid). Once we have a progression that looks like it's close enough to what we want, we can assign

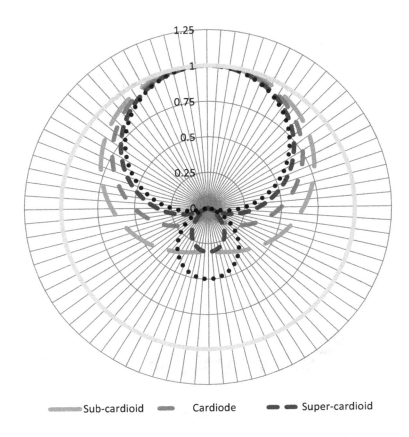

Sub-cardioid   Cardiode   Super-cardioid

FIGURE 16.3   Comparative polar patterns (magnitude gain, not dB).

an arbitrary ordinal value from one end of the progression to the other, and then derive a mathematical formula via a (most likely) nonlinear regression.

As it turns out, you just need one set of capsule parameters (I picked P_{ZF} and P_{GF}) to go from an omnidirectional pattern to a hyper-cardioid pattern, as the other capsule is only strictly necessary to generate a perfect bidirectional pattern.

Table 16.2 and Figure 16.4 show a progression that I found empirically that works quite well.

16.4.3 Regressing Analysis to Find the Morphing Function

At this point, we have a polar pattern generator that's simpler than where we started, and we have a set of parameter values for P_{ZF} and P_{GF} that will give us the five configurations that we're looking for. What we're missing

TABLE 16.2 P_{GF} and P_{ZF} Progression from an Ordinal Value of 1–5, Expressed as Exact Ratios

Directivity Q	P_{ZF}	P_{GF}
1	2	$2 - 2 = 0$
2	$\sqrt{2}$	$2 - \sqrt{2} \approx 0.59$
3	1	$2 - 1 = 1$
4	$\dfrac{1}{\sqrt{2}}$	$2 - \dfrac{1}{\sqrt{2}} \approx 1.29$
5	$\dfrac{1}{2}$	$2 - \dfrac{1}{2} = 1.5$

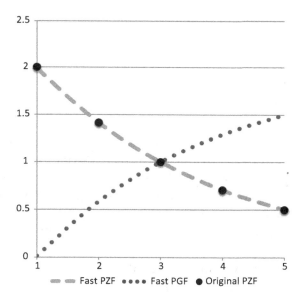

FIGURE 16.4   The same P_{ZF} and P_{GF} progression shown graphically.

is a morphing function that transforms those two parameters according to those preferred values as we vary the directivity Q.

A good solution is a polynomial fit as it's the sort of mathematical template that can be calculated with the simple operators {add | subtract | multiply | divide}, and especially because these operators can be grouped together in SIMD instructions—making them very CPU efficient. I'm going to skip the part where I explain how I do the polynomial fit (as this would be a chapter in itself) suffice to say I normally use Microsoft Excel with the "Analysis Toolpak" enabled. In other words, I don't need any exotic tools.

Based on the observations we have to regress, we'll use a third-order polynomial that takes this form:

$$f(x) = \left[x^0 k_0 + x^1 k_1 + x^2 k_2 + x^3 k_3 \right]$$

Naturally, $x^0 = 1$, so we often ignore that operator. In this case, I've kept it there to remind us later to initialize the first unit of the first SIMD block with 1.0. I also recommend that you avoid any math power function calls by using in-line multiplies since we know the powers are whole numbers and never change. In other words, where you see x^2 or x^3, your non-SIMD-optimized code should replace the power function with a hard-coded multiplies like this:

```
float calcPZF(float x)
{
    float x2 = x*x;
    float x3 = x2*x;

    return k0 + x*k1 + x2*k2 + x3*k3;
}
```

We're going to replace this function with a SIMD-optimized version later on, so I've left it here as a non-encapsulated method with the k constants declared in a wider scope for simplicity. In the event that SIMD isn't available on your platform, ultimately you should implement this version of the function and constants within the scope of a class (e.g. as a private method and members).

The coefficients from the third-order polynomial fit of P_{ZF} are shown in Table 16.3.

Since $P_{GF} = 2 - P_{ZF}$, we only need to calculate the polynomial for P_{ZF} and then infer P_{GF} using the same $2 - P_{ZF}$ conversion.

Table 16.4 shows the resulting progression for P_{ZF} and P_{GF} by substituting Q for x.

As you can see, we've now got almost the same morphing behavior without using any expensive mathematical operations. The overall function then looks like this:

$$g(\theta, Q) = \left| \frac{f(Q) + (2 - f(Q))\cos\theta}{2} \right|$$

TABLE 16.3 All Four "k" Coefficients for the Polynomial Fit of P_{ZF}

k_0	k_1	k_2	k_3
2.74873734152917	−0.871494680314067	0.113961030678928	−0.00592231765545629

TABLE 16.4   The Polynomial-Fitted Version of P_{ZF} and the Inferred P_{GF}

Q	Q²	Q³	Original P_{ZF}	3rd Order Poly-Fit P_{ZF}	Inferred P_{GF}
1	1	1	2	1.985281374	$2 - 1.985281374 = 0.014718626$
2	4	8	$\sqrt{2} = 1.414213562$	1.414213562	$2 - 1.414213562 = 0.585786438$
3	9	27	1	1	$2 - 1 = 1$
4	16	64	$\dfrac{1}{\sqrt{2}} = 0.707106781$	0.707106781	$2 - 0.707106781 = 1.292893219$
5	25	125	$\dfrac{1}{2}$	0.5	$2 - 0.5 = 1.5$

Since the attenuation of super and hyper-cardioid mics can go negative, I've added a modulus operator to the whole equation to make sure we only get values of g in the range $\{0 \le g \le 1\}$. This will make things simpler if we want to use this equation for an emphasis control value.

16.4.4 Optimizing for Cosine

There's just one niggle left, and that's the use of cosine. Trigonometric functions are very expensive operations, so executing them at frame or sample rate is a no-no. Thankfully, we don't need that much accuracy as provided by a native CPU instruction, and our input range will never exceed the limits of $\{0 \le \theta \le \pi\}$ because we're going to be using as input the converted radian value of a dot product in the range $\{-1 \le d \le +1\}$. We can, therefore, safely approximate $\cos \theta$ with a low-order Taylor series polynomial.

$$\cos\theta \approx 1 - \frac{\theta^2}{2!} + \frac{\theta^4}{4!} - \frac{\theta^6}{6!} + \frac{\theta^8}{8!}$$

Now, we can't use it as-is yet, because we need to make a few minor adjustments so we can turn those $1/x!$ parts into constant coefficients we can just multiply with. Table 16.5 shows these coefficients. Figure 16.5 shows the difference between the cosine function and the Taylor expansion; as you can see, they are very similar.

So, now we compute a new function $h(\theta)$ that approximates $\cos \theta$ using coefficients c_1, c_2, c_3, and c_4:

$$h(\theta) = \left[1 + c_1\theta^2 + c_2\theta^4 + c_3\theta^6 + c_4\theta^8 \right]$$

TABLE 16.5   All Five "c" Coefficients Needed to Approximate
Cosine Using Taylor Series

Coefficient Label	Factorial Ratio	Substitute Coefficient
c_1	$-\dfrac{1}{2!}$	-0.5
c_2	$\dfrac{1}{4!}$	0.041666667
c_3	$-\dfrac{1}{6!}$	-0.001388889
c_4	$\dfrac{1}{8!}$	$2.48016E{-}05$

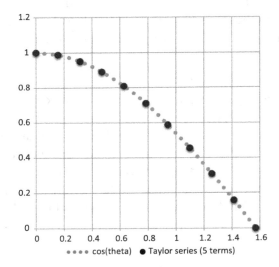

FIGURE 16.5 $\cos\theta$ and its five-term Taylor series equivalent.

Later on, I'm going to show you how to SIMD-optimize this function, but for now your non-SIMD-optimized code for this function should look something like this:

```
float taylor5cosine(float t)
{
  float t2 = t*t;
  float t4 = t2*t2;
  float t6 = t4*t2;
  float t8 = t4*t4;

  return 1.0f + c1*t2 + c2*t4 + c3*t6 + c4*t8;
}
```

Again, we're going to replace this code with a SIMD-optimized version later on, so I've shown the function here as a nonencapsulated method with the c constants declared in a wider scope for simplicity. If SIMD is not available on your platform, you should implement this function and constants within the scope of a class (e.g., as a private method and members).

Finally, we can substitute cos θ with our new function $h(\theta)$ into our final equation like so:

$$g(\theta,Q) = \left| \frac{f(Q) + (2 - f(Q))h(\theta)}{2} \right|$$

16.4.5 Converting Between the Dot Product Direction Test and Theta

Remember that although we're testing source orientation with respect to the listener, we're actually going to apply the emphasis to the source, so we need to view the orientation from source's perspective (Figure 16.6).

For this to work as seen from the source, you'll first need to generate the normalized direction vector from the source to the listener like this:

$$n_{source\text{-}to\text{-}listener} = \frac{p_{listener} - p_{source}}{\left\| p_{listener} - p_{source} \right\|}$$

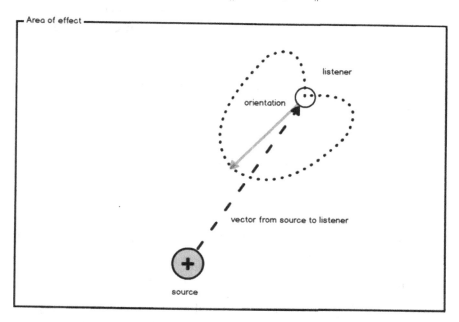

FIGURE 16.6   The listener when viewed from the source.

$n_{source\text{-}to\text{-}listener}$	Normalized direction from the source to the listener
p_{source}	Position of the source in cartesian space
$p_{listener}$	Position of the listener in cartesian space

$\|p_{xz}\| = \sqrt{\left[p_x^2 + p_z^2 \right]}$: the magnitude of the vector along the x and z axes (normally the azimuth plane, adjust according to whatever axis convention your engine uses).

Second, you'll need to perform a dot product with that normalized direction vector and the listener's orientation (which is also a normalized direction vector you should already have).

$$d = n_{source\text{-}to\text{-}listener} \cdot n_{listener}$$

d	Scalar rotation factor
$n_{listener}$	Listener orientation vector (normalized direction vector)

Note: You should consider the dot product of $a \cdot b$ to be equivalent to $a_x b_x + a_z b_z$ if we consider those axes to be the azimuth plane.

When the listener is pointing directly at the source, the result will be −1, while when the listener is pointing directly away from the source, the result will be +1. When the two normalized direction vectors are orthogonal, the result will be 0. Converting this number range to radians is a straightforward linear conversion from the range $\{-1 \le d \le +1\}$ to $\{0 \le \theta \le \pi\}$ and looks like this:

$$\theta = \frac{(d+1)\pi}{2}$$

Code-wise you could implement it as in inline method like this:

```
inline float DirectionalEmphasis::directionTestToRadians(float d)
{
    return 0.5f * ((d + 1.0f) * c_PI);
}
```

Assume c_PI is a constant brought in via a header or as a protected member of the class (or its base).

16.5 IMPLEMENTING SIMD OPTIMIZATIONS

SIMD is a feature of modern CPUs to facilitate multiple numerical operations in single calls. Typically, these function calls are hardware dependent, so using them normally involves the use of intrinsic code woven into your C/C++ source. For the purposes of this chapter, we'll assume that we're using an x86_64 CPU or similar.

16.5.1 SIMD Optimizing the Function $f(x)$

As you may recall, we need to implement this function:

$$f(x) = \left[x^0 k_0 + x^1 k_1 + x^2 k_2 + x^3 k_3 \right]$$

Rather than calculating P_{ZF} twice (the second time for $P_{GF} = 2 - P_{ZF}$), we opt here to take a reference to placeholders of both P_{ZF} and P_{GF} so that they can be calculated together:

```
#include <pmmintrin.h>

static const __m128 DirectionalEmphasis::k_constants =
  _mm_set_ps(
    2.74873734152917f,
    -0.871494680314067f,
    0.113961030678928f,
    -0.00592231765545629f);

void DirectionalEmphasis::fastPZFandPGF(
  float Q, float& PZF, float& PGF)
{
  float Q2 = Q*Q;

  __m128    x_values = _mm_set_ps(1.0f, Q, Q2, Q*Q2);
  __my_m128 f_values;

  f_values.m128_v4 = _mm_mul_ps(k_constants, x_values);
  f_values.m128_v4 = _mm_hadd_ps(f_values.m128_v4, f_values.m128_v4);
  f_values.m128_v4 = _mm_hadd_ps(f_values.m128_v4, f_values.m128_v4);

  PZF = f_values.m128_f32[0];
  PGF = 2.0f - PZF;
}
```

Since the k values are constant, we calculate them once and store them as a 4x float vector within the scope of the class. For clarity in context, I've initialized the k_constants member just ahead of the encapsulated method that uses it, but in your complete class implementation should probably initialize all the static constants in the same place (e.g. at the top of the .cpp file), most likely as protected members.

Directivity Q is squared once and put temporarily on the stack so it can be used twice locally with the function. A 4x float vector for the x values is then loaded with 1.0 and the power permutations of Q. Another 4x float vector for the f values is then returned from the point-by-point multiply of the x values with the k constants. Finally, the contents of the f vector are summed horizontally. This has to be done twice as that particular SIMD instruction sums adjacent pairs of elements and updates both element pairs with the result. Feeding the vector through twice will make all the elements of vector f retain the total sum, so we just read out the first element. Microsoft have added a union with 16-byte alignment that allows you to index the elements like an array, but this does not exist in the GCC version of <pmmintrin.h> so I've used an agnostic union called __my_m128 that works for either compiler and added some preprocessor to determine which version gets compiled. You can do the same like this:

```
#include <pmmintrin.h>

    typedef union
#if IS_GCC_COMPILER
        __attribute__((aligned(16)))
#elif IS_MICROSOFT_COMPILER
        __declspec(intrin_type) __declspec(align(16))
#endif
        __my_m128
    {
        float    m128_f32[4];
        __m128   m128_v4;
    } __my_m128;
```

Note: If you use this type for a member of a class or struct, be sure to override the container's new and delete operators with an aligned allocator suitable for that platform.

For example, from <mm_malloc.h>
`_mm_malloc(size_t    bytes,    size_t    align)` *and*
`_mm_delete()`

16.5.2 SIMD Optimizing the Function $h(\theta)$

$$h(\theta) = \left[1 + c_1\theta^2 + c_2\theta^4 + c_3\theta^6 + c_4\theta^8\right]$$

```
#include <pmmintrin.h>

static const __m128 CDirectionalEmphasis::c_constants =
  _mm_set_ps(
    -0.5f,
    0.041666667f,
    -0.001388889f,
```

```
       0.0000248016f);

float DirectionalEmphasis::fastTaylor5cosine(float t)
{
   float t2 = t*t;
   float t4 = t2*t2;
   float t6 = t4*t2;
   float t8 = t4*t4;

   __m128    t_values = _mm_set_ps(t2, t4, t6, t8);
   __my_m128 h_values;

   h_values.m128_v4 = _mm_mul_ps(c_constants, t_values);
   h_values.m128_v4 = _mm_hadd_ps(h_values.m128_v4, h_values.m128_v4);
   h_values.m128_v4 = _mm_hadd_ps(h_values.m128_v4, h_values.m128_v4);

   return 1.0f + h_values.m128_f32[0];
}
```

This function works in a very similar way to `fastPZFandPGF()` with the exception that I've chosen to implement a fourth-order polynomial, which is five operators. This still fits into the 4x float vector paradigm though, as the zeroth-order term is always 1.0—you can just add that to the result at the end. Again, for clarity in context I've initialized the `c_constants` member just ahead of the encapsulated method that uses it, but in your complete class implementation should probably initialize all the static constants in the same place.

16.6 THE OVERALL IMPLEMENTATION SO FAR

So, to implement the overarching method that computes this equation:

$$g(\theta,Q)=\left|\frac{f(Q)+(2-f(Q))h(\theta)}{2}\right|$$

we just need to do something like this:

```
float DirectionalEmphasis::calculate(
   float directionTest, float directivityQ)
{
   float PZF = 0.0f;
   float PGF = 0.0f;

   fastPZFandPGF(directivityQ, PZF, PGF);

   float theta = directionTestToRadians(directionTest);

   return std::fabsf(0.5f * (PZF + PGF * fastTaylor5cosine(theta)));
}
```

This method brings together the other methods we've seen so far and returns the emphasis control value that we intend to apply to our emphasis processor. Note that neither input variables are clamped within their suitable ranges—you should definitely consider doing this somewhere in your code.

16.7 LISTENING TO THE RESULT

Using the emphasis control value as a simple linear attenuator does yield some vaguely interesting results for directivity $Q = 2$ (i.e., sub-cardioid), but take it too far and some sources will disappear from the mix completely! Using the emphasis control value to blend/morph between transparent and de-emphasized filtering sounds more interesting (much like the government lobby scene from "The Matrix" as mentioned in the introduction), but without some serious source-state management you could have the issue of important cues such as NPC speech becoming unintelligible whenever the player isn't looking directly at them. For example, a source-state management system could drop the directivity Q to 1 whenever a source needs to be heard no matter what.

The conclusion, then, is that you can't leave the directivity Q of these sources at some preferred value without occasionally landing on unwanted results.

16.8 AN ARRANGEMENT THAT NEEDS LESS MANAGEMENT

Let's consider a different orientation measure. What about when an NPC is pointing at the player? This is typically quite important as an NPC will typically turn toward the player to say something, or indeed when the NPC is shooting at them. This is something we can definitely work with (Figure 16.7).

In these circumstances, we should already have a collection of normalized direction vectors we can use—the listener and source orientations. Testing these vectors with a dot product will yield their relative direction to one another:

$$d = n_{source} \cdot n_{listener}$$

d	Scalar rotation factor
n_{source}	Source orientation vector (normalized direction vector)
$n_{listener}$	Listener orientation vector (normalized direction vector)

Note: You should consider the dot product of $a \cdot b$ to be equivalent to $a_x b_x + a_z b_z$ if we consider those axes to be the azimuth plane.

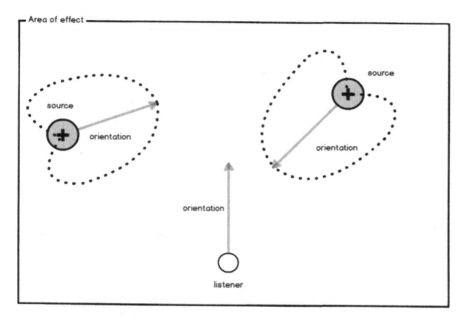

FIGURE 16.7   Viewing the source orientation from the listener perspective.

d will still be in the range $\{-1 \le d \le +1\}$, but now NPCs can manage their own emphasis/de-emphasis based on their orientation to the listener. Assuming the game's AI is set up to work as we expect it to, the AI might do all the emphasis management for you!

16.9 A FINAL WORD ON AZIMUTH AND ZENITH ORIENTATION HANDLING

So far, I haven't really given a concrete definition as to what I've meant by orientation in a 3D game world, other than to pretend we were only interested in one plane (the azimuth plane) in Section 16.4.5. Truth is, the polar patterns are the same shape in either plane, so you can follow the same pattern if you need to emphasize/de-emphasize sources in both planes simultaneously. In that instance, a dot product across all three axes may suffice, so with

$$d = n_{source} \cdot n_{listener}$$

d will still be in the range $\{-1 \le d \le +1\}$, but

$$a \cdot b \equiv a_x b_x + a_y b_y + a_z b_z$$

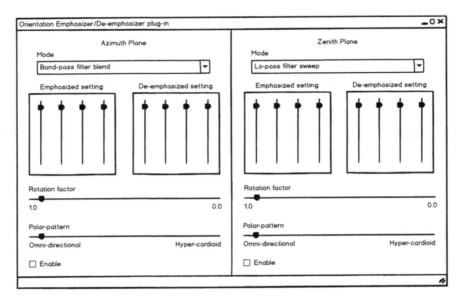

FIGURE 16.8 How you might layout the controls for orientation support in both planes (the rotation factor and polar-pattern controls being automatable via game syncs).

Consider though that you may want to use a different type of emphasis, and possibly a different polar pattern for the two planes.

For example, an NPC pointing away from the player might have a band-pass filter cut into the mid frequencies of its gun to lessen the "aggressive" tone of gun fire, i.e., to make it soundless "dangerous" to the player. The sound designer might want to use a relatively wide polar pattern for the azimuth plane as the player is still in relative danger. Conversely, they might want a narrower polar pattern when the NPC is pointing their gun into the sky as this means the NPC isn't tracking the player, therefore, presenting less of a "danger." In either plane, the sound designer might want a different type of filtering—maybe have a low-pass filter sweep in for when NPC guns are elevated? You could cascade the two filters to aggregate their effects. Figure 16.8 illustrates what the UI for a plug-in that performs this aggregate effect might look like. By handling each plane's orientation as a separate case, you will build a more flexible system overall.

16.10 CONCLUSION

What we've established in this chapter is that we can

a. Model the polar patterns of microphones in a way that varies smoothly from omnidirectional to hyper-cardioid.

b. Use this polar pattern variable as an emphasis control for a bespoke filtering process decided at design time.

c. Apply the orientation of sources to the listener in some different ways, and get some very useful results (even when they seem at odds with realism).

d. Calculate the rotation in separate azimuth and/or zenith planes, giving the designer a flexible solution that applies different types of emphasis behavior depending on the plane of rotation. In some cases, you may only need to apply one plane of rotation, but this separation approach scales up to both planes of rotation, if necessary. This also allows different types of emphasis filtering to be applied to the two planes of rotation.

Note that the emphasis control value is quite cheap to calculate (once certain optimizations have been performed), so if necessary the polar pattern shape and orientation can be updated very regularly: every game update, or even at sample rate.

Certainly, some experimentation is required to suit the game you're working on, but hopefully you will quickly see the benefit of applying one or two mixing rules based on orientation to the listener.

CHAPTER 17

Obstruction, Occlusion, and Propagation

Michael Filion

Ubisoft

CONTENTS

17.1 INTRODUCTION

As consoles become more and more powerful with each iteration, more processing, memory, and disk storage are allocated to audio. With these extra resources comes the advantage of being able to add more and more realism to modern video games that simply wasn't previously possible.

The added processing power of modern game consoles has enabled the creation of larger and larger open-world games, including two of the series that I have worked on *Assassin's Creed* and *Tom Clancy's The Division*. With these open-world games, relying on a systemic approach as the foundation of the audio becomes all the more important.

If game audio programming means being responsible for the bleeps and the bloops in a game, obstruction, occlusion, and propagation are a few methods of ensuring that those elements are all the more realistic. Employing these principals allows us to emulate the real world to help immerse the player in our game world.

In this chapter, we'll take a look at what are obstruction, occlusion, and propagation along with the high-level considerations of what a system that implements these methods requires.

17.2 CONCEPTS

In this chapter, we'll use listener to represent the movable position in the world where the sound is being perceived from. Generally, this will be the player or camera. Before delving into the questions about how to design the system, we first need to define obstruction, occlusion, and propagation.

17.2.1 Obstruction

When discussing obstruction, there are two examples I like to think of: the first is of standing on one side of a rock and having the sound on the opposite side, a distance away from the rock (Figure 17.1). In this case, we will still hear the sound from the sides of the rock, the same way that water would spill around a rock. The other example is being able to see a sound source through a door, where not all of the sound will be able to reach the player.

In a real-world model of obstruction, there are several components to the behavior of how sound is obstructed. These include deflection and absorption by the obstacle, and transmission through the obstacle. However, for the purposes of this chapter we'll limit the definition of obstruction to deflection and separate the modeling of transmission through obstacles to occlusion. In addition, we'll ignore the reflections that could be generated by obstruction. The reason for this is that many DSP reverb effects allow for the modeling of these reflections.

17.2.2 Occlusion

When thinking about occlusion when it relates to game audio, I can't help but think of the example of the thin walls in an apartment building that has seen better days. If you were to place the spawn point of your main character in a room in this building, what would be the first thing he would

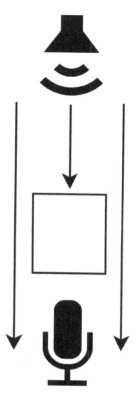

FIGURE 17.1 A listener with an obstacle directly between the source and the listener's position and a listener with a direct line of sight through an opening.

hear from outside of the room? If we were in a busy apartment block, the sound of the neighbor's TV with the higher frequencies attenuated from the wall could be present. The argument of the neighbors on floor above, with the man's deeper voice being easier to hear through the ceiling.

Occlusion can be defined as the effect of a sound being modified by being perceived exclusively through an object, such as a wall. These sounds usually have a volume attenuation and/or a low-pass filter affecting them.

To determine the volume attenuation of your sound, we can calculate the mass m of a concrete floor with density 2300 kg/m^3 and thickness 0.15 m can be calculated as

$$m = 2300 \text{ kg/m}^3 \times 0.15 \text{ m} = 345 \text{ kg/m}^2$$

By looking up 345 kg/m² in Figure 17.2, we can estimate that the attenuation is 48 dB. In the real world, the different frequencies of a sound would

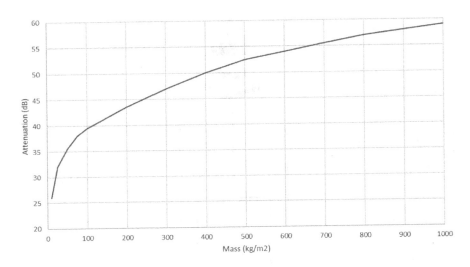

FIGURE 17.2   Mean attenuation through a mass.

attenuate differently: lower frequencies would attenuate less than higher frequencies. In my opinion, the same results can be achieved through an artist choice of how the low-pass filter and the volumes are reduced, depending on the nature of sound that you are occluding.

17.2.3 Propagation

While the broad definition of propagation is quite large, for the purposes of this chapter we'll define it as the relocation of the dry signal of a sound, affected only by volume attenuation that would normally occur.

In Figure 17.3, we can see that a direct line of sight to the original sound (the black speaker) doesn't exist. However, there is a point where we can expect some of the original sound to propagate from, the gray speaker. Given the wavelike properties of sound, the propagation location would not be omnidirectional. Rather, in a fully realized simulation, the greater the angle from the propagation point (using a forward vector created from the difference between the original position and the new propagation point), the more the volume attenuation and low pass that would be applied to the sound. While the realistic simulation would demand this, it is again an artistic and/or performance question whether to implement this additional detail.

In the rest of this chapter, we'll examine in more detail how to implement a propagation system.

FIGURE 17.3 An example of sound propagation in a corridor.

17.3 ENVIRONMENTAL MODELING

An important question to answer is how we will model the environment for this system.

If processing power is not a concern, using the same geometry as the lighting or collision meshes are potential options. The primary advantage of using preexisting environment information reduces the amount of work that the sound designers (or other team members) are required to do.

However, with the constraint of processing time allocated to audio, using complex geometry like lighting, or even collision meshes, may prove not to be the best choice.

Given the image of a top-down view of a room in Figure 17.4, the complexity of the world geometry (solid line) versus the proposed geometry (dotted line) for use in our system yields some big differences. To illustrate the point, let's take a quick look at the difference in code between detecting whether or not a point is inside the different pieces of geometry.

```
bool IsPointInsideCube(const Vector3& point, const Cube& cube)
{
  return
    point[0] >= cube.GetMinX()
      && point[0] <= cube.GetMaxX()
      && point[1] >= cube.GetMinY()
      && point[1] <= cube.GetMaxY()
      && point[2] >= cube.GetMinZ()
      && point[2] <= cube.GetMaxZ();
}
```

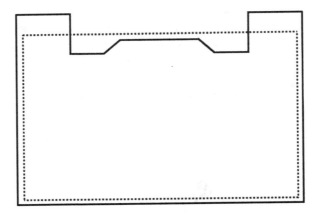

FIGURE 17.4   An example of game geometry.

```
bool IsPointInPolygon(
  const std::vector<Vector3>& vert,
  const Vector3& pt)
{
  bool result = false;
  for (unsigned int i = 0, j = (vert.size() - 1);
    i < vert.size();
    j = i++)
  {
    //First test the X & Y axis
    if(((vec[1] > pt[1]) != (pVec[1] > pt[1])) &&
        (pt[0] <
          (vert[j][0] - vert[i][0]) * (pt[1] - vert[i][1]) /
          (vert[j][1] - vert[i][1]) + vert[i][0]))
    {
      result = !result;
    }

    //Now test the Y & Z axis
    if(((vec[2] > pt[2]) != (pVec[2] > pt[2])) &&
        (pt[1] <
          (vert[j][1] - vert[i][1]) * (pt[2] - vert[i][2]) /
          (vert[j][2] - vert[i][2]) + vert[i][1]))
    {
      result = !result;
    }
  }
  return result;
}
```

To simplify the code examples, I've ignored floating point inaccuracies, assumed that the geometry is axis-aligned, and written the code to facilitate readability in book format. In addition, the function

`IsPointInPolygon()` is a simple 3D adaption from W. Randolph Franklin's PNPOLY[1] algorithm and may not necessarily be the most optimal solution to this problem. Comparing these two code examples side by side we can clearly see that `IsPointInsideCube()` is less expensive than `IsPointInPolygon()`. Some quick profiling showed a ~50% increase in time for one call to `IsPointInPolygon()` versus `IsPointInsideCube()`.

In many cases, the optimized proposal will be perfectly acceptable. Whether or not we can accept this geometry will be based on a few questions: Can the player ever reach any of the areas where the optimized geometry doesn't cover? Is it possible, and how often, for sounds to be located in or pass through the areas that the optimized geometry doesn't reach?

Should using the lighting or collision meshes still prove to provide information that is too precise (in terms of required CPU cycles), and manual implementation is not an option, there still lies the option to use automatic generation from pre-existing data. You can use a voxelization algorithm to simplify the original geometry (the source geometry can be visual, physics, or another source) to a point where the quality/performance ratio is acceptable. An even easier implementation is to use the bounding volumes associated with the objects you wish to be sound occluders. In both cases, it's important to exclude geometry from objects that aren't static or important, such as small props in the world.

No matter how the geometry is provided for the audio systems to use, it is always important to remember that there will be exceptions to the rule. The tools for the sound designers to make an exception based on artistic choice, a bug, or optimization is important.

17.4 PATH FINDING

With the concepts out of the way and having decided how to model the environment for our system, now comes the important part: pathfinding. Pathfinding is the cornerstone of determining the input parameters for our propagation function. There are several ways to go about finding the paths, be it implementing A* or using a third-party solution and integrating into the game engine. Of course, the benefit of using an algorithm implemented on the game engine side is that you can always optimize the performance yourself, while third-party solutions are often black boxes. However, using a third-party solution (that has already been included in a few shipped games) will generally already have been the target of some optimizations, therefore, reducing the burden on the game engine side.

An important item to remember is that the shortest path is not always the best path. This means that calculating several different paths from the listener to the sound to evaluate the best choice is important to help combat popping issues. You'll see popping issues in situations like standing in the middle of the room and moving to the left or right. The shortest path may only be 1 or 2 units less on one than the other, but if the resulting calculation from all of the contributing factors isn't taken into account, you can suddenly jump from something relatively audible to something mostly inaudible as a result.

Given the example in Figure 17.5, moving toward or away from either the door on the left, or the window on the right, would cause the shortest path to change relatively easily. Because the size of the each of the portals is different they would not add the same amount of obstruction to the sound. Additionally, should either of those portals be closed, the obstruction value would be different. Therefore, simply using the shortest path doesn't always provide the most accurate result.

The other path information that we will want is the direct path between the listener and the sound source. What we need from this is to collect all the occluder information to make our occlusion calculation. Doing a ray cast from the listener's position to the sound's position and collecting any collision information can generally yield the correct information.

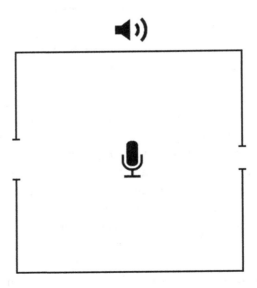

FIGURE 17.5 An example of potential popping issue.

How exactly this will be implemented will definitely depend on how much is precomputed and how much you'll want to compute at runtime. For instance, using precomputed information will simply require you to identify which object was touched, and given that object you'll know what the occlusion value that should be applied.

One important caveat that must be taken into consideration before computing offline is that the thickness and the density of the material can have a significant impact on the final value. With a slight variation in thickness for a dense material, your occlusion value could be quite different. These thickness differences can be produced by having a wall in between the listener and the sound source and the distance between the two being rather substantial.

17.5 ADDING PROPAGATION USING PATH FINDING INFORMATION

Now, given the path(s) from the listener to the sound, we can determine where we want to add the propagation point. This point should generally be at the end of the first segment of the path, starting from the listener. With the hard work of determining the path already calculated, all that we need to determine is the volume of the sound at the new location. The volume will change with the listener's proximity to the sound, because we should hear more and more of the original source (or propagated position along the path) the closer that we approach position. This ensures that we won't have a popping issue the moment we see the first segment of the path disappear.

17.6 INTERFACING WITH THE AUDIO ENGINE

My personal experience with third-party middleware is mostly limited to Wwise. With Wwise, the API defines several functions for setting the obstruction and occlusion values on each sound emitter. They are well documented and relatively easy to use. However, there is one significant limitation with the Wwise: only one obstruction and one occlusion curve is permitted for the entire project. This means that the built-in obstruction and occlusion functions have no ability to have different volume attenuation or LPF/HPF values for different types of sounds. One possible solution for this is simply to use RTPCs, but there are associated challenges with this as well (such as the managing of the RTPC data throughout the entire project).

In addition to the obstruction and occlusion, another issue to tackle is propagation and double-decoding. When adding propagation, you'll need the original source to play at the propagated location, as well as a filtered sound that plays at the original position. The simple solution to this is to play the sound twice, incurring all of the costs twice. However, this incurs all the costs and synchronization headaches of playing the sound twice. One potential option to alleviate this issue is to decode once and then share the decoded buffer between both sounds. While this doesn't remove all the duplicated costs, it will help. With Wwise, you could use a source plugin to provide the buffer for the audio engine to play. In addition to this, with the latest version of Wwise you have access to the concept of a 3D bus which seems to serve as a building block for a propagation system.

17.7 TESTING AND VALIDATION

As with any development, it is important that the system be tested and validated after any work has been done. Using test cases in a controlled environment will definitely help speed up validations that new features or bug fixes affect the world in the predicted manner. However, pay special attention that the system is validated in real use-case scenarios in game. Not doing so can lead to not finding small-edge cases or them being found late in the development cycle. In an ideal world, all members of the development team, and not just those directly implicated in sound, would notice and help identify bugs and problem areas. However, because of the detail that is involved with development and implementation of obstruction, occlusion, and propagation elements some of the bugs and weird-edge cases may escaped the untrained ear. While this may lead some people to say "good enough," we must be careful that we don't end up in an uncanny valley where the implementation is close, but not quite correct and leads to an under-appreciation of all audio in the game as a result.

17.8 CONCLUSION

This chapter aimed to address some of the potential challenges and considerations required when employing obstruction, occlusion, and propagation to create more realistic game audio. Hopefully, this chapter has given you some insights into the different challenges of creating your own system while also providing inspiration for your own solution.

NOTE

1 W. Randolph Franklin, PNPOLY—Point Inclusion in Polygon Test (https://wrf.ecse.rpi.edu//Research/Short_Notes/pnpoly.html).

CHAPTER 18

Practical Approaches to Virtual Acoustics

Nathan Harris

Audiokinetic

CONTENTS

18.1 MOTIVATION

18.1.1 Immersive Experiences and Virtual Reality

There has never been a more exciting time to be an audio professional in the video game industry. The maturation of the virtual and augmented reality market has made everyone realize something us audio nerds knew all along: sound matters. A true sense of immersion is a fragile experience. The brain relies on subtle cues to give us a sense of being, of placement in our environment. Human perception relies more heavily on visual rather than auditory sensory input, and because of this the gaming industry has for a long time been preoccupied with computer graphics, which has become a mature field with well-established best practices. Visuals, however, only tell part of the story—the part that is directly in front of us. Audio software engineers are now looking toward many years of graphics technology for answers to similar problems and adopting similar terminology to paint the rest of the picture. With the advent of VR comes an audio renaissance, allowing us to finally get the resources, and hopefully the recognition, we always knew we deserved.

18.1.2 Why Virtual Acoustics?

Virtual acoustics is the simulation of acoustic phenomena in a virtual environment. That sounds good, but we must stop and ask ourselves: what are we really trying to achieve? We have two primary objectives—first, to enhance the expressiveness of the room or environment so that it mimics the virtual environment that the player is in. Each environment has a unique tonal signature and can be thought of, in a sense, as a musical instrument. This objective is for the most part solved with a well-recorded impulse response or with a carefully tuned high-quality reverb effect. The second, more difficult objective is to position sounds in their virtual world and carefully manipulate them so that they fool the player into thinking they are coming from the correct place in the environment. Doing so effectively goes a long way toward heightening the player's sense of immersion, which is easier said than done in a dynamic real-time simulation.

18.1.3 Addressing Computational Complexity

There is a large body of fascinating research on acoustic simulation which we lean on heavily for inspiration, broadly separated into two categories: wave-based and geometric. In practice, we are forced to deviate from pure theory to address practical concerns because video games have limited resources with which to simulate in a real-time environment.

This deviation is a recurring theme in this chapter. Even with the ever-increasing transistor count of modern CPUs and with larger memory budgets than ever before, video game programmers must always write code with performance in the front of their mind.

Wave-based approaches to acoustic simulation, where one calculates the solution to the wave equation at each point on a discrete grid, are becoming frighteningly realistic, but are more or less off the table for real-time simulations. Not only do we need an enormous amount of memory to store the data, but the CPU time taken to calculate the results is often measured in hours or even days depending on the accuracy required. However, given sufficient time and resources, wave-based techniques can be successfully applied offline by pre-processing game geometry to generate impulse responses. Such a technique was applied by the Coalition studio in Gears of War 4.[1]

In this chapter, we will explore geometric-based approaches applied in real-time, where sound is simulated as set of discrete rays. Savioja and Svensson provide an excellent overview[2] of existing research on this approach. Even with geometric techniques, we still have to pick our battles carefully and pull some strings to make sure our computation results fit into a typical game frame.

Another often-overlooked aspect of acoustics in video game audio is simply that we are not actually simulating reality. Rather, we are simulating an environment that is inspired by reality—perhaps heavily so. But in the end, we are creating entertainment. We always need to give sound designers the tools to create an exaggerated, cinematic experience when desired. For this reason, we veer away from physics equations when needed to, and this allows us to further cut some computational corners.

This chapter will present a framework for virtual acoustics that strikes a balance between realism and artistic expression of sound. We introduce some ideas and concepts that can be used to dial in a hyper-realistic sound, but also tweaked to be as exaggerated or as subtle as desired. As audio programmers, we need to serve our sound designers and ultimately our players, in order to deliver a truly emotional experience.

18.2 SIGNAL CHAIN CONSIDERATIONS

For any interactive audio simulation, audio programmers and sound designers need to sit down, discuss, and layout a signal chain that accomplishes various technical and creative goals. There will always be trade-offs between CPU, memory, and creative intent, and therefore, it is impossible to present a definitive guide. The following is a set of recommendations for designing a signal chain that balances these trade-offs with the desire for acoustic realism. Figure 18.1 shows an example signal chain which depicts a single sound emitter and listener routed into various spatial audio effects.

To model the straight-line path between the sound emitter and the listener, we need little more than a sound emitter and a 3D panner (send "a" in Figure 18.1). We call the sound wave that travels directly between the emitter and the listener without bouncing off or bending around any objects the *direct path*.

To place the emitter within a virtual room, we add a send to a reverb effect (send "b" in Figure 18.1). The effect has been designed to model the

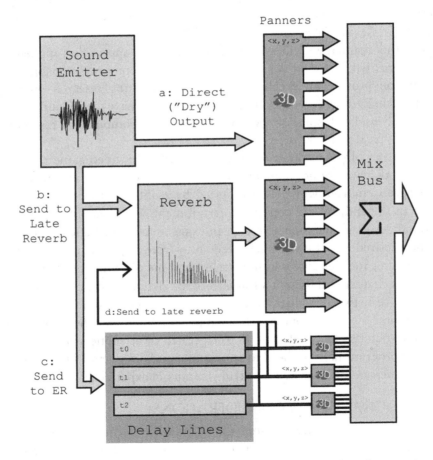

FIGURE 18.1 An example signal chain diagram for routing a sound emitter into an early reflections unit and late reverb effect.

acoustic environment, perhaps parametrically, or perhaps by applying a recorded impulse response. Multiple emitters in the same environment may send to the same reverb effect. Sharing the effect in this way reduces the total number of effect instances but also reduces flexibility. The effect cannot render reflections that are specific to the position of any given emitter, and in truth, most popular off-the-shelf reverb effects are not designed to do so. For these reasons, we split the reverb chain into two modules, and relegate this reverb effect to what we call the *late reverb* or *diffuse field*. The diffuse field is the sound energy in an environment that has bounced off enough surfaces that it appears to come from all directions.

The second reverb module, which must be specific to each emitter in order to take its position into account, is called the early reflection (ER) unit (send "c" in Figure 18.1). The ER unit is responsible for rendering, at the correct angle, amplitude, and delay time, the first few prominent reflections of the sound off of nearby geometric features. ER simulation is a well-studied geometric approach to virtual acoustics and adds a crucial element of space and dimensionality that is otherwise missing from traditional, static reverb plug-ins. Figure 18.1 shows an ER module with three delay lines. In a real implementation, the number of delay lines and corresponding delay time will vary depending on proximity to nearby geometric features. The ER module does not go through the same 3D panner as the dry path (or the late reverb), as each reflection must be individually panned according to its *image source* (IS) location—the apparent position of the "source of the reflection" relative to the listener. Note the additional send from the ER module to the late reverb module (send "d" in Figure 18.1), which helps to smooth the auditory transition from discrete, localizable reflections into a diffuse reverb bed. The result is a denser reverb tail overall.

The final novel feature of the presented signal-flow diagram is the additional 3D panner located after the reverb unit. It is useful to think of environmental (i.e. room) reverbs as objects in the virtual world, as we do for sound emitters, and instantiate one reverb for each room. When the listener is in the same room as the emitter, then the room reverb object should have the same position as the listener, but with an orientation fixed to the world. However, when the emitter is in a different room than the listener then we model the transmission of the diffuse field from one environment to another through an acoustic portal. In this situation, the reverb itself can be thought of as an emitter positioned at the portal between the two environments. Decomposing the signal chain components into emitter–listener pairs is a useful abstraction and is a recurring theme when simulating virtual acoustics which occurs in every section of this chapter.

18.3 EARLY REFLECTIONS

Dynamic geometrically based early reflections are one of the most important auditory cues that the brain relies on for positioning a sound in 3D space. Surprisingly, early reflections are largely absent from today's video games. I expect this to change rapidly going forward and here we look at a simple approach to ER calculation.

18.3.1 Calculating Image Sources

As the sound travels from emitter to listener it will bounce off a number of surfaces. This number we call the *order* of our reflection calculation. Early reflection calculation is often dismissed as impractical because the computational complexity increases exponentially with the order of the reflections. For games, this means we have to stop calculating after the first or second reflection and call it a day. Fortunately, the relative importance in determining the directionality of a sound also decays with each successive reflection because the relative volume decreases as the density increases. So long as we have a well-tuned late reverb effect that provides a dense layer of diffuse echoes following the early reflections, we still get a huge bang for our buck if we only calculate first- or second-order early reflections.

An IS refers to a virtual sound emitter—the position of the reflected sound, as if it is itself an emitter. The position of a single IS is determined by mirroring the emitter's position across a reflecting surface. Each surface generates a reflection, and therefore, there is one IS for each surface. Figure 18.2 shows an emitter, a listener, two walls, and the first- and second-order image sources.

To calculate a second-order IS, the first-order IS becomes the emitter that is reflected over each wall, excluding the wall that was used to generate the previous IS. To readers familiar with the subject of algorithmic complexity, the exponential growth of the procedure becomes evident. For each additional reflection order that we want to calculate, we must take each of the previous N ISs and reflect them over $N - 1$ surfaces, which will generate $N*(N - 1)$ additional virtual sources for the next step. The number of Kth-order ISs for N surfaces is $N(N - 1)^{(K-1)}$, and the summation of this expression from 1 to K gives us the theoretical maximum number of ISs.

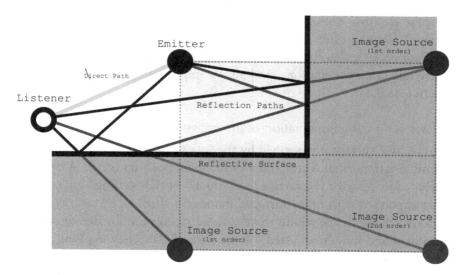

FIGURE 18.2 A sound emitter's reflections off of two surfaces are calculated by mirroring its position over each wall to generate ISs.

18.3.2 Validating Image Sources

Calculating the reflection of a point about an infinite plane is a relatively cheap and straight forward operation (refer to `Reflect()` in the following code example). Unfortunately, planes are not typically infinite in real life. To deal with these pesky non-infinite planes, we must *validate* ISs that we calculate by checking that the ray between the listener and the IS actually intersects the plane within its defined boundaries. Afterward, if the IS is determined to be valid, one last step is necessary. The path along which the sound travels must be constructed, and must be checked for other occluding surfaces along each segment. For computing reflections against arbitrary geometry, we require a full ray-tracing engine capable of performing a large number of ray-surface intersection tests.

18.3.3 Rectangular Rooms

If we are able to constrain our geometry to convex rooms, we can skip the costly occlusion checking ray casts, as doing so renders occlusion of reflections impossible. Furthermore, if we constrain our geometry to rectangular rooms, we are able to skip both the above-described validation and occlusion checking steps, which removes the need for ray-surface intersection tests and makes for a sleek and practical implementation.

In practice, this works reasonably well (depending on the game's level design). We can often get away with rectangular approximations, even for non-rectangular rooms. At any rate, it is a great starting point for early reflection calculations, and a C++ implementation is presented in Section 18.3.4.

18.3.4 A C++ Implementation of the Image Source Algorithm

A reflective surface is described by the Surface struct, which contains a unit-length normal vector and a world-space position vector. A string is included to describe the surface (e.g. "floor," "wall," "ceiling," etc.), and is later appended with other surfaces' names (in GetPathString()) to describe the path the sound travels; these strings are for demonstrative purposes and may be omitted for the sake of efficiency. As long as the surfaces form a rectangular room—and are therefore all either parallel or perpendicular to one another—no further validation of the ISs generated by CalcRoomReflections() is necessary.

The algorithm will, however, generate some duplicate ISs, only one of which will arise from a valid path. Consider Figure 18.2 again as an example. There are two perpendicular walls which we will call "right" and "down." The second-order IS generated with the sequence of reflections, "right" then "down," is the same as the one generated with the sequence "down" then "right," and it is depicted in the bottom-right corner of the figure. If we re-trace the path between the emitter, the two walls, and the listener, we find that only one of the two sequences ("right" then "down" vs "down" then "right") is actually possible from a particular emitter and listener position. Duplicate ISs are not handled by the presented algorithm and should be filtered out in a final implementation.

```cpp
// Maximum number of reflections to be calculated.
const unsigned int kMaxOrder = 4;

// Unbounded reflective surface
struct Surface
{
  Vector3D normal;    // surface normal (length 1.0)
  Vector3D position;  // any point on the plane in world space.
  std::string name;   // name, for identification
};

// Reflect the point 'source' over the plane 'surface' and
// return the image source.
Vector3D Reflect(const Surface& surface, const Vector3D& source)
{
```

```
  Vector3D sourceToSurface = surface.position - source;

  // project on to the surface's normal Vector3D.
  // Assumes that surface.normal has length 1.
  float projection = DotProduct( sourceToSurface, surface.normal );

  // the result is 2x the projection onto the normal Vector3D,
  // in the opposite direction.
  Vector3D result = -2.f * projection * surface.normal + source;
  return result;
}

// Construct a description string for a path of reflections
// defined by a list of surfaces.
std::string GetPathString(const std::list<const Surface*>& path)
{
  std::string str;
  for (const Surface* s : path)
    str += s->name + " ";
  return str;
}

// Recursive version of CalcRoomReflections() function.
// Calculates image sources for an array of surfaces.
// The results are appended to the array 'imageSources'
void CalcRoomReflectionsRecursive(
  // IN: Emitter position or previous image source position.
  const Vector3D& sourcePos,
  // IN: A std::vector of surfaces to reflect off of.
  const std::vector<Surface>& surfaces,
  // OUT: a std::vector of (path description, image source) pairs.
  std::vector<std::pair<std::string,Vector3D>>& imageSources,
  // IN: Previous surface that was reflected off of, or NULL
  // if this is the first call.
  const Surface* prevSurface,
  // IN: Working depth. Initially 1.
  unsigned int order,
  // IN/OUT: Working path of reflective surfaces, up to this call.
  // Initially, this is an empty list.
  std::list<const Surface*>& path
  )
{
  for (const Surface& s : surfaces)
  {
    if (&s != prevSurface)
    {
      path.push_back(&s);

      Vector3D imageSource = Reflect(s, sourcePos);

      imageSources.push_back(
        std::make_pair( GetPathString(path), imageSource ));

      if (order < kMaxOrder)
      {
```

```
                    CalcRoomReflectionsRecursive(
                      imageSource,
                      surfaces,
                      imageSources,
                      &s,
                      order + 1,
                      path
                      );

                }

            path.pop_back();
          }
       }
}

// CalcRoomReflections
// Calculates image sources for an array of surfaces.
// The results are appended to the array 'imageSources'
// This is stub function that exists only to call
// CalcRoomReflectionsRecursive() with the correct initial
// parameters.
void CalcRoomReflections(
  // IN: Emitter position.
  const Vector3D& sourcePos,
  // IN: A std::vector of surfaces to reflect off of.
  const std::vector<Surface>& surfaces,
  // OUT: a std::vector of (path description, image source) pairs.
  std::vector<std::pair<std::string,Vector3D>>& imageSources,
  )
{
  std::list<const Surface*> path; //empty list
  CalcRoomReflectionsRecursive(
    sourcePos, surfaces, imageSources, NULL, 1, path);
}
```

18.3.5 Rendering Reflections with Delay Lines

Once we have calculated the positions for all our ISs, we need to manipulate the source audio in such a way to make it sound like it is emitting from the IS locations. Once again, modeling the ISs as sound emitters gives us some insight into what kinds of manipulations need to take place. We encounter the usual suspects for rendering 3D audio: volume attenuation and filtering simulate dispersion and absorption from air, and 3D panning plays the sounds from the correct speakers. Most importantly in this case, the sound must be delayed by the time it takes for sound to propagate from the IS to the listener. And, because the sound source can move, we need to incorporate a delay-line that can interpolate between different delay times, called a *time-varying* delay.

When the delay time does change, the delay buffer must either playback at a faster or slower rate than real time, resulting in a change of pitch. In physics, this described change of pitch actually occurs, known as the Doppler effect, but it can sometimes sound odd or undesirable in the digital realm, so we may need to limit the rate of movement for each individual IS.

The delay time for each IS is calculated by dividing the distance between the IS and the listener with the speed of sound in air—approximately 343 meters per second. Note that the direct sound from the emitter will also have a propagation delay calculated similarly, and it is important to take this into account. Even though it is physically accurate, it is sometimes reported by players as sounding "wrong" when we introduce a propagation delay on the direct sound, because it does not match the expected cinematic experience. If the direct sound is not delayed, it is crucial to subtract the direct propagation delay from the reflected sound so as to maintain the same relative delay time, otherwise the result will be noticeably skewed. This effect is particularly jarring when the listener is close to one or more surfaces generating loud reflections, but far away from the emitter such that the direct sound is relatively quieter.

18.4 DIFFRACTION

One recurring problem in many video games is how to render sounds that are behind obstacles. Diffraction plays an important role in finding a solution to this problem, but first we will motivate our discussion of this important acoustic phenomenon by looking at issues with traditional approaches to the problem of rendering sounds behind obstacles. We will then show how these issues can be mitigated by coming up with a model for diffraction.

18.4.1 Spatial Continuity

Most game engines can determine if a point-source sound is visible or obstructed by an obstacle by using a ray test, a service that is often offered by the game's physics engine. The binary hit/no-hit result of this ray test, however, raises two more issues which need not be dealt with in the realm of graphics, and are often poorly handed in the realm of audio. First, what should we do if an object is obstructed, and second, how should we transition between visible and obstructed states.

For the first issue, we can apply an attenuation and low-pass filter to the sound and get adequately realistic results. The second issue is much more difficult to solve and perhaps the worst decision to take would be to perform a time-based fade between visible and obstructed states. Only if the player happens to be moving away from the source at exactly the same rate as the fade, will he be fooled. Acoustics in games must strive to be *spatially continuous*, meaning that any change made to the way sound is manipulated is continuous and based solely on the position of the listener, with respect to the emitter. If not, the player will have a tendency to attribute this change to a change at the source. We will show that instead by modeling sound behind obstacles as diffracting around them based on the position of the listener and emitter and the angle to the obstacle, we achieve spatial continuity.

18.4.2 Obstruction and Occlusion

When audio programmers and sound designers refer to occlusion and/or obstruction of sound, these two terms are traditionally defined as follows. Obstruction occurs when the dry path of a sound is blocked by an obstacle; however, the wet path is able to find a way around (namely, reflections off of nearby surfaces), because the listener and the emitter are in the same acoustic environment. Occlusion, however, occurs when the listener and the emitter are in separate environments, and therefore, both the wet path and the dry path are blocked.

Defining and using occlusion and obstruction as such is at odds with our acoustic models for a number of reasons. Going forward, I generally recommend that these terms be put aside in favor of the acoustic phenomena they attempt to describe. For example, obstruction is more accurately described by the phenomenon of *diffraction*, where sound waves are filtered and attenuated as they bend around an obstructing object. The term *occlusion* is vague, and even harder to pin to an acoustic phenomenon; setting this value in your audio middleware usually applies a filter and attenuation to both the dry path and the wet path (auxiliary send). Wwise, in particular, behaves this way. Occlusion may in some cases be used to model the phenomenon of acoustic *transmission*, where sound travels through a solid object. Regardless, we get more precise results if we model the wet path as an independent source from the direct path (as described in Section 18.2), and control the volume and filters independently.

18.4.3 The Physics of Diffraction

When thinking about diffraction, we often visualize sound waves bending around an object. But physically speaking, diffraction is best described as the perturbation of an incident waveform by a boundary edge, causing a secondary wave front that emanates spherically outwards from the edge of diffraction. Keller's *geometrical theory of diffraction* (GTD),[3] which was later extended by the *uniform theory of diffraction* (UTD),[4] is a notable contribution to the field which introduces the concept of diffraction rays. Diffraction rays originate at excited edges in a manner analogous to reflected rays described by the IS algorithm. The GTD is originally in the context of geometrical optics and is only valid for sufficiently high frequencies. However, we can nevertheless study it to gain insight into how diffracted sound can be rendered as secondary sources originating at the diffraction edge.

Figure 18.3 shows the interaction of a pure sine wave with an infinite rigid edge, as predicted by the GTD. A diffraction wave front originates at the edge in the center of the diagram and expands outwards in all

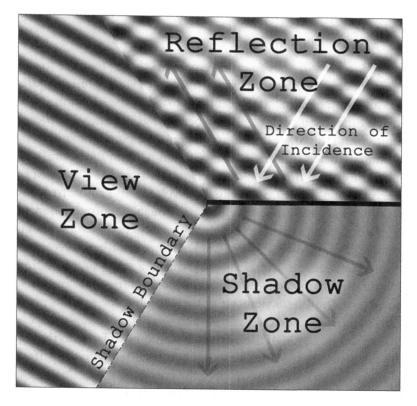

FIGURE 18.3 Diffraction and reflection of an incident wave at 60° to a rigid surface.

directions. The space is divided into three distinct zones: the reflection zone, the view zone, and the shadow zone. In the reflection zone, we primarily observe an interference pattern caused by the interaction between the incident and reflected wave. In the view zone, the amplitude of the incident wave greatly outweighs that of the diffracted wave; however, it is interesting to note that in theory, the diffraction wave is indeed present. These former two zones are modeled by our direct path and our early reflections unit as described in the preceding sections, and the effect of diffraction is small enough that it can be ignored.

In the shadow zone, we clearly observe how the edge mimics a point-source sound emitter with the waveform dispersing outwards, and this is the primary zone of interest when simulating diffraction in video games. The amplitude of the diffracted wave depends on the frequency of the incident wave. Going back to our intuitive definition of diffraction, we can think of lower frequency waves being able to bend further around corners than higher frequency waves.

18.4.4 Auralizing Diffraction

At this point, we will once again diverge from theory in order to address practical concerns when auralizing diffraction in video games. Figure 18.4 depicts an emitter behind an object that obstructs the sound from the listener. The diffraction angle is taken to be the angle into the shadow zone of the emitter, and this angle is used as our control input to the sound engine. When unobstructed this angle is zero; the maximum theoretical angle is 180°, but the critical transition occurs between 0° and 15°. For each sound emitter, mapping the diffraction angle to volume and cutoff frequency of a first-order low-pass filter provides a reasonable approximation of the effect of diffraction. Furthermore, giving a sound designer a set of curves to tweak (e.g. angle to volume and angle to low-pass filter) leaves the door open for creative expression. In reality, this is a gross simplification: we ignore the angle of incidence, the size and shape of the edge, and the interference effects from reflections off of the edge, but the result is plausible, spatially continuous, and relatively easy to compute for simple shapes.

The correct direction of the diffracted sound ray relative to the listener can be calculated by moving the sound emitter directly to the diffraction edge. However, we also want to apply the correct distance attenuation so we place the virtual source as shown in Figure 18.4.

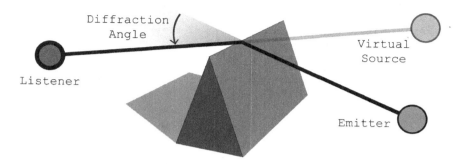

FIGURE 18.4   Diffraction of a sound emitter: the diffraction angle relative to the shadow boundary and the placement of a virtual source.

18.4.5 Calculating Diffraction Angle from Edge Geometry

Here, we present a method to test for and find the diffraction angle if it exists, given an emitter position, listener position, and a diffraction edge. This code should be executed after detecting a ray hit (i.e. there is no line of sight) between the emitter and the listener, and can be executed iteratively against a set of possible diffracting edges. The edges are represented by an origin point, an edge direction vector, a scalar edge length, and two normal vectors. The normal vectors are the vectors perpendicular to the two surfaces that intersect to form the edge, defined in such that they face away from the acute angle formed by the two planes. All vectors should be normalized to unit length.

The method, `InDiffractionShadowRegion()`, first determines if the emitter and listener are positioned such that diffraction occurs about the edge. This can be used as an efficient way to filter out invalid edges. Afterwards, the method `FindDiffractionPoint()` calculates the diffraction point along the edge. The diffraction point is taken as the closest point on the edge to the ray between the emitter and the listener. A detailed explanation and derivation of this formula, along with a plethora of other relevant information, can be found in Christer Ericson's "Real-Time Collision Detection"[5] Finally, `GetDiffractionAngle()` calculates the angle in degrees. Note that this implementation is limited to diffraction from a single edge and does not attempt to find pathways between multiple edges.

```
struct Edge
{
  // World-space point at the beginning of the edge.
  Vector3D origin;

  // Unit-length direction vector for the edge.
  // Should be standardized such that
  // CrossProduct(n0,n1) == direction
  Vector3D direction;

  // Length of the edge.
  float length;

  // Normal vector for first plane intersecting the edge.
  // Normals are defined such that n0 and n1 always point
  // away from each other.
  Vector3D n0;

  //Normal vector for second plane intersecting the edge.
  Vector3D n1;
};

bool InDiffractionShadowRegion(
  const Edge& edge,
  const Vector3D& emitterPos,
  const Vector3D& listenerPos)
{
  Vector3D to_emitter =  emitterPos - edge.origin;
  Vector3D to_listener = listenerPos - edge.origin;

  float e_dot_n0 = DotProduct(to_emitter, edge.n0);
  float e_dot_n1 = DotProduct(to_emitter, edge.n1);
  float l_dot_n0 = DotProduct(to_listener, edge.n0);
  float l_dot_n1 = DotProduct(to_listener, edge.n1);

  bool emitter_front_of_plane0 = e_dot_n0 > 0;
  bool emitter_front_of_plane1 = e_dot_n1 > 0;
  bool listener_front_of_plane0 = l_dot_n0 > 0;
  bool listener_front_of_plane1 = l_dot_n1 > 0;

  // The listener and the emitter must be on opposite sides of
  // each plane.
  if (listener_front_of_plane0 == emitter_front_of_plane0 ||
      listener_front_of_plane1 == emitter_front_of_plane1)
    return false;

  // The emitter and listener must each be in front of one plane,
  // and behind the other.
    if (emitter_front_of_plane0 == emitter_front_of_plane1 ||
        listener_front_of_plane0 == listener_front_of_plane1)
      return false;

  // Project to_emitter and to_listener onto the plane defined
  // by edge.origin and edge.direction.
  // This is the plane that is perpendicular to the edge direction.
  Vector3D to_emitter_proj =
```

```
      emitterPos -
        edge.direction * DotProduct(to_emitter, edge.direction) -
        edge.origin;
    to_emitter_proj = Normalize(to_emitter_proj);

    Vector3D to_listener_proj =
      listenerPos -
        edge.direction * DotProduct(to_listener, edge.direction) -
        edge.origin;
    to_listener_proj = Normalize(to_listener_proj);

    // p is the vector that is parallel to the plane with normal n0,
    // pointing away from the edge.
    Vector3D p = CrossProduct(edge.n0,edge.direction);

    // Project to_emitter_proj, and to_listener_proj along p so that
    // we may compare their angles.
    float a0 = DotProduct(to_emitter_proj, p);
    float a1 = DotProduct(to_listener_proj, p);

    if (-a0 < a1)// The listener is in the diffraction shadow region
        return true;

    return false;
}

bool FindDiffractionPoint(
  const Edge& edge,
  const Vector3D& emitterPos,
  const Vector3D& listenerPos,
  Vector3D& out_diffractionPt)
{
  Vector3D rayDirection = Normalize(listenerPos - emitterPos);

  Vector3D r = edge.origin - emitterPos;

  float a = DotProduct(edge.direction, edge.direction);
  float b = DotProduct(edge.direction, rayDirection);
  float c = DotProduct(edge.direction, r);
  float e = DotProduct(rayDirection, rayDirection);
  float f = DotProduct(rayDirection, r);
  float d = a*e - b*b;

  float s = 0;

  bool inRange = false;
  if (d != 0) // if d==0, lines are parallel
  {
    s = (b*f - c*e) / d;
    inRange = s > 0 && s < edge.length;
  }

  out_diffractionPt = edge.origin + edge.direction * s;

  return inRange;
}
```

```
float GetDiffractionAngle(
  Vector3D& diffractionPt,
  const Vector3D& emitterPos,
  const Vector3D& listenerPos)
{
  Vector3D incidentRayDirection =
    Normalize(diffractionPt - emitterPos);
  Vector3D diffractedRayDirection =
    Normalize(listenerPos - diffractionPt);
  return
    acosf(
      DotProduct(diffractedRayDirection,
                 incidentRayDirection)) * 180.f / M_PI;
}
```

18.5 FINAL REMARKS

The code examples provided in this chapter are by no means comprehensive and should not be regarded as standalone units, but rather as a base to build on. For further inspiration, I suggest you head over to Lauri Savioja's excellent website[6] and play around with his interactive applets. He gives a detailed explanation of various geometric and wave-based techniques for virtual acoustics, and also dives into a number of other fascinating subjects.

We covered a relatively broad range of subject matter and present practical applications of complex acoustic phenomena. It is, however, only possible to scrape the tip of the iceberg in a single chapter on virtual acoustics. If nothing else, take with you the idea that it is indeed possible to achieve workable, efficient solutions on today's hardware, in today's games, and it is absolutely worth the time and effort involved.

NOTES

1 N. Raghuvanshi and J. Snyder, "Parametric wave field coding for precomputed sound propagation," ACM Transactions on Graphics (TOG) 33(4), 38, 2014.

2 L. Savioja and U. P. Svensson, "Overview of geometrical room acoustic modeling techniques," Journal of the Acoustical Society of America 138, 708–730, 2015. doi:10.1121/1.4926438.

3 J. Keller. "Geometrical theory of diffraction," Journal of the Optical Society of America 52(2), 116–130, 1962.

4 R. Kouyoumjian and P. Pathak, "A uniform geometrical theory of diffraction for an edge in a perfectly conducting surface," Proceedings of the IEEE 62(11), 1448–1461, 1974.

5 C. Ericson, "Real-Time Collision Detection," Boca Raton, FL: CRC Press; 1 edition, December 22, 2004.

6 L. Savioja, Room Acoustics Modeling with Interactive Visualizations, 2016. http://interactiveacoustics.info/.

CHAPTER 19

Implementing Volume Sliders

Guy Somberg

Echtra Games

CONTENTS

19.1 THE CURRENT STATE OF THE WORLD

In the past, video game options screens included a wealth of settings and controls for audio. Often, these settings existed in order to control performance. For example, reducing the mixing sample rate could change the performance of a game from a slideshow to an acceptable play experience. In some competitive games, a few extra milliseconds of time per frame could mean the difference between victory and defeat.

The world has progressed since those days. We no longer embrace hardware audio mixing, the tools we use to build the games have become more like DAWs, and the performance difference of mixing at 48,000 Hz is no longer meaningful on most platforms. With the advances in hardware and software, the audio settings menus in games have become more and more sparse. In many cases, the only settings left are volume controls.

Unfortunately, many games implement volume controls entirely incorrectly. Let's see what this incorrect method is, and what the end user's experience will be with it.

19.2 THE WRONG WAY

Let us say that you have a volume control for the master volume for your game; the slider controls the volume of the master bus in your engine's middleware, and your middleware provides you with a function to set the volume percent of the bus. In FMOD, this will be either `FMOD::Studio::Bus::setVolume()` or `FMOD::ChannelGroup::setVolume()`, depending on whether you're using the Studio API or the low-level API, but other middleware solutions will look similar. The input to the function is a floating-point number from `0.0f` to `1.0f`. We need to hook up our slider control to this function.

Easy, right? Just set the left side of the slider to 0, the right side of the slider to 1, and linearly interpolate. Then just send the value off to the middleware. And we're done!

Right?

```
void SetBusVolume(FMOD::Studio::Bus* pBus, float ControlPercent)
{
    pBus->setVolume(ControlPercent);
}
```

19.2.1 The End-User Experience

Except that this ends up being a terrible user experience for the players. Let's examine the actual behavior. In Figure 19.1, we note various points

FIGURE 19.1   Volume slider with linear interpolation.

along the volume slider; let us examine the perceived volume level at each one. At point A on the far right, the game is at full volume.

Our player has decided that the game is too loud, so she wants to reduce the volume. She slides the control about half way to point B, only to find that the volume has hardly changed. In desperation, she continues to slide the control to the left until it actually has a meaningful audible effect. She finally finds a range of meaningful volume changes close (but not all the way over to) the far left of the volume slider, between points C and D. The entire range between points D and E is effectively silent, and anything to the right of point C has no meaningful effect on the volume.

Unfortunately, this range is only about one-tenth of the total range of the volume slider, which can be especially problematic if the slider is relatively short or has a coarse precision level. In extreme situations, there may be just one or two pixels' worth of meaningful volume in the control.

19.3 WHAT'S GOING ON

Why does this happen? Why is the volume control so nonlinear? We've done a linear interpolation of the volume as the thumb goes across the slider. Why isn't the perceived audio level also linearly interpolating? What gives?

The short answer is that the volume control is nonlinear because audio volume is nonlinear. It's right there in the formula for converting decibels to percent: our sensation of loudness is logarithmic.

$$dB = 20\log_{10}(V)$$

$$V = 10^{dB/20}$$

Figure 19.2 demonstrates what's going on. On the X-axis is linear amplitude—the value of the slider control. On the Y-axis is perceived loudness. When we select a portion of the curve toward the right side (A_1), we can see that it represents a small change in perceived loudness (A_2). Contrariwise, when we select a portion of identical size from the left side (B_1), it represents a much larger difference in perceived loudness (B_2).

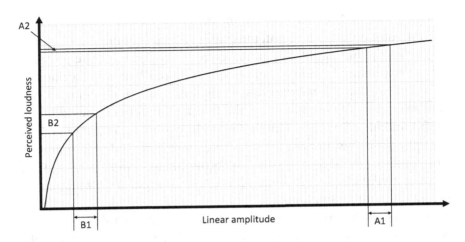

FIGURE 19.2   Curve showing perceived loudness to linear amplitude.

19.4 HOW TO FIX IT

In order to fix our volume slider, we must make its behavior exponential, rather than linear. This will give us the linear change in perceived loudness that we desire because

$$e^{\ln(x)} = x$$

and

$$\ln\left(e^x\right) = x$$

What we want is a formula which will return a linear curve when we take the log of it, and which also passes through the two end points of our volume curve: full volume at the far right and silence at the far left. In order to create this exponential relationship, we must find the appropriate values for a and b in the relation:

$$y = ae^{bx}$$

Where y is our desired volume percent, and x is our linearly interpolated input value from the volume slider. We have an equation with two unknowns in it—we, therefore, need to find two points along the curve in order to find the values of a and b. Fortunately, we have those values at the end points of our slider. This makes our two end points (0, 0) and (1, 1).

Sort of. Let's start with (1, 1), and then we'll explore why (0, 0) isn't exactly what we want.

At the end point (1, 1), we need to find a relationship between a and b. Plugging the values in gives us

$$1 = ae^{1 \cdot b}$$

Or

$$a = \frac{1}{e^b}$$

Now, onto the (0, 0) point. The problem with this point is that it is infinitely far along the curve. The logarithmic curve that we have is tangential to zero, so it will never actually reach it. Furthermore, getting the full range of volumes is not meaningful or helpful. You can get a lot more nuance out of the 6 dB range between 0 dB and −6 dB than you can out of the 6 dB range between −48 dB and −54 dB.

What we need to do is select a value that is close enough to silence for our purposes. As we'll see later, selecting a dynamic range that is too large is every bit as problematic as using a linear volume control, and selecting a dynamic range that is too small also has audible artifacts. In my experience, a dynamic range of 30–40 dB is appropriate for a game setting. So, rather than (0, 0), the second point that we will use as input to our formula is actually (0, $10^{-R/20)}$, where R is our dynamic range. For a dynamic range of 40 dB, our point is (0, $10^{-40/20}$) = (0, 10^{-2}) = (0, 0.01).

Now we can plug it into our formula:

$$10^{-R/20} = ae^{0 \cdot b} = ae^0 = a$$

Let's rewrite that in positive terms:

$$a = 10^{-R/20} = \frac{1}{10^{R/20}}$$

Great! That gives us our value for a. We calculated the relationship between a and b earlier. We can finally get our value for b by plugging this value into that formula:

$$\frac{1}{10^{R/20}} = \frac{1}{e^b}$$

Cross-multiplying:

$$e^b = 10^{R/20}$$

Which gives us:

$$b = \ln\left(10^{R/20}\right)$$

19.5 SHOW ME THE CODE!

Enough with the math! We have now solved our system of equations, and we can write the code for them. Note that both of the terms for a and b include a common term: $10^{R/20}$, which we can split out into an intermediate variable. Furthermore, all of these values are constant and only dependent on the chosen dynamic range, which allows us to move the contents out and only calculate them once. Our code is now a direct translation of the formula:

```
static const float dynamic_range = 40.0f;
static const float power = powf(10.0f, dynamic_range / 20.0f);
static const float a = 1.0f / power;
static const float b = logf(power);

void SetBusVolume(FMOD::Studio::Bus* pBus, float ControlPercent)
{
    float VolumePercent = a * expf(ControlPercent * b);
    pBus->setVolume(VolumePercent);
}
```

In this example, we have put the constants into a static global scope, but it may also make sense to put them into static class scope, or some sort of compile-time calculated machinery.

The initial temptation for compile-time machinery is just to prepend constexpr to the declarations. Unfortunately, that does not work (at least as of C++17) because powf and logf are not constexpr themselves. So, in order to make these declarations constexpr, we need constexpr versions of powf and logf. Whether it is possible to implement these functions (and what those implementations might look like) is outside the scope of this chapter.

19.6 EDGE CASE

There is one edge case that we should call out: when the volume slider is on the far left (at $x = 0$), then the intent of the player is that the volume should be silent. In that case, we can just set the volume to 0, which makes the final code:

```
void SetBusVolume(FMOD::Studio::Bus* pBus, float ControlPercent)
{
  float VolumePercent;
  if(ControlPercent == 0.0f)
  {
    VolumePercent = 0.0f;
  }
  else
  {
    VolumePercent = a * expf(ControlPercent * b);
  }
  pBus->setVolume(VolumePercent);
}
```

19.7 SELECTING THE DYNAMIC RANGE

Now that we have the correct formula, all that remains is to select an appropriate dynamic range. As I said before, I have found that 30–40 dB is an appropriate level, at least as a starting point. You can probably select a value in that range blindly and move on. However, if you do want to experiment with the various values, it will be valuable to have an idea of what the consequences are.

Let us first examine a dynamic range that is too small. Figure 19.3 shows the interesting points in such a setup. We get a nice smooth volume curve from full volume at point A all the way at the right, down to a quieter (but still audible) volume at point B on the left, just before the end. However, because we're clamping down to silence at point C on the far left, we end up with a pop in the volume when transitioning between B and C. Also, when the dynamic range is not high enough, the volume difference from full volume to just before the pop to silence can be insufficient for the players to find an appropriate listening volume.

FIGURE 19.3   Volume slider with a dynamic range that is too small.

FIGURE 19.4   Volume slider with a dynamic range that is too large.

On the other end of the spectrum, we might end up with a dynamic range that is too large. Figure 19.4 shows the interesting points in such a setup. We get a nice smooth volume curve from full volume at point A all the way at the right, down to effective silence at point B, about a quarter of the space of the control. The remaining three-quarters of the volume slider between points B and C are all effectively silent. This curve is basically the opposite of the original linear curve, where a small portion of the slider on the left side was actually usable. Here only a small portion of the slider on the right side is actually usable.

The challenge, therefore, is to find the "goldilocks" value for the dynamic range: not too high and not too low, but just right. The value that we picked in Section 19.4 (40 dB) was found by trial and error—different systems may have different effective dynamic ranges, so finding the appropriate value for your platform may require some experimentation.

19.8 SELECTING VOLUME CONTROLS

The above math formulas and code are the one true, proper, and correct way to implement volume sliders. If you're using any other formula for it, you're probably doing it wrong. Now the question is which volume controls to surface to your players.

Traditionally, games have put volume sliders for each of the major buses in a game: master, sound effects, music, voice, and maybe one or two others such as UI or ambiences. It is relatively cheap to add to the settings panel, and it is technologically easy to hook up to the appropriate buses in the middleware. Why not do it?

The answer to that question is that you shouldn't expose volume controls to your player that are not meaningful to them. Does your player really care what the balance between music and voice is? Are they likely to turn off everything except for the UI sounds? Under what circumstances does it make sense for a player to reduce the volume of the voices, but leave the sound effects and music untouched? Players will either ignore these controls and leave them at their default values, or they will fiddle with them and destroy your game's mix. Or, worse, they will adjust the values by accident and then be unable to fix them back to their appropriate values.

Instead of trusting the player to control their own volume, the proper thing to do is to mix the entire game properly. Make sure that the music and the voices and the sound effects and everything that is happening in the game all balances properly and can be heard. Make it so that your players don't *want* to adjust the volume of the game.

In the extreme, there is actually an argument for not having volume control in your game at all. After all, game consoles already have a master volume control built-in: it's called the TV remote! Similarly, phones and tablets already have a system-wide master volume control with easily accessible hardware buttons to adjust it.

PCs also have an OS-level master volume control, but the breadth of hardware makes in-game volume controls more meaningful there. Not all PCs have easily accessible volume control buttons, and because PCs are also general purpose computers, players don't necessarily want to adjust their hardware volume because they have it adjusted properly for the other activities that they do on their computer. So, for PCs, you will definitely want to add a volume control to your game.

19.9 WHICH VOLUME CONTROLS TO HAVE

Given the above discussion, what controls should you actually have in the audio panel of your game? Of course, every game is different, but the default that I use in my games is to expose only one single volume control to players: the master volume.

In addition to the master volume slider, it is also important for games to have a "mute music" checkbox available to players. As of this writing, all major consoles, phones, and tablets support player-music playback, where the owner of the devices can select an alternate source of music from the device's library or another app. Similarly, PC players can simply run their music player of choice with their own custom library of music. Your game may have been authored with relaxing classical music, but if the player wants to listen to her Swedish Death Metal, then the game should allow that and mute the music.

That discussion notwithstanding, your players will have different tolerances for music. They may want to have the game's music playing, but decide that it is too loud, or they may leave the slider alone, or mute the music entirely. It may, therefore, be prudent to add a music volume slider. But if you do have enough control over your game's moment-to-moment mix (maybe in a story-driven adventure game), think about whether you can omit the music slider entirely and go with just a checkbox.

19.9.1 Optional Voice Control

By default, then, the only two controls on the audio settings panel should be a master volume slider and a mute music checkbox (or a music volume slider). However, if your game is very dialog-heavy, then there is one extra control that I encourage you to add: a "mute voice" checkbox.

Several jobs ago, I was working for a company that made heavily story-driven games with full dialog and voice acting which were released episodically. During my tenure at this company, we made the switch from volume controls per bus (master, music, sfx, and voices) to the master-volume-only scheme described in this chapter. This transition was a success technologically, and we thought nothing of it after releasing a few episodes.

However, at some point we received a piece of fan mail from a couple who were enthralled by our games. So much so that they implored us to bring back the voice control for the volume. The way that they played the games was that they would read the text of the dialog aloud: she would read the lines for the female characters and he would read the lines for the male characters.

I found this concept so delightful that I resolved to include a "mute voices" option for this couple whenever the opportunity arose.

19.10 CONCLUSION

Writing proper volume controls is not difficult, but it does require some understanding of what's going on. Using the code in Section 19.5 will always give you a proper perceptibly linear volume control—the only choice to make is what dynamic range you will use. A good starting point is 40 dB, but a little bit of experimentation will help to zero in on the appropriate value.

Before filling your game's audio settings page with volume sliders, though, take a step back and think about whether your player should actually have control over that part of the mix. A properly mixed game will not need anything more than a single master volume slider and a mute music checkbox (or music slider). And, of course, a "mute voices" checkbox in honor of the couple who reads the dialog aloud.

SECTION IV

Music

CHAPTER 20

Note-Based Music Systems

Charlie Huguenard

Meow Wolf

CONTENTS

20.1 WHY SEQUENCERS?

Currently, the most popular methods of composing music for games are the two provided by many audio middleware engines right out of the box: "horizontal" and "vertical" composition. They work as in Figure 20.1. Horizontally composed music plays one piece of music at a time. When the state of the game changes, a new piece of music is swapped in, usually with a transition stinger in between. Vertically composed music fades in

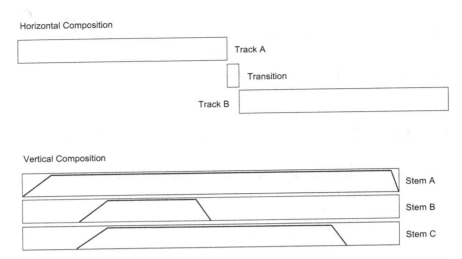

FIGURE 20.1   Diagram showing horizontal and vertical music composition.

and out a collection of stems—groups of instruments mixed to a single audio file—in response to game state changes. Both rely on prerecorded pieces of music and offer handy ways to vary a game's score without sacrificing much of the composer's control over the mix and arrangement.

But what if you want to change the timbre of the synth pad or the articulation of the flute player based on the anxiety level of your main character? It's certainly possible to make a complex cross-fading system with one of the above methods, but the amount of content required could explode to an unmanageable level. And what if you wanted to change the tonality or slow down the tempo of the whole score at any time? Even with the availability of high-quality time-stretching and pitch-shifting algorithms, you'll be hard-pressed to find a way to do that without a very angry mix engineer.

These sorts of runtime adjustments are trivial if you're working with notes and sound generators, and the thought process isn't much different from what many composers are already doing in a DAW to create their finished pieces. Details such as letting the tails of notes ring out beyond a transition or swapping instrumentation on the fly are also straightforward when using note-based music systems. But perhaps most interesting is the potential for designing evolving scores that are appropriate for the current situation—even situations you didn't plan for. When you're working with notes and instruments, improvising at runtime becomes a possibility, and generating new music for new situations is within reach.

20.2 DESIGN CONSIDERATIONS

As with all game systems, it's important to consider your goals and constraints when designing a music sequencer system. If all you need to do is vary the tempo, you can probably get away with making a MIDI file player and a clock to drive it. If you also need control over articulation of notes, you might need to add in the ability to change note lengths, velocities, and instrument parameters. And if you want the system to improvise or reharmonize a theme, you'll need a way to define and respond to scales and chords.

You'll also need to find out what your creative team wants to use. Some composers are perfectly comfortable in a node-based modular environment, while others prefer to work with a global timeline. Ultimately, you're making a tool for someone else, and it's important to tailor it to their preferences and expectations. That said, sometimes your game calls for a system that your creative team isn't used to. In those cases, it's your job to teach and support them as they venture out into new territory.

20.3 LET'S MAKE IT!

In this chapter, we will make a simple, extensible sequencer system and build it up along the way. Example code will be provided in C# using the Unity3d game engine. Optimization, user interface, and clever code will be avoided for clarity when possible. The full source code is in the supplemental materials for this book, which can be downloaded from www.crcpress.com/.

20.3.1 The Clock

To get the whole thing moving, we need something to use as a timing base. A clock—or metronome, timer, or pulse generator, depending on your preference—can help us do that. A clock generates ticks at an interval related to the music's tempo and passes them on to sequencers, modulators, and other components that want to synchronize with music.

MIDI sequencers use a unit called "pulses per quarter note" (PPQN), which is typically set at 96, but is often configurable. The higher the PPQN, the higher the timing resolution, which can help make sequences sound more "human." If all you're using is step sequencers, you could safely set the clock's tick size to the size of the smallest step. For example, if the composer is just using 16th note step sequencers, then the clock's tick duration could be one 16th note, or four PPQNs.

Let's build a clock with a configurable tempo and tick duration:

```
public class Clock : MonoBehavior
{
   [SerializeField] private double _tempo = 120.0;
   [SerializeField] private int _ticksPerBeat = 4;

   // the length of a single tick in seconds
   private double_tickLength;

   // the next tick time, relative to AudioSettings.dspTime
   private double_nextTickTime;

   private void Recalculate { ... }
   (some wiring to call Recalculate on reset, etc.)

   private void Update() { ... }
}
```

Then, we can derive the tick duration from a tempo and a number of ticks that should occur within a single beat:

```
private void Recalculate()
{
   double beatsPerSecond = _tempo / 60.0;
   double ticksPerSecond = beatsPerSecond * _ticksPerBeat;
   _tickLength = 1.0 / ticksPerSecond;
}
```

Once we know the length of a tick, we can determine when we should schedule ticks using the following process:

1. Get the current time. We're using the audio system timer in the example code, which gives us elapsed time in seconds since the audio system started up.

2. Look ahead one update frame. We get the time the *last* frame took and use that as our look-ahead time.

3. Schedule any ticks that would happen before the end of the look-ahead window and pass them on to listeners.

```
// this gets called on the main thread every game frame
private void Update()
{
   double currentTime = AudioSettings.dspTime;

   // Look ahead the length of the last frame.
```

```
    currentTime += Time.deltaTime;

    // There may be more than one tick within the next frame.
    // Looping until the look-ahead time will catch them all.
    while (currentTime > _nextTickTime)
    {
        // pass the tick along
        DoTick(_nextTickTime);

        // increment the next tick time
        _nextTickTime += _tickLength;
    }
}
```

This will result in our clock ticking with precision close enough to make music. But you may notice that there is a problem if one frame takes a significantly longer time than the one before it—the next frame could end up with a pile up of notes that all play at the same time. Because we don't know how long *this* frame is going to take, we have to make a guess based on the last frame. One way to handle those note pileups is to rate limit ticks. But if we rate limit at the clock stage, we'll end up throwing out ticks in our sequencers, which affects the phase of every sequencer down the chain, so it's better to do that at the instrument stage instead.

This update is happening in the main game loop, which is also something to consider. Moving the update code to the audio thread would allow us to count the samples in the audio buffers being processed, which gives us an easy way to ensure we're in sync. But for the sake of clarity, we will leave that topic for a future volume.

20.3.2 Step Sequencer

Now that we have a clock to drive our sequencer system, we need a way to trigger notes. Let's say our sequencer should

- Listen for a tick from a clock to advance

- Have a configurable number of steps to allow odd lengths for polyrhythms

- Listen for a tick from another sequencer to allow "chaining" of sequences

A step sequencer contains some number of steps which are active or inactive (notes or rests). It listens for an incoming tick, sends out a tick of its own if the current step is active, and then advances to the next step. If the current step is the last one in the sequence, the sequencer starts over from the beginning. Here is that process in pseudocode:

```
When a tick is received
{
  If current_tick is active
  {
    Send tick
  }
  Increment and wrap current_tick
}
```

Because we want to be able to chain sequencers, it will be helpful to be able to treat both a Clock and a Sequencer as valid tick sources. One way to do that in C# is to have both inherit from a generic Ticker class, which defines an event that tells listeners a tick has happened:

```
public abstract class Ticker : MonoBehaviour
{
  public delegate void TickHandler(double tickTime);

  public event TickHandler Ticked;

  // call this in your class to send a tick
  protected void DoTick(double tickTime)
  {
    if (Ticked != null)
    {
      Ticked(tickTime);
    }
  }
}
```

In order to do polyrhythms, we'll let our composer define an arbitrary number of steps. Our Sequencer class ends up as:

```
public class Sequencer : Ticker
{
  // Information about a step in the sequencer
  [Serializable]
  public class Step
  {
    public bool Active;
  }

  // The "Ticker" we want to listen to
  [SerializeField] private Ticker _ticker;

  // The list of steps in this Sequencer
  [SerializeField] private List<Step> _steps;
```

```
  private int _currentTick = 0;

  // Subscribe to the ticker
  private void OnEnable()
  {
    if (_ticker != null)
    {
      _ticker.Ticked += HandleTicked;
    }
  }

  // Unsubscribe from the ticker
  private void OnDisable()
  {
    if (_ticker != null)
    {
      _ticker.Ticked -= HandleTicked;
    }
  }

  // Responds to tick events from the ticker.
  public void HandleTicked(double tickTime)
  {
    int numSteps = _steps.Count;

    // if there are no steps, don't do anything
    if (numSteps == 0)
    {
      return;
    }

    Step step = _steps[_currentTick];

    // if the current step is active, send a tick through
    if (step.Active)
    {
      DoTick(tickTime);
    }

    // increment and wrap the tick counter
    _currentTick = (_currentTick + 1) % numSteps;
  }
}
```

This gives us a step sequencer we can hook up to a clock and a sound generator to make rhythms. And thanks to the Ticker construct, we can easily create other kinds of sequencers to add to the set (more on that later).

20.3.3 Making Noise

Speaking of sound generators, it would be hard to know if our sequencer system is working without some sound. Now that we have the structure of the sequencer system in place, let's make a sampler instrument. Simply put, a sampler plays a sound—usually a sound file loaded from disk—in response to a trigger message. There are many additional features that could be added to make a more useful and musical sampler instrument, such as velocity mapping, volume envelopes, and looping. We will stick to the basics for now.

Unity provides a quick and easy way to load sound files and play them back—the AudioSource component. All you have to do is attach the component to a GameObject, drag in a sound file, and tell it to play from your code. A simple sampler using the AudioSource component might look like this:

```
[RequireComponent(typeof(AudioSource))]
public class Sampler : MonoBehaviour
{
  // the Ticker we want to listen to
  [SerializeField] private Ticker _ticker;

  // the attached AudioSource component
  private AudioSource _audioSource;

  private void Awake()
  {
    _audioSource = GetComponent<AudioSource>();
  }

  private void OnEnable()
  {
    if (_ticker != null)
    {
      _ticker.Ticked += HandleTicked;
    }
  }

  private void OnDisable()
  {
    if (_ticker != null)
    {
      _ticker.Ticked -= HandleTicked;
    }
  }

  private void HandleTicked(double tickTime)
  {
    // play the sound at the tick time,
    // which is now or in the future
    _audioSource.PlayScheduled(tickTime);
  }
}
```

Some of the code looks familiar. Listening for ticks in the `Sampler` code works the same as in the `Sequencer`. But in this case, when it gets a tick, it tells the attached `AudioSource` to play a sound, and does not pass the tick through.

This sampler instrument will work fine for basic testing, but what if a tick arrives while a sound is still playing? With this setup, it will go ahead and play the new sound, but the currently playing sound will stop immediately. This will usually cause clicks and pops, and it would sound much nicer if each sound was allowed to play to the end. To solve this problem, we need more than one *voice* in the sampler. This doesn't require much more work. Instead of playing the sound on the sampler object, we'll make a separate `SamplerVoice` class, and the `Sampler` can create and manage as many of them as we want:

```
[RequireComponent(typeof(AudioSource))]
public class SamplerVoice : MonoBehaviour
{
  private AudioSource _audioSource;

  public void Play(AudioClip audioClip, double startTime)
  {
    _audioSource.clip = audioClip;
    _audioSource.PlayScheduled(startTime);
  }

  private void Awake()
  {
    _audioSource = GetComponent<AudioSource>();
  }
}
```

In the `Sampler` code, we will add a reference to a `SamplerVoice` prefab, along with the logic to rotate between some number of voices:

```
public class Sampler : MonoBehaviour
{
  [SerializeField] private Ticker _ticker;
  // The audio file to play for this sampler
  [SerializeField] private AudioClip _audioClip;
  // The number of voices this sampler will have
  [SerializeField, Range(1, 8)] private int _numVoices = 2;
  // A prefab with a SamplerVoice component attached
  [SerializeField] private SamplerVoice _samplerVoicePrefab;

  private SamplerVoice[] _samplerVoices;
  private int _nextVoiceIndex;
```

```
private void Awake()
{
  // create the sampler voices
  _samplerVoices = new SamplerVoice[_numVoices];

  for (int i = 0; i < _numVoices; ++i)
  {
    SamplerVoice samplerVoice = Instantiate(_samplerVoicePrefab);
    samplerVoice.transform.parent = transform;
    samplerVoice.transform.localPosition = Vector3.zero;
    _samplerVoices[i] = samplerVoice;
  }
}

...

private void HandleTicked(double tickTime)
{
  // play the clip on the current voice
  _samplerVoices[_nextVoiceIndex].Play(_audioClip, tickTime);

  // rotate to the next voice (which will be the oldest)
  _nextVoiceIndex = (_nextVoiceIndex + 1) % _numVoices;
}
}
```

Now our sampler can play a few sounds at the same time.

20.3.4 Adding Pitch

Music isn't usually very interesting without varying the pitch of instruments, so let's add pitch to our sequencer. Depending on the kind of sound generator, pitch could be specified as frequency (oscillators, resonators, etc.) or playback speed (samplers and other waveform playback sources). It would be much easier to use a standard unit to cover these two cases as well as others that may arise. One simple solution is to use something already familiar to many musicians: MIDI note numbers. MIDI specifies a note number as an integer in the range of 0–127 (although we can ignore that range limitation if we want). Translating note numbers to the units preferred by sound generators is straightforward. The sampler can be updated to handle MIDI notes with these changes:

```
(Sampler.cs)

// Helper to convert MIDI note number to pitch scalar
public static float MidiNoteToPitch(int midiNote)
{
   int semitoneOffset = midiNote - 60; // offset from MIDI note C4
   return Mathf.Pow(2.0f, semitoneOffset / 12.0f);
}

...

private void HandleTicked(double tickTime, int midiNoteNumber)
{
   float pitch = MidiNoteToPitch(midiNoteNumber);
   _samplerVoices[_nextVoiceIndex].Play(_audioClip, pitch, tickTime);

   _nextVoiceIndex = (_nextVoiceIndex + 1) % _numVoices;
}

(SamplerVoice.cs)

public void Play(AudioClip audioClip, float pitch, double startTime)
{
   _audioSource.clip = audioClip;
   _audioSource.pitch = pitch;
   _audioSource.PlayScheduled(startTime);
}
```

Let us now add note numbers to our sequencer system. First, we modify our Ticker class to include MIDI note numbers:

```
public abstract class Ticker : MonoBehaviour
{
   public delegate void TickHandler(
     double tickTime, int midiNoteNumber);

   public event TickHandler Ticked;

   protected void DoTick(double tickTime, int midiNoteNumber = 60)
   {
     if (Ticked != null)
     {
       Ticked(tickTime, midiNoteNumber);
     }
   }
}
```

Then, we add a note number field in our sequencer's step info:

```
[Serializable]
public class Step
{
```

```
    public bool Active;
    public int MidiNoteNumber;
}
```

And finally, we modify the sequencer's tick handler method to accept and pass on note info:

```
public void HandleTicked(double tickTime, int midiNoteNumber)
{
  int numSteps = _steps.Count;

  // if there are no steps, don't do anything
  if (numSteps == 0)
  {
    return;
  }

  Step step = _steps[_currentTick];

  // if the current step is active, send a tick through
  if (step.Active)
  {
    DoTick(tickTime, step.MidiNoteNumber);
  }

  // increment and wrap the tick counter
  _currentTick = (_currentTick + 1) % numSteps;
}
```

And now the MIDI note number is sent through. In our delegate, we can hook it up to the generator and make some melodies.

20.3.5 Playing in Key

Specifying notes directly works just fine, but if we want to be able to change the tonality of a piece, we need a way to set the key. Shifting the root is simple: you just add to or subtract from the MIDI notes coming through the system. But tonal changes are usually more than simple transposition. For example, in a C Major scale, you have these notes: C, D, E, F, G, A, and B. In C Aeolian (a common minor scale), you have C, D, E♭, F, G, A♭, and B♭. There is no way to simply add or subtract a fixed amount to the note numbers to change C Major into C Aeolian.

A more abstract way to represent a scale is to list the semitone intervals between the tones in the scale. You can then apply that pattern starting with any root note to derive the scale. This sort of representation is also helpful with programming music. In this notation, a Major (Ionian) scale would be [2, 2, 1, 2, 2, 2, 1] starting with the interval between the first- and second-scale tones and ending with the interval between the seventh-scale tones and the first. Aeolian would be [2, 1, 2, 2, 1, 2, 2].

Using this interval notation, we can write a system that allows us to compose with scale tones instead of explicit notes. For ease of explanation, we will use the modes of the major scale. If you're not familiar with modes, it's equivalent to playing the white keys on a piano and shifting where you start. If you start on C, you get the first mode—Ionian, more commonly called Major. If you start on D, you get Dorian, which has more of a minor tonality. The rest, if you follow that pattern in order, are Phrygian, Lydian, Mixolydian, Aeolian, and Locrian.

An additional component is required to tell the sequencer system what scale to use, which we'll call the `KeyController`:

```
public class KeyController : MonoBehaviour
{
  public enum Note
  {
    C = 0,
    Db,
    D,
    Eb,
    E,
    F,
    Gb,
    G,
    Ab,
    A,
    Bb,
    B
  }

  public enum ScaleMode
  {
    Ionian = 0,
    Dorian,
    Phrygian,
    Lydian,
    Mixolydian,
    Aeolian,
    Locrian
  }

  // The root note of the current scale
  public Note RootNote;

  // The mode of the current scale
  public ScaleMode Mode;

  // Converts a scale tone and octave to a note in the current key
  public int GetMIDINote(int scaleTone, int octave)
  {
```

```
    . . .
    }
}
```

The meat of the work in this component is the `GetMIDINote()` function. What we need to do is use the root note and mode of the key we're in to translate a scale tone and octave to a MIDI note that our sound generators can play. We can represent the intervals of the Ionian mode starting with the interval *before* the root of the scale (between the seventh and first tones when wrapping around):

```
private static int[] INTERVALS = { 1, 2, 2, 1, 2, 2, 2 };
```

We can derive a semitone offset using this array by adding up all the intervals on the way to the scale tone we want, but not including the first-scale tone, because it has no offset from the root note. In the simplest case, where we want scale tone one of any mode, we get no offset from the root note. If we want scale tone three of Ionian, we add up the second and third intervals in the list to get a semitone offset of 4. If we want a different mode, we shift the point at which we start adding intervals by the offset of the mode from Ionian—Dorian is offset by 1, Phrygian is offset by 2, and so on.

```
// add semitones for each step through the scale,
// using the interval key above
int semitones = 0;
while (scaleTone > 0)
{
    int idx = (scaleTone + (int)Mode) % 7;
    semitones += INTERVALS[idx];
    scaleTone--;
}
```

The entire function with input cleaning and octave calculations is:

```
public int GetMIDINote(int scaleTone, int octave)
{
    // scaleTone is range (1,7) for readability
    // but range (0,6) is easier to work with
    scaleTone--;

    // wrap scale tone and shift octaves
    while (scaleTone < 0)
    {
        octave--;
        scaleTone += 7;
    }
    while (scaleTone >= 7)
```

```
{
  octave++;
  scaleTone -= 7;
}

// C4 = middle C, so MIDI note 0 is C-1.
// we don't want to go any lower than that
octave = Mathf.Max(octave, -1);
// shift to minimum of 0 for easy math
octave++;

// add semitones for each step through the scale,
// using the interval key above
int semitones = 0;
while (scaleTone > 0)
{
  int idx = (scaleTone + (int)Mode) % 7;
  semitones += INTERVALS[idx];
  scaleTone--;
}

return octave * 12 + semitones + (int)RootNote;
}
```

We need to make some modifications to our step sequencer in order to specify the scale tone and octave instead of directly inputting MIDI note numbers. First, our step info changes to

```
[Serializable]
public class Step
{
  public bool Active;
  [Range(1, 7)]
  public int ScaleTone;
  [Range(-1, 8)]
  public int Octave;
}
```

Then, we add a reference to a KeyController and use it to translate a scale tone and octave to a note number in the HandleTicked() function:

```
if (_keyController != null)
{
  midiNoteNumber =
    _keyController.GetMIDINote(step.ScaleTone, step.Octave);
}
DoTick(tickTime, midiNoteNumber);
```

With this setup, we can specify scale tones instead of directly inputting notes, which allows us to change the key of an entire piece of music at runtime.

20.3.6 Game Control

We can make music with what we've built so far, but it's not yet *interactive*. The real power of note-based music systems is in the myriad opportunities for changing the music in response to game state or player input. Let's add some ways to manipulate the music.

A good starting point is changing the tempo. Let's say we want the music to get faster as the player approaches a goal. It is usually most convenient to manage the state of the music in a central location, so let's start filling in a `MusicController` to handle our game-to-music mapping:

```
public class MusicController : MonoBehaviour
{
  // game-modifiable fields
  public float playerDistance;

  // references to things we want to control
  [SerializeField] private Clock _clock;

  // mapping settings
  [SerializeField] private float _playerDistanceMin = 1.0f;
  [SerializeField] private float _playerDistanceMax = 10.0f;
  [SerializeField] private float _tempoMin = 60.0f;
  [SerializeField] private float _tempoMax = 130.0f;

  private void Update()
  {
    // map the player distance to tempo
    // we'll assume the settings are reasonable,
    // but in the wild you really should clean the input
    float amount = (playerDistance - _playerDistanceMin)
                 / (_playerDistanceMax - _playerDistanceMin);

    // we flip the min and max tempo values because
    // we want the tempo to go up as distance goes down
    float tempo = Mathf.Lerp(_tempoMax, _tempoMin, amount);

    _clock.SetTempo(tempo);
  }
}
```

Set the distance and tempo values to the ranges you want, and the tempo will increase as the player gets closer to the goal.

Now let's say we generally want to be in a major key, but if the player gets spotted by an enemy, the music should shift to a minor key until the player returns to safety. All that is needed is to set the scale mode in the `KeyController`, like so:

```
public class MusicController : MonoBehaviour
{
  // game-modifiable fields
  ...
  public bool playerSpotted;

  // references to things we want to control
  ...
  [SerializeField] private KeyController _keyController;

  // mapping settings
  ...
  [SerializeField] private KeyController.ScaleMode _safeScaleMode;
  [SerializeField] private KeyController.ScaleMode _spottedScaleMode;

  private bool _lastPlayerSpotted;

  private void Update()
  {
    ...

    // if the player's "spotted" state changed, update the key
    if (playerSpotted != _lastPlayerSpotted)
    {
      _keyController.Mode = playerSpotted
                          ? _spottedScaleMode
                          : _safeScaleMode;
      _lastPlayerSpotted = playerSpotted;
    }
  }
}
```

As a finishing touch, let's also introduce an "excited" sequence that should turn on when the player is spotted, and back off when they return to safety. You could just enable or disable the sequencer GameObject completely, but it would no longer receive ticks from the rest of the system, and could get out of phase with the other sequencers. Instead, let's add a "suspended" mode to the Sequencer class, which continues to keep its place, but doesn't pass ticks down the chain.

```
// in the class definition
public bool suspended;

// in the HandleTicked function
Step step = _steps[_currentTick];

// if the current step is active, send a tick through
// skip if this sequencer is suspended
if (step.Active && !suspended)
{
  ...
```

```
}

// increment and wrap the tick counter
_currentTick = (_currentTick + 1) % numSteps;
```

Now, we can add a reference to the sequencer to the `MusicController` class and toggle the sequence:

```
// in the class definition
[SerializeField] private Sequencer _excitedSequence;

// in the Update function
// if the player's "spotted" state changed...
if (playerSpotted != _lastPlayerSpotted)
{
    ...

    // ...also toggle the "excited" sequence
    _excitedSequence.suspended = !playerSpotted;

    ...
}
```

And now we have a piece of music that follows along a little more closely to what the player is doing.

20.4 EXTENDING THE SYSTEM

With this basic system, we can make some music, and have it respond to what is happening in the game. But there's much more musical nuance and interesting behavior that could be added. This could be done by continuing to improve the `Sequencer` class, but another option enabled by this chainable sequencer structure is to create note processors that can be placed in the chain to modify what passes through to the instruments. Let's try a little of each.

20.4.1 Probability

One way to add some variation to a piece is to periodically leave out some notes. A simple probability processor could look like this:

```
public class NoteProbability : Ticker
{
    [Range(0.0f, 1.0f)] public float probability;

    // The "Ticker" we want to listen to
    [SerializeField] private Ticker _ticker;

    /// Subscribe to the ticker
```

```
private void OnEnable()
{
  if (_ticker != null)
  {
    _ticker.Ticked += HandleTicked;
  }
}

/// Unsubscribe from the ticker
private void OnDisable()
{
  if (_ticker != null)
  {
    _ticker.Ticked -= HandleTicked;
  }
}

public void HandleTicked(double tickTime, int midiNoteNumber)
{
  // roll the dice to see if we should play this note
  float rand = UnityEngine.Random.value;
  if (rand < probability)
  {
    DoTick(tickTime, midiNoteNumber);
  }
}
}
```

This could be placed between a sequencer and an instrument to randomly skip some notes, or between sequencers for some chaotic phasing of certain parts of the music.

20.4.2 Note Volume

Musical phrases tend to sound a bit stiff if every note is played with the same volume. MIDI sequencers generally include a per-note *velocity* to control volume and other parameters, and drum machines have usually provided an "accent" setting to increase volume for certain notes. It's straightforward to add modifiable volume to the sequencer system. First, each ticker needs to know the volume. We add that like so:

```
public abstract class Ticker : MonoBehaviour
{
  public delegate void TickHandler(
  double tickTime, int midiNoteNumber, float volume);

  public event TickHandler Ticked;

  protected void DoTick(
    double tickTime, int midiNoteNumber = 60, float volume = 1.0f)
  {
```

```
    if (Ticked != null)
    {
      Ticked(tickTime, midiNoteNumber, volume);
    }
  }
}
```

In addition, each `Ticker` in the system will need its `HandleTicked` function updated to take a volume parameter. From there, the `Sequencer` class needs a concept of volume, which can be added to the step information:

```
[Serializable]
public class Step
{
  public bool Active;
  [Range(1, 7)]
  public int ScaleTone;
  [Range(-1, 8)]
  public int Octave;
  [Range(0.0f, 1.0f)]
  public float Volume;
}
```

And to apply the volume, we just send it along in the `HandleTicked` function:

```
public void HandleTicked(
  double tickTime, int midiNoteNumber, float volume)
{
  ...

  if (step.Active && !suspended)
  {
    ...

    DoTick(tickTime, midiNoteNumber, step.Volume);
  }

  ...
}
```

One final addition is to make the sound generators actually use the volume. In the `Sampler`, these updates will make it respond to volume:

```
// in Sampler.cs
private void HandleTicked(
  double tickTime, int midiNoteNumber, float volume)
{
  float pitch = MidiNoteToPitch(midiNoteNumber);
  _samplerVoices[_nextVoiceIndex].Play(
    _audioClip, pitch, tickTime, volume);

  _nextVoiceIndex = (_nextVoiceIndex + 1) % _samplerVoices.Length;
}

// in SamplerVoice.cs
public void Play(
  AudioClip audioClip, float pitch, double startTime, float volume)
{
  _audioSource.clip = audioClip;
  _audioSource.pitch = pitch;
  _audioSource.volume = volume;
  _audioSource.PlayScheduled(startTime);
}
```

Now we can specify volume per note in the sequencer system.

But what if we want an easy way to modify the volume of all notes going to a sound generator? We can take the "processor" approach as in the probability example and make a volume processor:

```
public class NoteVolume : Ticker
{
  public enum Mode
  {
    Set,
    Multiply,
    Add
  }

  [Range(0.0f, 1.0f)] public float volume;
  public Mode mode;

  ... (ticker subscribe/unsubscribe)

  public void HandleTicked(
    double tickTime, int midiNoteNumber, float volume)
  {
    float newVolume = 0.0f;
    switch (mode)
    {
    case Mode.Set:
      newVolume = this.volume;
      break;
    case Mode.Multiply:
      newVolume = this.volume * volume;
      break;
```

```
    case Mode.Add:
      newVolume = this.volume + volume;
      break;
    }

    DoTick(tickTime, midiNoteNumber, newVolume);
  }
}
```

For a little extra control, this `NoteVolume` processor lets us specify whether the volume change is direct, additive, or multiplicative.

20.4.3 Bonus Round: Euclidean Rhythms

Adding more sequencers to the system can further increase the algorithmic variation of the resulting sound. In 2004, Godfried Toussaint discovered that applying the Euclidean algorithm to steps in a sequence of notes would result in traditional music rhythms. In short, distributing some number of triggers (such as MIDI note on messages) over another number of steps as evenly as possible will usually create a rhythm you've heard before. As an example, five triggers distributed over sixteen steps would produce the familiar *Bossa-Nova* rhythm, shown below as an array of triggers (1) and rests (0):

```
[1, 0, 0, 1, 0, 0, 1, 0, 0, 1, 0, 0, 1, 0, 0, 0]
```

Tap along and you'll probably recognize the feeling. Toussaint detailed this phenomenon in a paper, "The Euclidean Algorithm Generates Traditional Musical Rhythms."[1]

One way to implement a Euclidean Rhythm generator is to loop through each step and turn that step "on" if multiplying the step's index by the number of triggers and wrapping it results in a number less than the total number of triggers:

```
stepIsOn = (i * numTriggers) % numSteps < numTriggers

step by step: euclid(3, 8)
index 0: 0 * 3 % 8 = 0, less than 3, on
index 1: 1 * 3 % 8 = 3, not less than 3, off
index 2: 2 * 3 % 8 = 6, not less than 3, off
index 3: 3 * 3 % 8 = 1, less than 3, on
index 4: 4 * 3 % 8 = 4, not less than 3, off
index 5: 5 * 3 % 8 = 7, not less than 3, off
index 6: 6 * 3 % 8 = 2, less than 3, on
index 7: 7 * 3 % 8 = 5, not less than 3, off

resulting rhythm:
[1, 0, 0, 1, 0, 0, 1, 0]
```

Using the above, we can make a `EuclideanSequencer` that looks like this:

```
public class EuclideanSequencer : Ticker
{
  [Range(1, 16)] public int steps = 16;
  [Range(1, 16)] public int triggers = 4;

  private int _currentStep;

  ... (ticker subscribe/unsubscribe)

  public void HandleTicked(
    double tickTime, int midiNoteNumber, float volume)
  {
    if (IsStepOn(_currentStep, steps, triggers))
    {
      DoTick(tickTime, midiNoteNumber, volume);
    }

    _currentStep = (_currentStep + 1) % steps;
  }

  private static bool IsStepOn(
    int step, int numSteps, int numTriggers)
  {
    return (step * numTriggers) % numSteps < numTriggers;
  }
}
```

This simple sequencer can be connected anywhere in the chain of sequencers, and modifying the number of triggers and steps at runtime can create some interesting rhythmic variation and phasing while generally staying on the grid of the music.

20.5 CONCLUSION

Note-based music systems open up all kinds of new interaction and reaction possibilities for music in games. With a simple framework like the one in this chapter, you can create a set of tools to allow your composers to get their hands on the *behavior* of music as well as the sound. And building on it to create new behavior is quick and easy, leaving time and energy for thinking about the creative possibilities.

You can take this system much further than is practical to show in this chapter. Adding a polished and intuitive UI will allow your creative team to work quickly and efficiently. Further encapsulation of the tick generator and tick receiver classes can make it even easier to add new functionality.

And as mentioned earlier, higher timing precision can be achieved by moving sequencer and processor logic to the audio thread. Hopefully, the information and examples provided will get you closer to your ideal music system.

NOTE

1 Godfried Toussaint. School of Computer Science, McGill University. The Euclidean Algorithm Generates Traditional Musical Rhythms. http://cgm.cs.mcgill.ca/~godfried/publications/banff.pdf.

CHAPTER 21

Synchronizing Action-Based Gameplay to Music

Colin Walder

CD Projekt Red

CONTENTS

21.1 INTRODUCTION

21.1.1 The Goal of Synchronizing Action and Music

Music is a medium that is inherently emotional, and it is one of our key tools when it comes to evoking and communicating emotion to our players. By making a connection between the music and the game action we can effectively tell our audience what to feel. Consider an action sequence scored with fast, powerful music compared to one scored with a slow, melancholy piano. The first score gives the scene a feeling of energy and intensity by supporting what's happening on the screen with a complementary emotional message: classic high-octane action. The second score, however, provides an emotional contradiction with the action, switching the audience's perception of the scene completely. Perhaps, they are led to empathize with the hero's mounting despair in the face of insurmountable odds.

We can have a big impact on the emotional content of our musical message and the effectiveness of our communication by our choice of synchronization. Achieving this first level of emotional impact is a (relatively) simple case of choosing the appropriate music to play along with our gameplay, according to the emotion we want to evoke. If we want to deepen the connection between the action and the music, we need to have a stronger synchronization between what the player is seeing and what they're hearing. In linear media (such as film and television), the practice of synchronizing elements of action with hits and transitions in the music to deliver an emotional narrative is well established and commonly used. In fact, our audiences are so used to this communication that when we remove music completely from an action sequence it can be disturbing in a way that, when used sparingly, can increase the tension.

21.1.2 Audio Engine Prerequisites

The approach to synchronization in this chapter is based on the use of Audiokinetic Wwise to provide callbacks at musically significant points for tracks implemented using the interactive music authoring tool. A full description of implementing the required audio engine features is beyond the scope of this chapter but it should be possible to achieve similar results with other middleware libraries either using the built-in mechanisms, or by calculating the sync points yourself based on the elapsed time of the track, tempo, time signature, and entry point. Be careful to use the elapsed time based on the audio data consumed rather than a timer in your code as these will almost certainly drift and become desynchronized.

21.2 INTERACTIVE SYNCHRONIZATION

21.2.1 The Challenge of Interactivity

In narrative-based games, we have broadly similar goals to a film or TV show in that we want to draw our audience (our players) in and connect them with the story and with the emotions of our characters. In some respects, we have advantages over linear media: we provide a feeling of agency to the player through interactivity that can immerse and involve players in ways that are unavailable to traditional linear media. When we compare the musical techniques employed in games we typically see synchronization of a more basic type, where a score or backing track supplies the broad emotional context for a scene. Perhaps there is a dynamic response to what is happening in the game, but only rarely will the action be synchronized closely with the music.

While interactivity gives us extra opportunities to connect with our audience, it also poses unique challenges. In linear media, there is a fixed timeline in the end product, so the sound and image can be carefully crafted to mesh together for the maximum emotional impact at precisely the right points. In games, especially action games where there is a high level of player interaction, we do not have a fixed timeline since the player can act in their own time and the game world has to react appropriately. It is possible to force a more linear experience on the player by restricting the interactive choices available to them, or by using a cutscene where we present an entirely linear and hand-crafted section of the game with a fixed timeline. Cutscenes are an effective technique and make it much easier for us to synchronize our visuals and music, but the further we push in this direction the less our game can provide a feeling of agency and interactive immersion. Typically, we see alternating sections of action gameplay and cutscenes so the player can experience both sides of the coin. We can involve the player more with semi-interactive cutscenes using "quick time events" where the player has to respond to the cutscene with some simple time-sensitive interaction in order to progress, or to choose from a number of branches the cutscene may take. Ideally though, we would be able to use music synchronization alongside interactive action to get the benefit of both together.

21.2.2 Seeking Opportunities

The answer to this challenge is a compromise based around finding opportunities for synchronization that already exist within the gameplay. Action gameplay can be highly predictable with fixed timings and actions that the player needs to learn, or be random and procedural, testing the player's ability to react to an unpredictable situation. Often a modern action game (especially one with cinematic aspirations) will include elements of both styles: fixed/predictable gameplay loops to give depth to the gameplay mixed with randomization to give an organic feeling and keep the player on their toes. An example might be a shooting game where the design allows the player to force enemies to take cover by using a certain set of actions. The intention is that the player is learning the cause and effect nature of these actions, and can apply them in different situations rather than simply learning by rote the sequence and timing of buttons to press at a certain point of the game.

For gameplay that is very fixed timing-wise, synchronizing to music can provide a powerful and interesting way for the player to learn and master complex timings. This requires the gameplay to be designed from the beginning around the music, and so is more likely to be found in a music-based game than in an action game. At the same time, it's possible that gameplay which is highly focused on rhythm action will also lend itself more toward an arcade experience, rather than a cinematic experience. When there is an overt and mechanical relationship between the gameplay and music, there can be less freedom or room to use subtler (and perhaps more interesting) techniques.

On the other end of the spectrum, gameplay which is intended to feel organic or natural will have timings that are not fixed and can vary greatly based on a combination of the players' actions and randomness. In this case, it is unlikely that we have music as a foundational pillar of gameplay, so we must instead look for opportunities within the existing design. For these situations, randomness is a great place to start; any time there is randomness, we have a window of opportunity that we can use to achieve some level of synchronization with music. If an event can happen normally within a range even as small as one to two seconds, quantizing the event to a musical beat is likely to be possible without stepping outside the limits already accepted by the gameplay designers. In this way, we can begin to introduce musical synchronization for cinematic effect in a nondisruptive fashion.

As we'll see in the next section, finding nondisruptive opportunities for synchronization will be key in order to sell the idea to the rest of the team. We can usually find other opportunities for synchronization: additive animations on characters, visual effects, and lighting that are not tightly linked to gameplay and player action, and even the behavior of NPCs. At first, this may seem like it would violate the idea of hiding the mechanics; however, because we are looking for opportunities that already exist within the gameplay, we end up with an effect that can be surprisingly subtle.

In my first experience with synchronizing the attacks of a boss in The Witcher 3: Blood and Wine to music, we at first held back on the amount of synchronization, fearing that it would become too mechanical. In the end, we were able to push the level of synchronization to the limit of our tech, without feeling unnatural or overpowering. This aligns well with our goal because when we think about using the ideas and techniques of music synchronization that have been exemplified in cinema, these are approaches that are powerful precisely because they are subtle in such a way that the audience doesn't explicitly recognize them. Also, it's important to note that in seeking opportunities for syncing elements of the game to music, we still want to keep the traditional approach of syncing the music to the game too and so gain the benefit of both.

21.2.3 Selling it to the Team

In my experience, it can be a harder task convincing the rest of the team that it is worth spending time and resources to implement music synchronization technology than it is to actually implement it. It is common in games for sound and music to be thought of as part of the post-production stage: something that is added on at the end when all the other pieces are in place, so the idea of having the game react to the audio can be unexpected or even alien. They may be worried that introducing music sync will create a feeling of a rhythm game, which would go against what they want to achieve in their own areas.

While it is possible to create a presentation for your colleagues to describe the approach and techniques, I've found the best way is to simply do it and show the effect in-game. That said, it doesn't hurt to have some references on hand from games and films that do it well. The process of exposing music sync from middleware such as Wwise or FMOD to the game is relatively quick and easy, so start by adding this support to your music systems and expose it via tools and scripts. With this technology in place you need to find a designer who will be willing to experiment and put together a prototype. Favors come in handy here as do offers of help to fix that one annoying bug which has been sitting on a low priority for ages. Depending on your tools and engine, it may be possible for you to create a prototype yourself. Involving someone from the implementation team at this early stage, however, can help secure their buy-in to evangelize the idea within the rest of the team. Be sure to emphasize that your intention is to seek out opportunities for sync within their design and not change their design to fit the music.

Once team members see that implementing music sync can be done very easily on their side and that it doesn't break their designs to do so, I've found that the process gains its own momentum. Not only are they happy to implement your ideas for music sync, but they start to come up with ideas for how to interact with music themselves. Having members of other teams come to you excited about how they can use music in their features and designs is a really wonderful experience!

21.3 BASIC SYNCHRONIZATION

For basic synchronization, I start with bars, beats, and grid since it is trivial to prepare the interactive music to support these, and because they are the most straightforward to understand in terms of mapping to gameplay.

Beats are the simplest of all to implement: they are the most frequent point for synchronization and the most likely to be able to fit to gameplay without disrupting the design. They have a low impact effect in terms of experiencing the sync which means we can be quite liberal synchronizing elements. A single synchronized event by itself won't be enough to feel different from random events; it will take multiple actions on-beat for the sync to be felt. Synchronizing a single footstep animation wouldn't be noticed but having every footstep in a walk cycle sync could have a strong effect.

Syncing to the bar means having synchronization on the first beat of the measure. Depending on the tempo, bar synchronized events can also be relatively easy to tie to in-game events that happen often, but not constantly. For example, an enemy initiating an attack or performing a special maneuver, an environmental effect like a moving piece of machinery or some reaction from wildlife. Bar sync has a stronger impact than syncing to the beat, therefore, should be used to highlight more notable events and actions that you want to stand out and be associated with emotions in the music. It is important that the events don't need to be instantaneous, since they may have to wait several seconds for a sync point.

Grid is Wwise's term for a musical phrase, commonly four bars. The beginning beat of a grid is a very powerful point to sync at, since large accents, musical progressions, and the beginning of repeated sections often happen here. When an event is synchronized to the grid, it will have the most impact and connection to the music, so grid synced events should be used when you want the greatest emphasis. In Blood and Wine, we used this for the most powerful boss attack: something that posed a significant danger to the player and was worthy of being connected with the strongest musical accents. It also happened infrequently enough that the relatively long wait between grid points (over ten seconds in this case) was not a problem.

21.3.1 Music Timing Callbacks

The first thing you'll need to do to achieve music sync is to have your composer prepare the music in Wwise. The music needs to be implemented using the interactive music hierarchy, with the correct time signature and tempo and the media file aligned appropriately to the bars/grid in the editor. For full details on implementing music in Wwise, see the Wwise documentation. A "by-the-book" interactive music approach will suffice to allow for sync callbacks.

Next up is to register to receive callbacks for the bars beats and music from Wwise by passing in the appropriate flags and callback function when posting the music event:

```
AkPlayingID result =
  AK::SoundEngine::PostEvent(
    eventName,
    gameObjectId,
    AK_MusicSyncGrid | AK_MusicSyncBar | AK_MusicSyncBeat,
    eventCallback );
```

Where `eventCallback` is a function which parses the different callback types and notifies your music system that a sync point has occurred along with the current number of beats per grid, beats per bar, or beat duration depending on the callback type. This lets us adapt our synchronization in the case of changes in tempo and will be important later:

```
void eventCallback(
  AkCallbackType in_eType, AkCallbackInfo* in_pCallbackInfo )
{
  AkMusicSyncCallbackInfo *info =
    (AkMusicSyncCallbackInfo*)in_pCallbackInfo;

  Uint32 barBeatsRemaining =
    ( Uint32 )( info->fBarDuration/info->fBeatDuration );
  Uint32 gridBeatsRemaining =
    ( Uint32 )( info->fGridDuration/info->fBeatDuration );
```

```
switch ( eventType )
{
case AkMusicSyncBar:
  NotifyBar( barBeatsRemaining );
  break;
case AkMusicSyncGrid:
  NotifyGrid( gridBeatsRemaining );
  break;
case AkMusicSyncBeat:
  NotifyBeat( info->fBeatDuration );
  break;
default:
  break;
}
}
```

There are other music callbacks that can be registered for music sync in Wwise, such as user cue, but for now we'll stick to grid, bar, and beat. Here I'm assuming that we only register a single music track for sync callbacks, but if we did want to have multiple tracks providing separate sync in game, it is possible to use the data in `AkMusicSyncCallbackInfo` to differentiate between them.

21.3.2 Waiting for the Callback

Now that we have callbacks being returned for the sync points, we need to provide a way for the game to use these timings. Game systems may prefer to access this either by registering a callback or by polling each frame to see if sync is achieved. We should implement whichever the game will be able to use most readily—as the different game systems interact with the music, we'll probably end up needing to support both callbacks and polling.

At its most basic, a callback system is the simplest to implement on our end since all we have to do is keep a list of sync listeners and then trigger them upon receiving the appropriate sync notification. An example where we might want to make use of this feature for audio would be to trigger a sound effect to play in sync with the music, or to have a quest progress only at a synchronized moment.

For systems which prefer to poll, such as an AI tree that reevaluates its inputs each frame, we need to keep track of the most recent beat, bar, and grid, then compare the time when polling with the appropriate type and check if it falls within a specified epsilon. At first, this approach suffers some limitation of sync because it will only succeed if the poll falls just after the notification. If the epsilon is large, however, beat syncs lose their potency. As we will see in the next section, we will quickly want to develop this approach to allow for predicting future sync points.

21.4 SYNCHRONIZING ANIMATION AND AI

While not the simplest features to connect to music sync, AI and animation are actually a good place to start, since they can provide some of the most interesting and potentially powerful interactions. This is especially true if we want to orchestrate and coordinate epic moments of synchronization in the action. Furthermore, once AI has been shown to be possible to synchronize with music, it should be easier to connect other systems, both in terms of technology and in terms of buy-in from the rest of the team. We will need to start with something that is clearly visible so that it is apparent to the team that the synchronization is actually happening. We can introduce subtle elements later on, but it is hard to sell the idea that your teams should invest their time if they constantly need to ask if the sync is actually happening. One good option is to have the AI perform an action that involves an animation based on the condition of synchronization. There are two important subtleties to this tech: We need to have a safety mechanism so that the AI won't wait for a sync point that is too far in the future, and we will need to be able to specify an offset to the point of synchronization.

21.4.1 The Need for Predictive Synchronization

When we sync an action that involves an animation, we almost always want to have the sync occur partway into the animation. For example, with a large enemy trying to stomp on the player, we'd want to synchronize the foot landing, not when it is initially raised. In order to be able to do this we need to develop our music sync system so that we not only react to the callbacks from Wwise, but can predict when future callbacks will happen and apply a temporal offset. Conveniently, this also gives us the functionality to override if there is too long to wait before the next sync point.

In the case of an AI behavior tree, we can add a condition in front of specific actions that will return false unless the condition is tested at a sync point of the specified type. The function call to the music system might look something like this:

```
bool IsSynched(
   Uint32 syncType, float maxSyncWait, float timeOffset = 0.f )
{
   return
    AreClose( 0.f,
```

```
                 GetTimeToNextEventBeforeTime(
                    syncType, maxSyncWait, timeOffset, c_musicSyncEpsilon ) );
}
```

I used a c_musicSyncEpsilon of 0.1f, but you may want to tune this to your own situation (or even use a variable epsilon).

```
float GetTimeToNextEventBeforeTime(
   Uint32 syncType, float timeLimit, float timeOffset )
{
   float gameTime = GetTime() - c_musicSyncEpsilon;
   float soonestTime = 0.f;

   switch ( syncType )
   {
   case Bar:
     soonestTime = GetNextBarTime( gameTime, timeOffset);
     break;
   case Beat:
     soonestTime = GetNextBeatTime( gameTime, timeOffset);
     break;
   case Grid:
     soonestTime = GetNextGridTime( gameTime, timeOffset);
     break;
   default:
     break;
   }

   if(soonestTime > timeLimit)
   {
     soonestTime = 0.f;
   }

   return soonestTime;
}
```

Here, we start searching for the next event just before the actual current time, in case a sync point has just happened and we still want to trigger our action.

21.4.2 Computing Future Synchronization

Our GetNext() functions compute the time of the next sync point (offset included) after the specified time, and give us the flexibility to look into the future (and partially into the past) for sync points. Before we can perform the predictive calculation, however, we need to set up some additional data in the sync notifications from Wwise:

```
void NotifyBar( Uint32 beatsRemaining )
{
   float gameTime = GetTime();
   //Because Wwise sends the beat notification before the bar,
   //we need to add one beat to account for the subsequent -
   //in the NotifyBeat call
   m_beatsToNextBar = beatsRemaining + 1;
   m_lastBarTime = gameTime;
   m_currentBeatsPerBar = beatsRemaining;
}

void NotifyGrid( Uint32 beatsRemaining )
{
   float gameTime = GetTime();
   m_beatsToNextGrid = beatsRemaining;
   m_lastGridTime = gameTime;
   m_currentBeatsPerGrid = beatsRemaining;
}
```

The bar and grid notifiers are very similar: we reset counters for each that keep track of how many beats are left until the next expected sync point, as well as the time the sync point occurs, the current time signature, and phrasing in the form of beats per bar and grid. Our prediction functions are going to be based on counting down the beats rather than calculating the expected time directly. The time between bars and grids is long enough that there can be significant drift between the game and music. Basing our prediction on the beat time means that it is updated frequently by the beat notifications, which helps keep the sync accurate. Note that, because we receive the events from Wwise in a specific order, we need to artificially increase the bar beat count to account for the beat notification that follows immediately. The grid beat count does not need this increment.

```
void NotifyBeat(float duration)
{
   float gameTime = GetTime();
   m_currentBeatDuration = duration;
   m_lastBeatTime = gameTime;
   m_beatsToNextBar--;
   m_beatsToNextGrid--;
}
```

When we receive a beat sync we update the beat time as well as the duration, to account for any changes in music tempo, and decrement the beat counters for bar and grid.

Now we can implement the GetNext() functions for our sync points:

```
float GetNextBeatTime( float timeNow, float timeOffset )
{
  float currentTime = m_lastBeatTime + timeOffset;
  while( currentTime < timeNow )
  {
    currentTime += m_currentBeatDuration;
  }

  return currentTime;
}
```

Getting the next beat is the simplest of our prediction functions. We combine the time offset with the last time a beat sync was received, and then increment it by beat duration until we pass the "now" time that we want for the next beat.

```
float GetNextBarTime( float timeNow, float timeOffset)
{
  Uint32 beatsRemaining = m_beatsToNextBar;
  float currentTime = m_lastBeatTime+timeOffset;
  while(currentTime < timeNow ||
        beatsRemaining != m_currentBeatsPerBar)
  {
    currentTime += m_currentBeatDuration;
    if( beatsRemaining > 0 )
    {
      beatsRemaining--;
    }
    Else
    {
      beatsRemaining += m_currentBeatsPerBar;
    }
  }

  return currentTime;
}

float GetNextGridTime( float timeNow, float timeOffset )
{
  Uint32 beatsRemaining = m_beatsToNextGrid;
  float currentTime = m_lastBeatTime+timeOffset;
  while( currentTime < timeNow ||
        beatsRemaining != m_currentBeatsPerGrid )
  {
    currentTime += m_currentBeatDuration;
    if( beatsRemaining > 0 )
    {
      beatsRemaining--;
    }
    else
    {
      beatsRemaining += m_currentBeatsPerGrid;
    }
```

```
      }
      return currentTime;
}
```

The bar and grid functions look very similar. The both count down the remaining beats in the bar until it reaches 0. If the time has not passed the "now" point, we add on a full bar/grid worth of beats and continue until we reach a sync point (i.e., where beats remaining equals 0) and the "now" time has been passed.

We now have all the pieces in place in order to sync our AI-driven animations to music.

21.4.3 Visualizing the Timeline

Debug visualization is always important, and doubly so when dealing with music synchronization. Sometimes you will have very strong and obvious sync, but often the sync will be subtle or the music might be playing around with the beat. Couple that with the fact that we want to involve people from other teams who may not have much experience and knowledge of musical structure. I recommend displaying a debug timeline that shows the current time as a fixed point, and plots predicted beats, bars, and grids both into the future and a short time into the past so that they can be seen as they cross the current time.

Fortunately, we already have functions that allow us to compute the predicted sync points based on an arbitrary time:

```
float currentTime = m_lastBeatTime;
// Add a small delta each time to move us onto the next
// beat/bar/grid
while(currentTime < gameTime + maxFutureTime)
{
  xPos = xZero + ( ( currentTime - gameTime ) * timelineScale );
  DrawBeatDebug( xPos );
  currentTime = GetNextBeatTime( currentTime ) + 0.01f;
}
```

Starting from the last beat time, we draw the beat and then move forward to the next beat. We need to add a small overshoot to the time returned in order to nudge the loop past the sync point. Grid and bar sync points are visualized in the same way.

I also recommend displaying a visualization to indicate when the IsSynched() function returns true for the various sync types, as this will help to diagnose bugs where another system is syncing to music but has supplied an incorrect offset.

21.5 SYNCHRONIZING VFX

Once we have built the sync machinery for the AI and animation, we have a relatively easy path integrating to other systems. Ambient VFX, for example, lend themselves to being synchronized to the music and can use the system as-is, except that they likely have less need for sync offset and timeout. One thing that ambient effects want that we have not yet supplied, however, is the ability to synchronize to custom beats. While we usually want to sync animations to a strong beat, we may want to use the music sync system to choreograph a sequence of VFX, for example, to have lights flashing different colors on alternating beats.

We may want to sync to even or odd beats, for example:

```
float GetNextEvenBeatTime( float timeNow, float timeOffset )
{
  Uint32 beatsToNextBar = m_beatsToNextBar;

  float currentTime = m_lastBeatTime + timeOffset;

  while( currentTime < timeNow )
  {
    //When (beats per bar - beats remaining) is even we are on
    //an odd beat
    //so we need to skip it
    if( ( m_currentBeatsPerBar - beatsToNextBar ) % 2 == 0 )
    {
      currentTime += m_currentBeatDuration;
      beatsToNextBar -= 1;
      if( beatsToNextBar == 0 )
      {
        beatsToNextBar = m_currentBeatsPerBar;
      }
    }
    currentTime += m_currentBeatDuration;
    beatsToNextBar -= 1;
    if( beatsToNextBar == 0 )
    {
      beatsToNextBar = m_currentBeatsPerBar;
    }
  }

  return currentTime;
}
```

Or we may want to find a sync point at an arbitrary beat in a bar:

```
float GetNextBeatInBarTime(
  float timeNow, float beatOffset, float timeOffset )
{
```

```
float nextBarTime = GetNextBarTime(timeNow);

//First see if we still have a beat in the current bar
float prevBeatTime =
  nextBarTime -
    (m_currentBeatsPerBar - beatOffset) * m_currentBeatDuration +
    timeOffset;
if( prevBeatTime >= timeNow )
{
  return prevBeatTime;
}

//We've already passed the beat, use the next one
return
  nextBarTime + beatOffset*m_currentBeatDuration + timeOffset;
}
```

Also, the `GetNext()` functions can be exposed to other systems directly where they would prefer to be driven by a parameter rather than to sync at fixed points, for example, a light that gradually gets brighter throughout the bar.

21.6 TAKING IT FURTHER

The system we have seen here is already quite flexible in being able to synchronize different systems, but also has a number of ways that it can be extended without too much effort:

- For open-world games where there can be multiple sources of music, we could add support for being able to specify which music event the game wishes to sync to. Perhaps some NPCs will be reacting in time with a street musician while some VFX pulse in time with the quest score.

- Another next step would be to support the other music callback types provided by Wwise: `AK_MusicSyncUserCue` in particular could be used to great effect in custom situations while `AK_MusicSyncEntry`, `AK_MusicSyncExit`, and `AK_MusicSyncPoint` could be used when you have the game respond to changes in your interactive music.

- Adding additional `GetNext()` functions is an easy way to support the team when they have some very specific synchronization needs, and anything that makes it easier for people to implement sync in their system will pay dividends.

- The system described here only delivers sync in the direction of music to game, but at the same time we still have the traditional method of triggering music based on events in the game. A great feature to develop would be to have a sync mode that facilitated waiting for a point in the music that was appropriate for a stinger or transition, and then coordinated the game and music so that the music could support the game action with even more potency.

Beyond technical improvements to the system though, the most interesting thing to drive forward is how synchronization can be used interactively to provide effects that would be normally unavailable. We start with direct, visual synchronizations, but perhaps it is possible to go even further by matching the dynamics of the action with the dynamics of the music. Music has an inherent structure and rhythm, repetitions and progressions. Building an interwoven two-way relationship between gameplay and music could be beneficial in both directions.

21.7 CONCLUSION

When talking about synchronizing gameplay to music in action games, I have often been told that it is impossible because, unlike movies, games are interactive and can't be restricted to the fixed timings of music. I've found, and hopefully have shown here, that not only is it creatively possible to find a way to reconcile interactivity with music synchronization, but it is also not an overbearing technical challenge when using modern audio middleware.

By taking an attitude of looking for opportunities to sync to music in our game rather than arguing for it as a foundational principle, we can overcome the most significant blockers to integrating a synchronization system. We offer a built-in safety net so that game systems never have to compromise their timing more than they are willing to. In the worst case, we have a game that is the same without the sync system, but in the best case, we have something really cool.

It's important that we enlist the support of the other game teams in our endeavor and that we win their excitement and imaginations to our cause. Starting with a challenging but important system such as AI-driven animations gives us both an opportunity to win the interest of the team and a strong foundation to extend support to other systems.

Index

Printed in the United States
by Baker & Taylor Publisher Services